MW01039399

COP
COP

Breaking the Fixed System

of American Policing

MAC MUIR
AND **GREG FINCH**

zando

NEW YORK

zandoprojects.com

First Edition: April 2025

Design by Neuwirth & Associates, Inc.
Cover design by Christopher Brand

The publisher does not have control over and is not responsible for author or other third-party websites (or their content).

Library of Congress Control Number: 2025930898

978-1-63893-008-2 (Hardcover)
978-1-63893-009-9 (ebook)

10 9 8 7 6 5 4 3 2 1
Manufactured in the United States of America

Contents

Part I

HOW TO INVESTIGATE POLICE MISCONDUCT

Part II

BEHIND THE BLUE WALL

Part III

BREAKING THE FIXED SYSTEM

Note from the Authors

T his is a work of nonfiction. Most events depicted in this book occurred between 2016 and 2022. Except where otherwise indicated, these events were recounted to us by firsthand witnesses or drawn from moments we experienced ourselves. The facts in these investigations are precisely accounted for. Where applicable, facts have been carefully cross-referenced with an array of public records. However, the names and identifying information of the officers, complainants, witnesses, their children, their relatives, and any other New York City employees that appear in the book have been changed to protect their privacy unless such information was reported on or otherwise made public. The opinions expressed here are our own and not necessarily the policy of the Civilian Complaint Review Board (CCRB).

In our investigations, we sought to corroborate individual recollections. In instances where there were discrepancies between accounts and no video footage to settle the difference, we depict the most plausible version of events based on a "preponderance of the evidence," the CCRB evidentiary standard, and the standard burden of proof in civil court. When we were unable to determine what happened, we note as much.

We condense only those moments we experienced firsthand—snippets of interviews, trainings, and everyday office experiences—solely to make the reading experience more accessible, and we do so sparingly. However, we always include material facts and aim to capture the spirit of what happened, and the events depicted in this book are faithfully represented by using contemporaneous notes, the best of our recollections, and our skill sets as professional investigators.

We learned the facts of each case through the course of our official duties. What we saw included waste, inefficiency, corruption, criminal activity, and conflict of interest in the activities of New York City agencies. Motivated by a desire to improve our democracy, we wrote some of it down.

Prologue

S pring 2017. Parked cars line a sunny residential block in Harlem, New York City. Sirens blare. An SUV, hazard lights flashing, screeches to a halt. Ron Davis, a man in his early twenties, opens the driver-side door, jumps out, slams the door behind him, and sprints forward. He weaves through a maze of police vehicles, fire trucks, and emergency workers. When he reaches an ambulance's open rear doors, he leaps inside, knocking an EMT to the ground. The EMT's supervisor shouts in vain. Inside, Davis looks down at a stretcher. His six-month-old daughter looks up and wails. Davis pulls her from the stretcher restraints, cradles her against his chest, and sobs. "My baby! My baby! My baby!"

Ten minutes earlier, Davis had received a phone call from his mother, who told him that his baby daughter had been found unconscious in a bathtub. It was a miracle that she was still alive.

The EMT grabs Davis's shoulders and tells him to put her down.

"Fuck. You."

The EMT tries to assure Davis that his daughter will be all right. Tentatively, Davis hands her over and steps out of the ambulance. The EMT's supervisor stares at him, bewildered. Officers and firefighters spill out from the lobby of a brick building nearby, returning to their vehicles as if the incident were all over. Davis walks toward his car.

Davis's cousin, Terrence, emerges from the brick building. Spotting Davis, he bolts across the street and wraps a consoling arm around his cousin's shoulder.

"Who put her in the bathtub?" Davis asks.

Terrence says it was Davis's girlfriend.

Davis vents, a little louder than he intended, "I'm gonna fuck some-body up. I can't believe that bitch."

Nearby, an NYPD lieutenant sits in the front passenger seat of a blue-and-white sedan. He overhears Davis's venting, then groans. Tossing aside the report he's completing, he steps out of his cruiser, scans the maze of emergency vehicles, and strides toward the sound of Davis's voice. Two officers follow close behind.

Still distraught, Davis fumes to Terrence. "I mean, the fuck is wrong with her?"

The lieutenant emerges from behind a fire engine and advances toward Davis. "The fuck is wrong with you?"

IN A CRAMPED ROOM STALE with fluorescent light, an investigator pressed the space bar on his computer. A Pause symbol appeared over the center of the screen, and the surveillance footage stopped. The investigator knew what happened next in the video but still turned to the lieutenant and asked, "At this moment, what was happening?"

Across a cheap wooden table, the lieutenant sat flanked by two union attorneys from the LBA.* Another more tenured investigator was carefully taking notes in a spiral notebook.

On the table was an audio recorder, red light blinking. An old computer monitor displayed silent surveillance footage. Although the video had no sound, the investigator had interviewed ten civilians and officers to piece together the missing dialogue.

As always, the NYPD compelled this lieutenant to answer the investigators' questions, but he knew that his answers could not be used against him in criminal court. According to New York Civil Rights Law 50-a, all records of this incident would be hidden from

---

* Lieutenants Benevolent Association, the name of the lieutenants' union. In New York, officers, detectives, sergeants, lieutenants, and captains have their own unions.

the public. If the investigator were to recount this interview to a friend, let alone a member of the press, he could be fired and face misdemeanor charges.*

Of the few who would ever hear this lieutenant's testimony, the most important was a deputy commissioner in the NYPD. And the lieutenant knew his audience.

"At this moment, I was aware that my cops had just saved the life of a drowning infant and that an unknown individual was on the street, acting erratically, flailing his arms, and threatening to kill a woman."

"Was there anything else you observed?"

"I feared for my safety."

"Okay. Why?"

"I feared for my safety because this guy threatened to kill someone."

"Did you know who he threatened?"

"No."

"So, what about this threat caused you to fear for your *own* safety?"

One of his attorneys interjected. "This guy threatened to kill someone. What more do you want?"

In the dance of an officer interview at the CCRB, an investigator needed to prevent the union attorneys from throwing off the tempo. They were known to yell, scream, and interject with little recourse. Sometimes they tapped their officers' knees as a signal to say, "I don't recall." Other times they went for personal insults, calling investigators children, incompetent, a waste of taxpayer money, or worse. Investigators who were women and people of color were known to be treated with far less courtesy than their white male colleagues. Privately, this investigator believed that much of the attorneys' conduct could have led to censures from the New York State Bar Association, but how would the bar association ever find out? None

---

* New York City Civil Rights Law 50-a was repealed in June 2020.

of this was in the public record. Every interview unfolded in a secret, half-regulated universe.

These two LBA attorneys, however, were notably professional, just trying to get their lieutenant out of a jam.

"Counsel, please don't interrupt."

The attorney went quiet, and the investigator continued.

"Again, what about this threat caused you to fear for *your own* safety?"

"I think someone making any threatening statements in the street makes them a threat to everyone."

"Okay. Was there any other reason you feared for your safety?"

"A crowd started to form."

"Can you show me on the screen where the crowd is?"

"You can't see it in the video."

There was no crowd.

"Okay. Any other reason you feared for your safety?"

"No."

Sometimes, well after an interview, an officer might conveniently remember other factors that caused them to fear for their safety. Perhaps, a year later at trial, this lieutenant would remember a suspicious bulge, therefore fearing that Davis was armed. Maybe he would remember a threatening statement that no one could corroborate or refute. In light of these new memories, his conduct might appear much more reasonable, and the entire case could fall apart. So each time the investigator asked, "Any other reason?" and he replied, "No," the lieutenant locked himself into a statement he couldn't conveniently reassemble.

The investigator tapped the space bar, and the video continued. All eyes returned to the screen.

The lieutenant takes two quick steps toward Davis, who stands firmly in place.

The investigator paused the video, by this point certain that the lieutenant had never seen the footage. The agency had pulled it from a surveillance camera at a construction site. As usual, Internal Affairs hadn't bothered to do the same.

"Earlier, you stated Mr. Davis charged at you. Is that depicted here?"

"Yeah," said the lieutenant, pointing at the computer screen. "It's right there."

It wasn't.

"Understood."

The investigator tapped the space bar, and the footage continued. *They are close. Davis steps to his left, away from the lieutenant.*

Tap. Pause. "At this moment did you say anything?"

Three civilians had reported that the lieutenant yelled, "You little motherfucker." The other officers couldn't recall what he said but didn't deny it either.

"I said, 'What are you doing? We're trying to get your baby to the hospital.'"

"Did you say, 'You little motherfucker'?"

"I don't recall."

That wasn't a "No."

"And what did he say?"

"I don't remember exactly, but it was threatening."

"What do you mean?"

"Like I said, I don't remember, but whatever he said caused me to feel threatened. I became increasingly threatened by his presence, and the look in his eyes."

"How would you describe the look in his eyes?"

"Irate."

"Was there anything else threatening about his eyes?"

"Not that I recall."

One attorney asked if the investigator could play the video all the way through.

"No. Sorry."

The point was to get the lieutenant to account for his own memory, not what happened in the video. The investigator pressed Play.

The lieutenant takes one final step toward Davis.

The investigator paused again. "So, had anything changed since you were three steps away?"

"No."

"Okay."

One of the attorneys barked, "This guy Davis threatened an officer. Lieutenant, is it against New York State law to threaten a member of the NYPD?"

"Correct."

The investigator had more than enough evidence to determine that Davis hadn't threatened the lieutenant, so he ignored the attorney's commentary. Under the CCRB's rules, attorneys were forbidden from saying anything to interfere during these interviews, let alone conducting their own lines of questioning.[1] But in this world, a rule was only as good as its enforcement.

The investigator also needed to maintain a professional relationship with these union attorneys. There would be more interviews to come, and not every interjection needed a rebuttal. The investigator tapped the space bar again.

The lieutenant's hands shoot forward and wrap around Davis's neck. Davis gasps for breath and looks directly into the lieutenant's eyes.

The investigator paused the video.

"Can you describe what's happening here?"

"He stepped too close to me."

"And then what happened?"

"I pushed him away."

"How did you push him away?"

The lieutenant glanced toward his attorneys. One nodded.

"I pushed his chest."

"Where on his chest?"

"His upper chest."

"So where were your hands relative to, say, the center of his chest?"

"Two inches above the center of his chest."

"Okay, two inches above the center of his chest. And where were your hands relative to, say, his neck?"

The investigator glanced at the surveillance footage. The lieutenant's hands were frozen around Davis's neck.

"Two inches below the neck."

"Okay. So, two inches above the center of his chest and two inches below his neck, is that right?"

"Correct."

Both attorneys nodded.

"Are your hands on his neck?"

"No."

"Okay. For the record, in the surveillance footage it appears that your hands are around Mr. Davis's neck."

The attorneys erupted. They claimed that the investigator was putting words in the lieutenant's mouth, that he wasn't being fair. This was an important charade. Although the lieutenant had already lied, his attorneys needed to give him the impression they were still fighting tooth and nail to keep him out of trouble. Some suspected that these outbursts helped their law firm keep its contract with the union.

"I'm not putting words in his mouth, and I heard exactly what he said. For the record, the lieutenant has given his account, and he stated that his hands were two inches above Mr. Davis's nipple line and two inches beneath his neck. Is that correct?"

"Yes."

"And for the record, as the investigator handling this case, I'm telling you what I personally see. I see your hands wrapped around Mr. Davis's neck. That's simply what I see. I'm not saying that's your statement."

The attorneys relented.

"In this surveillance footage, are your hands wrapped around Mr. Davis's neck?"

"No."

"Did you place your hands on Mr. Davis's neck?"

"No."

"Did you choke Mr. Davis?"

"No."

"Okay," said the investigator. "That's your statement."

The investigator tapped the space bar again.

MOMENTS AFTER CHOKING DAVIS, the lieutenant challenges him to fight in the street. His own officers have to hold him back. A bystander would later describe the lieutenant as "thuggin' out." Davis and Terrence walk around the block to cool off. The lieutenant searches Davis's car and calls for a tow truck. Terrence returns and talks the lieutenant into letting him take the car. The lieutenant agrees, but only if Davis apologizes to him "like a man." Davis returns and apologizes. The lieutenant writes him a summons for disorderly conduct, then leaves.

A FEW HOURS LATER, the lieutenant learned that Davis had filed a complaint with Internal Affairs. Later that day, the lieutenant called the Administration for Children's Services and opened a child welfare investigation into Davis and his girlfriend, as required by New York State law. A week later, the lieutenant sent a group of detectives to arrest Davis for knocking over the EMT. That arrest was dismissed and sealed by the Manhattan District Attorney's Office.

When the CCRB interview was over, the investigator turned off his audio recorder, shook hands with the lieutenant and his attorneys, and left the room. One month later, he submitted a lengthy closing report with a series of substantiated allegations. Three months later, the CCRB board reviewed the case and agreed with the findings. The case was referred to the CCRB's Administrative Prosecution Unit (APU). The lieutenant would face Charges. His penalty could range from losing two to thirty vacation days. In the NYPD, the main currency for officer discipline was docking vacation days.

Six months later, the lieutenant's administrative trial was finally scheduled. It would be held in Trial Room A on the second floor of NYPD headquarters at One Police Plaza. But one gray afternoon, the investigator's boss told him that the lieutenant had retired before the trial could even begin. He would never be disciplined, let alone fired. This case would remain in the dark.

Prior complaints against the lieutenant revealed something more. Similar stories of alleged child neglect, in which the lieutenant would respond to a 9-1-1 call and in one way or another lash out at the offending parents.[*] In this case, the lieutenant had just held an unconscious child in his arms. She'd nearly drowned. But while the investigator empathized with both Davis's panic and the lieutenant's loss of control, that wasn't his job. His job was to hold the lieutenant accountable. And in that regard, it seemed he'd failed. Case closed, on to the next.

That year, the CCRB handled over 4,000 cases. It was a down year.

---

* New York State designates police officers as mandated reporters of suspected child abuse or maltreatment.

Introduction

> Those who don't study history are doomed to repeat it, and
> those who study policing know we don't study history.
>
> —FORMER NYPD DEPUTY
> COMMISSIONER JOHN TIMONEY

How often do you think about the police? When you do, who do you think of? Columbo? Chief Wiggum? Derek Chauvin? Do you think of individual officers, or do you think of the police as an institution? Do you wonder where it all started? Were they always here? Sometimes, it seems the police are timeless. From movies and television to everyday life, a police presence looms over most conflict. An argument over dinner. A drive through the city. An unanswered phone call. The police can show up at any moment.

Today, this is particularly true for Black Americans, for whom the suspense of policing is constant. Too often, the argument over dinner devolves into a 9-1-1 call from next door. The drive through the city leads to blue-and-red lights in the rearview mirror. The unanswered phone call ends with a door rammed open. Some of us are watched by the police. Others are chased.

The 2020 protests over the murder of George Floyd captivated America. Despite sweeping lockdowns and a global pandemic, millions poured into the streets. It was a moment of taking sides. "Black Lives Matter." "Blue Lives Matter." "No police." "More police." Was policing canceled? Or was it about to be reformed? Change was in the air. But America's focus on an age-old institution was on its present, not its past. So amidst fragmented news coverage of police unions, militarization, and systemic racism, many Americans remained hazy on the details of what cops had been doing all along.

In this book you will find a new framing of the history of American policing, as we tether a story that begins in the fields of Ireland and the plantations of Barbados, courses along the cobblestone paths of Charleston, South Carolina, and London, England, flows through the heart of New York City, and bleeds into the present day. This book isn't policing PR, which is much of what the public gets, and it's not just another call for reform. It's a message from behind the blue wall, but we're not cops.[*]

From early 2016 until late 2022, the two of us rose to become senior investigators at the Civilian Complaint Review Board (CCRB), the independent New York City agency of civilians who investigate allegations of misconduct by members of the New York Police Department (NYPD). In the depths of this strange government agency, it was our job to police the police. Mac left the CCRB on good terms in late 2022, and went on to become Executive Director of a similar police oversight agency in Oakland, California.[†] Greg remained at the CCRB until early 2025.

---

[*] As per London Business School, the blue wall of silence "refers to police officers' well-documented refusal to speak out against their own. From procedural errors, to serious crimes, officers will almost never report a colleague's misconduct. In the court room, officers rarely testify against each other, often going so far as to perjure themselves by feigning ignorance." The blue wall is the main reason the public remains in the dark about modern policing, as according to *USA Today*: "Around the country, police departments hunt down and silence internal whistleblowers to cover up misconduct with impunity. They've been fired, jailed and, in at least one case, forcibly admitted to a psychiatric ward." "The blue wall" is a separate concept from "the thin blue line."

[†] This book will not cover Mac's time as Executive Director of Oakland's Community Police Review Agency. Many of the records that were published in New York following the 2020 repeal of Civil Rights Law 50-a would still be considered confidential had they been generated in California. As of 2025, disclosures of law enforcement

The CCRB has been around in various forms since 1953. Until 1993, it was an official department within the NYPD. And although in that year Mayor David Dinkins and the City Council transformed the CCRB into an independent agency, it was effectively toothless until 2012, when it was first empowered to conduct administrative prosecutions. It is the largest civilian-run police-oversight agency in the United States, if not the world. The two of us joined before the widespread use of body-worn cameras (BWCs), when the best evidence still came from old handheld audio recorders and grainy surveillance footage. Our database looked like it predated the Reagan administration, and case files in thick manila folders were piled on every investigator's desk.

In New York City, from 2011 to 2019, there were on average about seven hundred and fifty arrests per day.[1] About half of those arrests were dismissed outright by district attorney's offices.[2] Of the cases that remained, roughly 95 percent were resolved before trial. Those cases, the arrests, and the stories within them were almost always sealed from public view. The simple truth was, and is, that most policing happens in the dark.

Still, there are illuminating moments. Complaints of NYPD misconduct still wound through the New York City bureaucracy, at times landing on our desks at the CCRB. A manila folder would open. An investigation would begin. The allegations ranged in severity—from discourteous language, stop-and-frisks, and bad arrests to sexual assaults, chokeholds, and homicides.

The CCRB wasn't, and isn't, a powerful institution. But it was a revelatory space—a policing observatory. In 2018, Professor Barry E. Friedman, Director of NYU School of Law's Policing Project, told our staff that CCRB investigators are "the only ones who know what's happening on the ground, who see the front lines of

personnel records in California are strictly limited, and the punishment for unlawful disclosure is a misdemeanor.

policing." From this position, we learned to use the tools of detective work to scrutinize policing itself.*

That the CCRB was created by the NYPD was an irony not lost on us. Our research revealed that this police-oversight agency had inherited the same paramilitary structure that made the NYPD so difficult to reform. With each passing month, we came to better understand officers' exasperations with their bosses, the mayor, and the public. Police bureaucracy, it seemed, was built to grind down everyone at the bottom. This seemed as true for our fellow investigators as it was for the cops we investigated.

As the two of us learned the craft of investigations, police oversight was at the center of the American political dialogue. From Ferguson to Staten Island, to Donald Trump's speeches and Democratic Party debates, it seemed everyone had a take on the future of policing. And while debates raged, we spent nearly every day interviewing victims of police misconduct, around 80 percent of whom were Black or Latino men, and the officers accused of doing it.[3] To us, Americans' debates about policing seemed disconnected from what was happening before our eyes.

THERE'S A REASON THIS BOOK wasn't written sooner. The job of investigating police misconduct is exhausting and time-consuming. For those who really know their cases, who dedicate themselves to mastering the material, the job takes over their whole lives. Most CCRB investigators are between twenty-two and thirty years old and resign within two years of starting. They spend their downtime getting to know New York City, cultivating relationships, and trying

---

* In the NYPD, as with most police departments, police officers can be promoted to the rank of detective. Detectives are "cops" (a term for the profession) but not "police officers" (a term for the rank).

to keep a healthy distance between their personal and professional lives. The same cannot be said about the two of us.

We met during training in early 2016. At first, we seldom worked together. That May, we spent a few days observing the same trainings at the NYPD academy, but by and large, we had discrete introductions to the job on different ends of our sprawling Lower Manhattan office. Mac was constantly looking for other jobs, but because he had an excellent boss, he kept putting off leaving. Greg loved the job from the start. After a year, we were both promoted. As our workloads grew and our cases became more consequential, we would spend late nights in the office working overtime. It was the only way to keep up.

By day, the two of us began doing fieldwork together, traveling across the city to places few tourists ever visit, from Rikers Island and Brownsville to the projects of the South Bronx. With every trip came another wild story. We started to write these stories down.

With each passing year, around 30 percent of investigators left the agency. Burnout was high. Fresh new investigators would either quit or be hardened with experience. With time, the two of us entered the ranks of the tenured investigators we'd once most admired.

We'd spend evenings swapping our mentors' stories and pieces of advice before they were forgotten. We might impart that same advice in a training the next day. Over the years, we researched the history of the agency, parsed through archives, and read NYPD officers' memoirs. During a workday, one of us might hear a rumor about the sergeants' union, and that night, after overtime, we'd try to learn whether that rumor was true. All along, we kept our private pastime hidden from an office filled with professional investigators. It was a strange time.

Writing was therapeutic. Greg felt pressured into exonerating a shooting. We talked out every aspect of the case, then researched the history of NYPD shootings. Mac had a complaint submitted by a violent domestic abuser. The details of the case were deeply upsetting, and the only space to really process was after work.

Writing together helped us better understand why cops wall themselves off, why most are publicly silent about the impact their work has on them, and why only few write memoirs. At various times, it seemed we were doing all three. Our lives became a secret buddy-cop show within a secret buddy-cop show.

No person alone could have accomplished the task of managing a CCRB investigator's workload, getting better as an investigator every day, getting promoted early and often, carefully and independently documenting every aspect of their own professional life, dodging the suspicion of a team of deeply suspicious professional investigators, getting a book to publication, and living a relatively healthy life. We had to do it together.

Over the course of seven years, together we interviewed well over a thousand police officers, hundreds of victims of misconduct, and countless other witnesses, policymakers, journalists, jailers, and gatekeepers who make the criminal-justice system's gears turn. We sat with the families and friends of slain Black men and interviewed the officers who had pulled the trigger. We parsed through case files and interviewed incarcerated people upstate. We befriended officers' union representatives, quietly attended underground NYPD boxing matches, and sat with the prosecution at the disciplinary trial of Daniel Pantaleo, the officer who killed Eric Garner.

The policing we saw sprawled throughout the five boroughs, and sometimes across state lines. Victims came to us in moments of abject desperation, hoping we could help them or at least prevent what had happened to them from happening to anyone else. In the officers, we saw people acutely aware that their disciplinary system was unfair, tilted toward nepotism and privilege, and rarely consistent from case to case. They were being policed. We were the cop cops.

Every time a plane crashes, an investigation begins. Air-crash investigators come to the scene. The first thing they do is go through the wreckage to find the black box, which is built to withstand any crash. It contains flight data and audio recordings from the airplane's cockpit. But that data doesn't tell the whole story. Air-crash investigators also search for the probable causes of the crash, from corporate culture and training to daily operations and individual flight-crew behavior. Using this information, investigating "man, machine, environment," they seek to determine how and why a crash took place and recommend procedures to best prevent it from happening again.[4]

This process does not happen in policing. There is crash after crash—death after death—and the root causes are lost in the fray. In 2020, America had a referendum on policing where very few conversations revolved around what the average police officer actually does. And the people most impacted—the family members of the dead—had their solution-oriented voices drowned out by punditry. It's no surprise that little changed. In this book, we aim to illuminate the culture crisis that shapes American policing and dooms most reform to failure. This larger investigation frames our six proposals for reimagining policing—concrete steps to create a criminal-justice system deserving of the word "justice."

In different ways, policing exacts a devastating toll on both the members of overpoliced communities and the cops themselves. But police shootings are not the defining feature of today's crises. As Joo-Hyun Kang, then director of New York's Communities United for Police Reform, noted in 2020, "Egregious police killings are just the tip of the iceberg. It's the daily humiliation, the daily abuse of authority."

Our work often covered the less sensational part of policing, the cycle of abuse and humiliation. And this was possible because we had direct access to one of the world's largest archives of such incidents, a singular and exceptional resource. Provided with the tools and official authority of investigators, we were given a rare opportunity to observe policing in a more practical, more precise way. By meeting directly with everyone involved, we became aware of the mind-boggling police presence in Black and brown communities in a way that, as two white men, only this job could show us.

Our careers began by absorbing the day-to-day and then progressed to the shootings. America had it the other way around: the killings, then the day-to-day. But the killings were so alarming, so shocking and enraging, that they distracted virtually all attention from what everyday policing is like. Individual officers were blamed and in some cases punished, but as the next new tragedy waited in the wings, policing largely stayed the same.

A PROBLEM WITH BOOKS ABOUT policing is that they're primarily written by people from one of three groups: academics, journalists, and cops.

Academics typically write about policing through inaccessible, statistics-driven theses. They tend to live in the world of theory. Sometimes, their theories are profound, but they're rarely compelling to a general audience. To most Americans, academia is either boring, condescending, or both. Critically, academics in our field usually rely on data collected by police departments. On the inside, we found that policing data—crime statistics, use-of-force reports, stop-and-frisk logs, and more—was subject to the priorities of politicians, department higher-ups, and the officers themselves.[5] Because it's so easily manipulated, most data about policing is unscientific.

Journalists tend to write about policing with a focus on conflict, not theory. They live in the world of story. The problem is that they often rely on sources who are unreliable narrators. Note this *New York Times* headline from July 17, 2014:

Staten Island Man Dies After Police Try to Arrest Him

The *Times'* initial article reporting this incident is six sentences long, citing only unnamed police sources. It reads like a game of telephone happened: The police tell the *Times*, and the *Times* tells the public, that a man from Staten Island named Eric Garner died. The police tell the *Times*, and the *Times* tells the public, that the police were trying to arrest him. The police tell the *Times*, and the *Times* tells the public, that Garner had previously been arrested multiple times, most recently for selling cigarettes. The police tell the *Times*, and the *Times* tells the public, that Garner weighed more than three hundred pounds.[6]

The article does not state, as the *Times* and other news organizations would later report after the arrest drew more public scrutiny, that a police officer named Daniel Pantaleo put Eric Garner in a chokehold, that the incident was captured on video, and that Garner's last words were "I can't breathe."

Although the *Times* and other outlets would later more thoroughly cover the incident and its fallout, the *Times'* initial article illustrates an indelible snapshot of the public's first understanding of what happened before the bystander video came out or any investigation took place. Five years later, at Officer Pantaleo's CCRB trial, his defense painted its picture with the same incomplete set of points—as if echoing what might have been the police talking points that informed the *Times'* initial article—from Garner's arrest history to his weight.

Police departments have a monopoly on the flow of information related to crime. "If it bleeds, it leads," as the reporting mantra goes, and cops can tell you where to find blood faster than anyone in the modern American city. Reporters know that if you want to maintain access to police sources, you better not piss off the police. If cops disapprove of your reporting, you might lose your access, and a journalism career is only as good as your access. Simply put, police frequently frame the stories that journalists need. And too often, journalists are reliant on their police sources, don't know much about policing, or both.

Cops, unlike academics and journalists, traditionally write about policing based on personal experience. Their stories become new episodes of the proverbial American cop show. Any writing that severely critiques either their fellow officers or the institution of policing risks an abrupt end to that writer's personal and professional relationships. Consequently, almost everything cops write becomes propaganda, intentionally or not, perpetually legitimizing the institution of policing in the process. But from *Blue Blood* to *Blue on Blue*, cop books capture the ironies and tragedies of policing as if cops were mere observers or even victims, rather than people whose central responsibility was to put other people into cages.* And as these writers tend to cast themselves as heroes, they struggle to see how sometimes, their presence is not helpful, or is even destructive.

While a few cops write derring-do stories, the majority remain silent. Academics and journalists advocate for an array of police reforms, including a more compassionate style of law enforcement, the removal of police from schools, and the end of racial profiling. But most fail to offer practical steps to achieve their proposed reforms. Academics and journalists usually fail to consider the consequences of a society with less or no policing for the hundreds of

---

* The book *Blue Blood* was written by NYPD detective Edward Conlon while he was an active member of the NYPD and, as per CBS's attorneys, has absolutely no relationship to the popular series *Blue Bloods*.

thousands of real people currently working in law enforcement. In general, they view rank-and-file officers as opponents in the battle for reform rather than potential partners.

TRYING TO CONTEXTUALIZE OUR INVESTIGATIVE experiences, we pored through a wide body of research, from NAACP legal briefs to cops' memoirs to the histories of English colonialism and the American West.* We shared snippets with friends and colleagues. But we found mind-boggling disparities between what each already knew about policing. "Oh, everybody knows that policing is really about Catholics and Protestants. I don't know if you need to put that in," said a Latina woman in her thirties, to our bewilderment. "That's common knowledge," said a white man in his twenties, referring to the widespread manipulation of crime statistics. It seemed that baby boomers had rarely heard the adage that American police came from slave catchers, while younger progressives seemed to consider it settled history. Outside of law enforcement, only a few people we knew had heard of CompStat. And outside the world of policing, it seemed everyone had forgotten about Jack Maple. History that was indisputable to one person was a strange revelation to another. As we tracked the national discourse on policing, we could see this was true across the political spectrum: Americans were working with dramatically different information.

In this book, we could include only a fraction of our cases. It would take several volumes to retell them all. But each individual case pointed us toward the same fundamental conclusions. By combining our unique perspectives as police-misconduct investigators with a relevant history of policing, we hope to offer newfound

---

* It turns out American policing has a lot less to do with cowboys than we initially expected.

insight into what policing really looks like, what the problems are, a vision for a better future, and practical steps to get there.[*]

<hr>

* In her updated 2020 preface to *The New Jim Crow*, Michelle Alexander addresses a question she receives on a regular basis: Why the focus on Black men? Readers, she notes, were sometimes concerned that she'd downplayed the impact of mass incarceration on other populations. In response, Alexander writes that in her experience working for the ACLU, "the vast majority of those who contacted my office to report being stopped, frisked, searched, or brutalized by the police were black men." The same was true for us. The vast majority of victims in our cases were either Black men or Latino men of Afro-Caribbean heritage. But often, to portray a Black person being subjected to violence is to play into a larger and more complicated trope than violence itself. Depictions of violence against Black people evoke emotions that are political, generational, and sometimes distracting from the literal violence at hand. We invite the reader to see these incidents through the lens of humans treating humans poorly.

A Brief History

1829—The Metropolitan Police, the first modern police department, is established in London, England. Its founder, Sir Robert Peel, models London's department after the Royal Irish Constabulary, a quasi-military force that governs Ireland.

1845—The NYPD is founded in the image of London's Metropolitan Police.

1894—The Lexow Committee is the first major probe into police corruption in New York City.

1894—Reformer William Strong is elected mayor of New York City. He appoints Theodore Roosevelt as NYPD commissioner.

1895—Based on complaints from the public, Roosevelt punishes fifty-seven officers for alleged misconduct.

1895–1953—Several American cities attempt to create boards or commissions where civilians review complaints against local police. Nearly all these boards are dissolved when police unions and politicians push back.[7]

1953—Community leaders in New York City establish the first incarnation of the Civilian Complaint Review Board to receive complaints of NYPD misconduct. It is run by three NYPD Deputy Commissioners.[8] There is no civilian representation.

1964—An NYPD lieutenant shoots and kills James Powell, a Black teenager. Harlem riots.

1964—Martin Luther King Jr. travels to Harlem and calls for the establishment of a "Civilian Complaint Review Board," where civilians, not officers, review complaints against the NYPD.

1965—Mayor John Lindsay appoints four civilians to the CCRB, establishing a civilian majority.

1966—The NYPD officers' union, the Police Benevolent Association (PBA), campaigns to disband the CCRB. Their television campaign highlights that:

> Only the policeman stands between you and [the] threat of mounting violence. Your life can depend on his swift and decisive action. He must not feel doubt. He must not pause. Even for an instant. If he fears that positive action may be misinterpreted by non-professionals at the Civilian Review Board, it could mean your life.[9]

1966—Senator Robert Kennedy campaigns to save the CCRB. He describes the PBA's advertising campaign as "most dangerous."

1966—New Yorkers vote in a landslide to remove civilians from the Civilian Complaint Review Board. The city's police-oversight system is paralyzed indefinitely.

1971—NYPD detective Frank Serpico testifies to the Knapp Commission of widespread extortion, payoffs, and corruption. He tells the commission:

> We must create an atmosphere in which the dishonest officer fears the honest one and not the other way around . . . Police corruption cannot exist unless it is at least tolerated at higher levels in the department.[10]

1987—Mayor Ed Koch appoints six civilians to the CCRB board. However, the staff is still entirely composed of police department employees.[11]

1992—Mayor David Dinkins, the city's first Black mayor, proposes to separate the CCRB from the NYPD.

1992—In response, former US attorney and then mayoral candidate Rudy Giuliani is joined by ten thousand protesting police officers as they encircle City Hall. Officers chant the N-word, block traffic throughout Lower Manhattan, damage property, and drink openly as they demand Mayor Dinkins's resignation.

1993—Over the officers' protests, Mayor Dinkins and the city council pass Local Law 1, amending the city charter to formally separate the CCRB from the NYPD. This new CCRB is an independent city agency with thirteen board members—five appointed by the mayor, five by the city council, and three by the NYPD Commissioner. The CCRB staff investigates allegations of police misconduct and presents findings to panels of three board members who vote as to whether officers should be disciplined. When the board members find wrongdoing, a disciplinary recommendation is sent to the NYPD commissioner. According to New York State law, the only person who can discipline a police officer is the chief of their department. As of early 2025, this law remains in place.

1993—NYPD Officer Michael Dowd testifies to the Mollen Commission that, throughout the 1980s, he participated in a widespread system of extortion, payoffs, and corruption. He tells the Mollen Commission that he considered himself simultaneously an employee of international drug traffickers and of the NYPD. He admits to regularly looting the neighborhoods he policed, often at gunpoint, for his own benefit.

1993—The Mollen Commission concludes that the NYPD has "failed at every level" to uproot a culture of corruption and has instead tolerated misconduct and concealed lawlessness. The commission notes, "Today's corruption is characterized by brutality, theft, abuse of authority, and active police criminality."

1994—Rudy Giuliani is sworn in as mayor of New York. Although he cannot repeal Local Law 1, he lays the groundwork to hamstring the CCRB for the foreseeable future.

1997—In the 70th Precinct stationhouse, Police Officer Justin Volpe sodomizes a prisoner, Abner Louima, with a broken broom handle. NYPD Internal Affairs, finding Mr. Louima's allegation too outrageous to believe, closes his complaint without any investigation. Officer Volpe was ultimately prosecuted and sentenced to thirty years in federal prison.

1999—Four plainclothes NYPD officers assigned to the Street Crime Unit shoot at Amadou Diallo forty-one times, striking him with nineteen bullets. They later insist that they recognized his dark figure as that of a serial rapist (he was not). A bystander testifies that the officers shot without any warning. NYPD Internal Affairs exonerates the officers, and they are ultimately acquitted at trial.

2002—In response to demands for reform, the NYPD dissolves the Street Crime Unit, where plainclothes officers patrol low-income neighborhoods in unmarked vehicles. This unit is promptly replaced by Anti-Crime units, which have precisely the same responsibilities as Street Crime Unit officers. Calls for reform are deflected.

2009—In Oakland, California, Oscar Grant is pinned to the ground by a police officer on a train platform and shot point-blank in the back. Grant's final day is later portrayed in the movie *Fruitvale Station*, one of Hollywood's first attempts to frame such an incident from the victim's perspective.

2014—Eric Garner is killed by anti-crime officer Daniel Pantaleo, who places him in a tighter and tighter chokehold as Garner yells, "I can't breathe." Mayor Bill de Blasio condemns Officer Pantaleo's actions.

2014—In Ferguson, Missouri, protests over the killing of Michael Brown spill into the national spotlight.

2014—Two NYPD officers, Rafael Ramos and Wenjian Liu, are killed by a man who claimed to seek revenge for the killings of Michael Brown and Eric Garner. At Officer Ramos's funeral, thousands of officers turn their backs on Mayor de Blasio as he delivers a eulogy. Police advocates claim that the mayor personally inspired the shooter by condemning Officer Pantaleo. Internal emails later show that the mayor was deeply affected by these allegations. From that point on, he largely abandoned meaningful police reform.[12]

Part I

HOW TO INVESTIGATE POLICE MISCONDUCT

1

Training Day

If cop shows looked like the real criminal-justice system, the real-life version wouldn't be nearly as fucked up. But then again, I'd probably stop watching.

—CCRB MANAGER

On his first day as a police misconduct investigator, Greg dressed in a suit and tie, took the subway in from Queens, and walked to the entrance of 100 Church Street, a nondescript twenty-two-story building nestled in the shadow of the new World Trade Center. He passed through a revolving door and stood in line at the front desk. A security guard took his photo with a small camera and printed out a paper nametag. The security guard handed Greg the nametag, pointed to a set of turnstiles, and said, "Go to the tenth floor."

The CCRB office was an off-white labyrinth. The receptionist directed Greg to Human Resources. In a small room stuffed with files and a few old desktop computers, the HR specialist told Greg that if he made it for six months, he'd automatically join the union, at which point it would be very hard to get fired. He didn't explain what Greg could possibly be fired for, but this seemed like a positive development.

Shuffling through a sprawling maze of file cabinets and cubicles,* the HR specialist shepherded Greg across the tenth floor, pointing to different units: Mediation, Policy, and of course Investigations, which took up three-quarters of the office. He told Greg who gave the best pension tips and how to sign up for a health-care plan. He warmly introduced Greg to the directors of each unit and, after about ten minutes of small talk, dropped Greg off at an empty desk and waved goodbye. They never spoke again.

Greg's empty desk was surrounded by five more, each one crammed with paperwork and case files. As the HR specialist strode away, Greg's new manager and four investigators stood up in unison, walked over, and welcomed him to Squad 16.

Like every new investigator, Greg would start on the bottom rung as a Level I investigator. There were two other Level I investigators on Squad 16, one Level II investigator, and one Level III. Level II and III investigators handled the most serious cases. The Level II investigator was a year younger than Greg but had been on the job since graduating college. Paul, a Level III investigator, was Greg's assigned mentor.

At the CCRB, your mentor shaped the type of investigator you became—for better or for worse. This was especially important because being a CCRB investigator wasn't like being a detective. You didn't have a partner. You didn't get to spend years learning the craft before you were assigned a case. The cases came swiftly, and at the beginning, this work felt like being handed a scalpel and told to perform surgery on day one of medical school.

A good mentor like Paul taught you everything. How to interview. How to close a case. What made the union attorneys, or "reps," tick. Which cops were the worst. Who to avoid. Who to befriend. Who to be scared of. Who you needed to know. What the rules were, which ones mattered, and how to break them without getting

---

* Described by one visitor as "just like the office from *The Matrix*."

caught. But most important, Paul joked, where to get the best lunch. It seemed that there was a small group of people at the CCRB who went above and beyond, and Paul was proud to be one of them.

MAC STARTED AT THE CCRB about a month later. He barely had time to shake his new mentor's hand—"Welcome to Squad 4"— before being rushed beyond a locked door, down a long hallway, and into a big gray conference room. It was the first day of training.

Mac's nine new classmates, including Greg, were seated at a row of desks in the back. He sat down where a paper nameplate bore his name in marker.

The ten of us came from a wide range of backgrounds. We'd all gone to college. Three had graduated the previous year. There was the summer-camp counselor from Brooklyn. A firefighter from Colorado. A Berkeley Law graduate. A clerk at Whole Foods. A UN interpreter. All but two were in their early- to mid-twenties. Over the next two months, we'd be frequently told we were the most qualified class of investigators in the history of the CCRB.

Greg grew up in Queens. After college, he spent years booking and promoting underground concerts. He had held a handful of odd office jobs: a video producer at *Cosmopolitan*, an executive assistant at a pharmaceutical company, a professional matchmaker. But at twenty-six, what Greg really wanted was a stable job. So when a friend emailed him a note that their little-known City agency was hiring new investigators, he applied.

Mac had been studying policing for a long time. He was raised in Oakland, California, home to one of the country's most infamous police departments. Growing up, he worked for community activists who would regale him with stories of police violence. After college, he went to work for the governor of Colorado. When he arrived in New York, the job he moved for fell through at the last minute. But a friend knew a friend who worked at the CCRB, and although they were hiring, she said it wasn't worth applying. It was an entry-level job with a ton of work for bad pay. Mac took the job figuring he'd leave in a month or two.

For every one of the ten new investigators sitting in that conference room, this was a new career in a largely uncharted profession. We were all recruited on the premise that this job would be a springboard to something greater—law school, grad school, a better job at another city agency. Everyone was ready to leave from the moment they arrived.

Dennis, a higher-up, stood before us wearing a dapper gray suit and a car salesman's smile. He paced in front of us and boomed in a thick Brooklyn accent:

"Welcome to your first day of training! You're taking on a very important and totally thankless job. Welcome to public service. Down the road, you can come to my desk and we can think through your cases. But right now, I want to go over the basics, so you at least have something to tell your friends when they ask what you do."

First, we got the riot act. Anything and everything said within this office was a secret. Not just because Dennis told us, but because of New York State Civil Rights Law 50-a, which made it a misdemeanor to reveal the details of our work to the outside world.

Then, we got the motivational speech*:

This is an independent government agency. We're not part of the P.D., Mayor's Office, or City Council. That means we're gonna piss all of them off. We're here because sometimes cops fuck up and no one else holds them accountable. We investigate what we can, with the power we have. And when we conduct excellent investigations, we make officers explain what

---

* Over the years, this speech evolved in our minds. We received it in several different forms at different times and, later, even delivered versions of it in our own trainings. This was the heart of Dennis's speech.

they did and why they did it. This holds them accountable for their actions. And frankly, that's a very new idea.

As investigators, you're gonna see some ugly things. You're gonna see officers treat people in terrible ways. You will certainly see trauma, and you may see death. You're going to ask people to relive the worst days of their lives. And once you get settled in and have a little experience, you're gonna go to the bar, turn to the investigator next to you, and ask, "Will police misconduct ever end?"

We loved this speech. But Dennis only hinted at a point that would rarely be discussed at our office. Police misconduct was as much a regular feature of America's criminal-justice system as crime was a regular part of American city life. Stop-and-frisks, shootings, and chokeholds were normal by-products of policing. Although they weren't exactly standard practices, where there was policing, these things seemed to happen like clockwork. And where these things happened most, people were terrified of the police.

In their own way, officers seemed terrified, too. *Morale is low. The job is dead. Any traffic stop could be your last. Do whatever you have to do to make sure you go home to your wife and kids.* These were the hallmarks of a police union speech. Anyone who'd dabbled in police culture knew that this bleak worldview prevailed, but it didn't seem like an ideal way to live.

In the NYPD, officer suicides were a regular topic of conversation. In June 2019, three NYPD officers killed themselves in a 10-day period.[1] One of them, a deputy chief, shot himself in his squad car, outside the stationhouse where his retirement ceremony was to be held a month later.[2] Less discussed than suicide or PTSD was life expectancy.[3] A 2013 study found that an officer's life expectancy is on average 21.9 years shorter than the average American's.[4*] Beyond that, 40 percent of law enforcement families reported living through domestic violence.[5†] The public didn't know it, but American policing was in more than one crisis.

Dennis concluded, "Being a cop means crime never ends. They handle everyone's hell, all the time. So, when you're at the bar, asking your buddy if police misconduct will ever end, I hope you remember the cop asking the same thing about crime. Crime can go way down, but cops will still have to deal with what's left. And misconduct may go way down, but we're still gonna be the ones to deal with what's left. It all comes down to perspective."

Of the ten new investigators who sat there in early 2016, three would leave within six months. By June 2020, the two of us would be the last ones from our training class still working at the CCRB.

OVER OUR FIRST TWO MONTHS, as we began working our first cases and conducting our earliest interviews, we also twisted and turned through the information deluge called CCRB training. About half of these days were spent in the gray conference room, staring at PowerPoints and memorizing acronyms. "CTS" was the Complaint Tracking System, our main investigative database. On its home screen was a list of all your cases, the docket. "IAs" were Investigative Actions, how we documented every step. "FADO" stood for Force, Abuse of Authority, Discourtesy, and Offensive

---

* Another 2021 study found that law enforcement officers are 54 percent more likely to die by suicide than the general population.

† This study was conducted in the early 1990s, but according to the National Domestic Violence Hotline, "More recent statistics on specific rates of domestic violence within law enforcement families are unavailable. Regardless of the actual numbers, it is concerning that the rate is so high."

Language, the catchall for the categories of misconduct in our jurisdiction.

There were "POs," or police officers—about 23,400 of them. "D-Ts," or detectives—about 5,200 of them. "SGT" stood for sergeant—about 4,500. "L-T" stood for one of the 1,700 lieutenants. And in the upper echelons, there were about 355 "CPTs," or captains; 150 "D-Is," deputy inspectors; 125 inspectors; 120 deputy and assistant chiefs; and of course, the chiefs—about 15 of them. To the NYPD, they were all "MOS," members of service. But to us, they were all "officers."* More than thirty-five thousand officers in over six hundred commands, and we could end up with a case involving any one of them.

We quickly learned that there were more parts of the NYPD than there were cop shows on television. There were seventy-seven precincts. Most New Yorkers had heard of those, or at least knew which one they lived in. But they weren't numbered one through seventy-seven—so it might take years to memorize each one.

Within each precinct, day or night, there were at least two uniformed NYPD officers patrolling each of the city's three-hundred-plus "sectors."[6] Each pair of officers would drive in one "marked" car,† with the blue-and-white NYPD logo painted alongside the motto *Courtesy. Professionalism. Respect.*[7]‡ Normally, sector officers were either responding to 9-1-1 calls or circling their designated areas. Officers worked in three shifts, or "Tours." Tour 1 was from midnight to 8:00 a.m. Tour 2 from 8:00 a.m. to 4:00 p.m.

---

* "i.e., How many officers are in the NYPD? A little more than 35,000."

† "Marked" police cars had visible emergency lights and the Department seal or badge visible on the glossy exterior, "unmarked" were generally black or gray.

‡ In 2024, under the Adams administration, the Department changed the decal slogan to "Fighting Crime, Protecting The Public." Despite the decal change, the NYPD's official motto since 1872 has remained "Fidelis Ad Mortem," which translates from Latin to "Faithful unto Death."

Tour 3 from 4:00 p.m. to midnight.* There was one detective squad in almost every precinct stationhouse, usually on the second floor.

After that, there were hundreds of miscellaneous units that seemed to do a little bit of everything. There were narcotics bureaus, gang squads, robbery divisions, patrol boroughs, strategic-response units, an aviation unit, emergency service units, counterintelligence, anti-terror, housing, transit, auto larceny, a horse-mounted unit, a scuba unit. There was the barrier unit, an entire division dedicated to assembling barricades around the city. There were beekeeping specialists who handled hornets' nests with the dexterity of bomb squad technicians.

Then there was the Internal Affairs Bureau (IAB). Ostensibly, they too policed the police. But IAB had a spotty record when it came to police accountability.[8] For example, back in 1997, a nurse at a Coney Island hospital called IAB to report her belief that NYPD officers had sexually assaulted a patient named Abner Louima. The IAB officer ignored her complaint, failed to record her call, and did not log any record into the IAB database. We were told that after years of litigation, and after the officer who had indeed raped Louima with a broomstick was sent to prison, IAB was required to refer most civilian complaints to the CCRB. It seemed that every rule in this bureaucracy had a story behind it much like this one. Many evoked *1984*.

AS WE MEMORIZED NYPD RANKS, the shapes and colors of officers' shields, and the meanings behind each radio code, we were introduced to an unexpected reality: many of the officers we were

---

* The precise times are 11:35 p.m.–7:35 a.m., 7:35 a.m.–3:35 p.m., etc., but they're often rounded up to the nearest hour when discussed.

going to investigate neither looked nor dressed like the ones we'd seen on television. They operated in a world of their own.

According to the NYPD, "plainclothes" officers were first introduced to New York in 1898.⁹ They weren't undercover officers, a common misconception. They wore streetwear, but unlike undercovers, they openly carried guns and badges and didn't try to conceal that they were police officers. Theoretically, the element of surprise made plainclothes officers better suited to stop and prevent the most serious crimes, and over the course of the twentieth century, they were increasingly deployed as a sort of "brute force" style of crime fighting.¹⁰

The plainclothes officers we would investigate tended to drive in unmarked vehicles, usually common brands of silver or black sedans—always American made, always with heavily tinted windows. They generally wore baggy jeans and hooded sweatshirts with bulletproof vests pulled over. Sometimes their guns were tucked into their waistbands, evoking a Bruce Willis in *Die Hard* aesthetic. As recently as 2022, the NYPD did not disclose the number of plainclothes officers who were out on the street.¹¹ But by our rough approximation, there were about two thousand, or 5 to 6 percent of the Department, patrolling the streets from 2016 to 2024.

In our cases, plainclothes officers seemed to rarely call dispatch before jumping into action. They were also disproportionately responsible for stops, frisks, and shootings citywide.¹² Many commands deployed plainclothes officers: the Strategic Response Group, Gang Squad, Narcotics, Borough Anti-Crime, and more. But the most prominent plainclothes officers were assigned to Precinct Anti-Crime, the plainclothes units that worked out of local precincts.

From 2016 to 2020, we knew there were about six hundred Precinct Anti-Crime officers working throughout the city. And we knew where they weren't—it was rare to find an Anti-Crime unit patrolling a wealthy neighborhood. Most were deployed to Black and brown communities. The poorest ones—the South Bronx, East New York, and their surrounding neighborhoods. There, precincts seemed crammed with Anti-Crime units. Where there were housing projects, there was Anti-Crime. Where gun violence and drug trafficking were highest, there was Anti-Crime. They were the officers poised to pose for pictures with dope on the table.

Anti-Crime officers were a central source of complaints against the NYPD.[13] Whenever there was a stray curse, a racial slur, a car stop, a stop-and-frisk, or worse, a plainclothes Anti-Crime officer was a prime suspect. It seemed Anti-Crime officers fueled Black and brown communities' animosity toward the police, but other New Yorkers scarcely knew they existed.

Outside of training, one could often find us looking over our mentors' shoulders. Mac's mentor was Castor. Six feet tall, twenty-five, born in a Soviet satellite state, and very quiet, he was the kind of coworker who never came to happy hours and was happier for it. Another hawk for a good lunch spot, he spoke deliberately, like a young Mr. Rogers, and he worked late nights not for the good cause, but because overtime pay was 50 percent higher. Being an investigator was just a job to him, but he valued being good at it.

Oliver would be Mac's manager for several years. He decorated his cubicle as if to claim this office as equal parts workplace and dorm room, and despite having almost ten years under his belt, he still loved the job.

For his Squad 4 investigators, Oliver had one rule that governed all others: "Everyone makes mistakes. If you tell me your mistakes, we can fix them. But I can't protect you from what I don't know."

Mac wondered, protect me from what?

An investigation is rarely as simple as a step-by-step formula. With each piece of evidence, new considerations come into play. For clarity, we've distilled the CCRB process into three main phases: Complaint, Investigation, and Closure, with a few stories scattered in to illustrate the process in motion.

THE THREE PHASES OF THE CCRB PROCESS
Phase 1: The Complaint

Every case began with a complaint from a civilian. Civilians, colloquially known as CVs ("see-vees"), were categorized into complainants, witnesses, and victims. In 2018, 44 percent of our complaints
were referrals from IAB.[14] Most people had heard of IAB from cop
shows, so it made sense that that's where around half of our complaints were filed. By contrast, CCRB struggled with name recogni-
tion among everyday New Yorkers.[15]*

Complaints came to our agency in many shapes and forms.
Sometimes they were very detailed: Once, a large but delicate
book, bound by brown yarn, arrived in the mail. On the front page
was a handwritten title, "*Complaint.*" The investigator unraveled
the yarn to reveal an elaborate anime-style comic book, twenty
pages, all drawn in pen. Each panel, in incredible detail, depicted
the journey of an old man labeled "Me." The remaining text was
in Chinese. As the panels went on, he went from selling hot dogs
in Times Square to being framed for theft by a competing vendor
to being wrongfully arrested. The last panel showed him weeping
in an alley after he was released from jail. The back page included
an index of times and locations, along with the officers' names and
shield numbers.

Some complaints were mysteries:

<Email received, Sunday, January 16, 2016,
info@ccrb.nyc.gov>

---

* In 2007, the New York Civil Liberties Union described the CCRB as "largely
invisible in the communities that are most in need of its services," adding that "even
members of these communities who may have heard of the CCRB often have little
understanding of its function and operations." Although in recent years the CCRB
has received local and national attention, from 2019 to 2023, over 50 percent of
CCRB complaints were initially filed with IAB.

\<Subject: None\>
An officer attacked me.

Phase 2: The Investigation

DOCUMENTS

Once a complaint was on our desks, it was time to collect evidence.* If we had the time, date, and incident location, the next step was finding out which officers were involved. Sometimes, CVs had already identified the officers. But often, we began without a name or shield number and had to go through a byzantine process of elimination—one that often took many months, sorting through hundreds of documents—to narrow down a group of potential subject officers who might've been present.

In every NYPD precinct, supervisors used a digital database to schedule each officer's daily assignment: the Automated Roll Call System (ARCS). Given that we all worked for the City of New York, the NYPD could have granted the CCRB access to this database.[16] But as was so often the case, NYPD did not grant direct access. We would instead produce a stream of signed document requests, each functionally a subpoena, many of which the NYPD would ignore for months on end.† Procedure required that we send every request to either an unsympathetic IAB detective

---

* Cases were assigned to investigators on a rotating basis. Investigators would generally receive three cases at a time and usually would receive new batches every two or three weeks.

† A few months before the COVID pandemic, the CCRB digitized its case management system. But before that time, each document request had to be typed by an investigator on their computer, printed, hand-signed by the investigator, walked over to a specific bin for each squad, put into a pile of other requests awaiting their manager's review, reviewed by a manager, scanned into the manager's computer, and emailed to our NYPD liaison. If someone found a typo, or thought you missed something you should have included or were perhaps sending an even slightly too broad

or the potentially hostile officer from the Department Advocate's Office (DAO) who worked down the hall.

It could take many months for photocopied documents like ARCS to trickle back to our desks in untidy stacks. Sometimes they'd send us paperwork for a completely unrelated incident, and we'd have to wait a few more months for them to correct their mistake. This system led to delays in our investigations and sometimes sank cases altogether.*

Our efforts to obtain police documents were subject to what some younger investigators wryly called the Thin Blue Razor[†]: wherever there were two ways of doing something and one way would be simpler, faster, and better for the CCRB, the NYPD made us do the exact opposite.

Meanwhile, the NYPD would complain to the newspapers that the CCRB was taking too long to conduct its investigations. They'd sabotage police oversight from both ends: crying wolf in public and jamming us up behind the scenes.[‡]

SURVEILLANCE CAMERAS

NYPD documents didn't always help us identify a subject officer, so investigators also set their sights on tracking down video footage. While footage was rarely perfect, it offered more information than any written or verbal account. And although New York was covered

---

request, they'd often kick it back to you, and the process would start at square one again. Type. Print. Sign. In the bin. And on and on.

* The delays in our cases would inevitably hurt the lives and careers of individual NYPD officers. But to the policymakers at police headquarters, that was a sacrifice they were clearly willing to make.

† A riff on "Occam's razor."

‡ In later chapters, we will discuss why the agency was rarely able to speak out about this type of bureaucratic sabotage. [Hint: sometimes the Mayor's Office, NYPD, and CCRB all relied upon the same lawyers.]

in cameras, getting the footage was painstaking for an NYPD detective, let alone a CCRB investigator.

In 2016, most surveillance cameras we dealt with were closed-circuit, and the footage wasn't backed up in the cloud.[17] In a bodega with street-facing cameras, the footage might've been stored on an old computer, hidden in a crevice behind the front counter, or forgotten in a back room closet. And the footage was going to disappear. Soon. Almost all surveillance footage was overwritten after fourteen days, thirty tops. That turned every case into a race against the clock. If time ran out, your coveted surveillance footage was deleted forever.[*]

The NYPD had its own surveillance cameras, too. VIPER[†] and TARU cameras were mounted on poles and scattered across the city, concentrated near housing projects, "high-crime" areas, and landmarks like the Empire State Building and Times Square. Other NYPD cameras covered every precinct stationhouse. Most NYPD footage expired after thirty days. During one several-month period during our tenure, IAB waited thirty-one days to respond to every surveillance-footage request we knew of with a bold, handwritten "EXPIRED."

Spring 2017. Mac had a case with a young woman at the 6th Precinct stationhouse in Greenwich Village. She'd been roofied at a West Village nightclub, and when she asked the bouncers for help, they called the police because she wouldn't leave. An officer arrived and grabbed her by the shoulders to calm her down. In a hazy panic, she punched the officer in the mouth. More officers arrived, placed her under arrest, and transported her to the stationhouse.

---

[*] We found that, most times, the only person who had access to that fateful computer was the store manager. If the manager forgot the password, or was out of town, your footage was gone forever.

[†] Video Interactive Patrol Enhancement Response

She later alleged that at the front desk, while still in handcuffs, officers lifted her into the air and threw her to the ground. Mac requested surveillance footage—there were cameras all over the building, and he was certain some of them pointed at that desk. Thirty-one days later he received a notice from IAB: "THERE ARE NO CAMERAS." But when Mac walked into a CCRB interview room to question the arresting officer, he noticed the officer, a tall blonde woman, and her union attorney were cackling as they watched a video on her cell phone. Mac sensed that the video showed something he wasn't supposed to see.

Innocently, Mac asked, "Something funny?"

The officer explained that she had a video from the arrest. It was really funny.

"Cool! Can I see it?"

The officer turned to her union attorney. He wouldn't have let most investigators see what was on that phone, but for whatever reason, he shrugged and said, "Screw it."

The officer laughed and showed Mac her phone. She pressed Play.

Techno music blared over surveillance footage set inside the 6th Precinct stationhouse Juvenile Room, a place for detaining minors where the Department, ironically, was prohibited from recording. Based on the timestamp in the top-right corner, this camera had been recording just moments after the young woman had allegedly been beaten. Mac could still see the young woman standing shoulder to shoulder with the tall blonde arresting officer. Every four seconds, the young woman slapped the arresting officer in the face. Then the video skipped and started from the beginning, playing on a loop. Someone had turned the footage into a musical GIF.

The officer and the union attorney couldn't stop laughing.

Mac played it cool, but this was an egregious violation of his CV's privacy. The worst night of her life had become a stationhouse meme, caught on a camera that wasn't supposed to record. Moreover, IAB had told Mac that the camera didn't even exist.*

"Can I have a copy?"

To Mac's surprise, the officer emailed him the video without a second thought. After the interview, he reported the situation to his supervisor, whose boss called the chief of IAB, who said he was horrified and asked us to refer the case over to him. A month later, Mac learned that the arresting officer had faced discipline—but not for saving a copy of the recording and cutting it to a techno remix. Instead, IAB objected to her giving the recording to Mac. IAB exonerated the officer for the force shortly thereafter. With no surveillance footage of the stationhouse floor, all Mac had was conflicting testimony, so the woman's allegations were Unsubstantiated. The case was closed.

CELL PHONE FOOTAGE

Cell phone footage was generally useful, but it wasn't always as helpful as one might expect. On the plus side, unlike surveillance footage, cell footage usually had audio. Also, it was usually from a civilian's perspective, with the benefit of being recorded outside of the officer's direct control. But for every Eric Garner or Philando Castile, there were thousands of incidents where the cell phone footage was not so clear. Apparently, it's hard to prioritize cinematography over safety.

---

* Later, an IAB detective explained that they wrote "There are no cameras" because, although there were cameras that captured the incident, they weren't supposed to have been recording.

BODY-WORN CAMERA FOOTAGE

When we started in 2016, the NYPD barely used body-worn cameras, but everyone knew this was destined to change. In 2013, a federal judge had ordered the NYPD to start a pilot program.[18] In 2014, the NYPD started out by issuing BWCs to fifty-four officers, but that program was discontinued in 2016.[19] For us, each week brought a new rumor about the vaunted BWCs and how they might change our work forever. More on that later.

CIVILIAN INTERVIEWS

In all our cases, we needed to get at least one sworn statement from a civilian who'd been present.* During our years at CCRB, we met a wide range of people. Some were from other cities, states, or countries. Others had rarely left the neighborhoods where they grew up. Each interview was a singular experience, a delicate exploration of memory. Most people who walked into the CCRB had never recounted the entire incident from beginning to end, let alone provided adequate context. They hadn't been heard. So our job was to listen until they'd said all they could.

By listening—not interrogating—we aimed to absorb someone's story without traumatizing them again. We couldn't cut them off. We couldn't cast judgment. And while some CVs yelled, cried, or told half-truths, whatever happened, we had to shut up, listen, then ask more questions. An investigator's job is to judge the facts, not the people that shape them.

The last question was always "Is there anything I haven't asked you about that you'd like to add to the record?" If we'd covered all our

---

* Until 2022, the New York City Charter stated that the CCRB's findings and recommendations could not "be based solely upon an unsworn complaint or statement." Since then, the CCRB has been able to initiate its own investigations.

bases, we'd note the time, add, "This interview is now concluded," and turn off the recorder. We'd shake hands, hand them a business card with their case number scribbled on the back, and in all likelihood, we'd never see them again.

Most CVs came in to be interviewed at 100 Church Street, but sometimes we had to go to them.

Summer 2017. We found ourselves headed to Rikers Island for Greg's first shooting case. The CCRB handled shooting cases with considerable care, so it was something of an honor to get one. But at this point, all Greg had to go on was a letter his CV had written: two years before, an officer had shot him in the back.

Aside from his letter, the only thing we knew about this CV was that in 1996 he'd been sentenced to life in prison for murder. He was out on parole when he was shot by the police. Now, he was back in jail.

The road to Rikers Island began at the mostly unassuming intersection of Nineteenth Avenue and Hazen Street in north Queens. It could have been mistaken for any other intersection in Queens were it not for stout blue-and-white sign fastened to a brick foundation at the northwest corner, framed by a cluster of twisted elms and broad-leaved maples. The sign read: *Department of Correction. Rikers Island. Home of New York's Boldest.* We pulled up to what looked like a haggard elementary school portable. We got out of the car and stepped up to a window. Bulletproof glass. Below it, a metal tray slid toward us. We placed our driver's licenses and badges inside. The tray slid back out of sight. Behind the glass, a correction officer, a Black woman in her thirties, scrolled on a computer to confirm that we were authorized to enter. After a few minutes, she slid our IDs and badges back, along with a placard that granted us full access to the island. She gestured toward the bridge. "You're good."

We got back into the car and drove onto a long narrow bridge that hung low over the water like a highway on a Louisiana bayou.

From the bridge's muted peak, with the LaGuardia Airport runway just a few hundred yards to the right, planes roaring overhead, and the Manhattan skyline off to the left, the view was quite striking. Ahead of us were the brutalist concrete buildings of Rikers Island. We drove up to a security checkpoint, and the correction officer waved us through.

From there, we drove through what might have been a sprawling industrial park, if not for the razor wire. Greg's CV was housed in the medical unit. We didn't know why. Upon arrival, we gazed at the ruddy brick façade of the North Infirmary Command. It was built in 1932, the same year Rikers opened as a jail. Inside, security had us empty our pockets. We could each only bring a pen, a notepad, and an audio recorder.

After twenty minutes, a correction officer led us down a hallway into a small room divided in half by what looked like a bank teller's window. The correction officer closed the door behind him, leaving us inside. Where the bank teller might have sat was a man in his thirties wearing a tan jumpsuit and thick glasses.

We introduced ourselves.

He smiled. "It's very nice to meet you guys." He brandished a bulging manila folder and slid it through a narrow space at the bottom of the glass. It contained all the defense's documents: testimony from the officers, paperwork from the district attorney's office, depositions, partial witness statements—there were even parts of the IAB case file.

He told us that he remembered running into the street and being shot. One bullet in the back, one in the side, a final shot grazing his left arm. The officers said he had a gun. He denied it.

"Can you show me where on your back?"

Pushing away from the desk, his chair glided backward, and in one moment we realized that he wouldn't be standing up.

"I was paralyzed from the waist down," he said, lifting his shirt and twisting to point at a scar on the left side of his lower back. He remembered hitting the ground. An officer kicked him in the side to see if he was alive.

"Why did you shoot me?" he asked.

"Relax, buddy," said the officer.

He blacked out. Hours later, a doctor placed a metal object into his back, extracting a bullet fragment from his spine.

The man explained that we were his last resort. He was on parole for life. If found guilty of possession of a firearm, his parole would be revoked, and he'd likely spend the rest of his life in prison. He insisted that the officers planted the gun after they shot him, and he wanted us to prove it.

As we drove back into the free world, we had to ask ourselves: Was the man lying, or were we about to uncover a criminal conspiracy?

POLICE INTERVIEWS

After civilian interviews—interviews of complainants, victims, and witnesses—the officer interviews began. Thinking back to all the infamous police incidents we'd seen on the news, there was one common thread: We'd rarely, if ever, hear from the officers. We'd heard from the police chiefs, who held somber press conferences. We'd heard from the mothers of victims, who demanded justice. We'd heard from the heads of the police unions, who almost universally insisted that the officers' actions were justified. We'd heard from the news pundits, who liberally speculated as to what went wrong and what might happen next. But at the CCRB, it was our job to hear from the officers themselves.

At the NYPD academy, cops were told two conflicting stories about the CCRB.

Story One: CCRB investigators were a bunch of bumbling liberal arts kids, straight out of college, who knew nothing about real police work.

Story Two: The CCRB was a place to be feared and avoided because all it could do was hold a cop's career back.

We were the boogeymen. Cops had many reasons to avoid our interview rooms. Not least of all because, for about an hour, they were required to answer all of our questions as a term and condition of their employment.

Normally, we'd walk into an interview room, and on the other side of the table might sit an Anti-Crime officer and one of the twelve or so attorneys from the officers' union, the PBA. One was Stewie Russo, a white man in his fifties with slicked back hair and a booming Long Island accent.

Stewie would bark, "Well, if it isn't my two favorite garbagemen!"

"Good morning, Stew," Mac would say.

These moments were off the record, usually lasting a minute or two as we set up our equipment. An opportunity for everyone to read the room. Stewie would want to feel how tense we were. If the case was more serious or the evidence more damning, we were usually more reserved. The officer would be curious, too. The two of us would try to keep it loose.

"How you guys doing?" Greg would ask.

Stewie would bellow something like, "We're doing great," and slap the officer on the back. If the officer didn't chime in, something was off.

Most people get a little nervous when they do something for the first time. If that was it, Stewie would tell us, "Go easy on him, boys. We got a virgin! You're gonna pop his cherry!" He was always delighted to do the virgin routine when male officers were being interviewed for the first time. And around 90 percent of CCRB subject officers were men.[20]

Some people thought Stewie was a clown. He cracked jokes, slapped officers on the back, and launched into long soliloquies that had nothing to do with why we were there. But that's what made him a great attorney. In a fun house, you can't quite tell where you are. And whether it was Stewie's fun house affect or his smoke and mirrors misdirection, he was very good at calming officers down and getting them out of trouble.

In interviews together, Greg would play good cop, and Mac would play bad cop. In his own interviews, Greg almost always played good cop. Mac would switch back and forth, depending on the type of interview and his second-seat's preference. Every investigator had a different style.

Before going on the record, Mac might rest his hand on the audio recorder and say, "You remember this incident?"

The answer here could tell us a lot. And it wasn't always as simple as a "Yes" or "No." Some officers wanted to know if we even had proof the incident happened at all. Did we have video footage they didn't know about? Was the case as simple as a he said, she said? Who had we talked to? A surprise witness? Maybe we had no clue what really happened. Sometimes that was true. They weren't supposed to ask us, but if they did, we wouldn't tell them. They had to give us a statement first.

Do you remember this incident?

When an officer answered this question, it was all about tone. Would they give us their story? If they looked us in the eyes and replied, "Yeah, I remember," they were primed to give a clear statement on the record. If they shrugged, looked at Stewie, and said, "I don't recall," maybe we had another thing coming. In those moments, Stewie might jump in before the officer could reply.

"He wasn't there."

Sometimes, we had evidence that he was.

"No problem. Let's get that on the record," Greg would say.

Then, the interview would begin.

An officer interview began a little differently from a civilian interview. They were told they could be fired for providing a "False Official Statement" and were asked to read their memo books about the incident into the record. Then, as with a civilian interview, we asked the open-ended question: "From beginning to end, can you tell me what happened?"

Their side of the story was rarely as forceful or emotional as a civilian's account, and it was usually shorter. When they finished speaking, we'd stay quiet for a few awkward moments. Occasionally, just like in a civilian interview, the officer would cough up some new details to fill the silence. Then we'd start back at the beginning.

Chronologically, we'd have the officer walk us through the incident from their perspective, asking follow-up questions about each of the specifics they had provided.

The goal was to step into an officer's shoes. Each line of questioning followed the same two-step format: What happened, and why? When an officer said they did something, we needed to understand their experience precisely—how they moved, what they saw, heard, and felt. What was the reasoning behind each action? In a good interview, you didn't fight the officer. You became them. And when you became the officer, their actions started to make a lot more sense.*

While most officers were forthcoming, there were major obstacles. Namely their attorneys, who sat in on every interview, paid for and backed by the most powerful police unions in the world.

There was a rotating cast of about twenty-five union attorneys. About twelve for officers (PBA), four for detectives (DEA), four for sergeants (SBA), four for lieutenants (LBA), and one for a stray captain here or there (CEA).† Most of them were professional, but a few were memorably abrasive. And whenever you walked into an interview room, you didn't know which one you'd get.

Sometimes, it'd be obvious that counsel had advised their officer to provide empty answers to our questions. But if we were truly seeing from the officer's perspective, we could pick apart an absurd

---

* Unless, of course, they lied. At which point their actions didn't make any sense at all.

† EA stood for Endowment Association. BA stood for Benevolent Association.

explanation. It just wouldn't make sense. Other times, the officer would deny that they were even present. That's what evidence was for—proving whether an officer was there. Sometimes an officer would hit us with the all-too-familiar "I don't recall." Then it was time to figure out what they did recall.

When we asked the toughest questions, these interviews could feel like verbal combat. But we didn't only ask tough questions. We asked basic questions. Questions like "Can you tell me more about that?" and "Can you help me understand what you mean?" And for the two of us, we tried to show the officers that we were reasonable people, that we could be trusted to see the world from their perspective, or at least something close to it.

In their eyes, most people who gave officers a hard time knew nothing about policing. But CCRB investigators knew a lot more about policing than the average person. Namely, that under the law, police officers were allowed to do far more than we'd previously imagined, and that nobody seemed to know their own rights better than a cop. So when our questions showed an officer that we knew their rights, sometimes they started to open up. Most importantly, the interview wasn't the time to judge whether the officer was right or wrong, legally or morally speaking. It was a time to listen, ask the right questions, and try to piece together what happened.

FIELD WORK

Spring 2016. Mac's first day in the field. On a humid afternoon in Harlem, he walked south on Lexington Avenue toward 115th Street dressed, as he would soon be told, like a Mormon missionary. A woman had alleged that an officer shoved her against a fence and said, "Fuck you, lady." The cases were simpler then. He scanned the intersection for surveillance cameras. Nothing on the corner where the incident took place. He looked inside a MetroPCS store on the opposite corner. He saw that there were cameras inside, but they pointed straight down to the sidewalk. No good. He went to the next corner, El Barrio Deli Superette. Their camera was aimed directly at the fence in question, but the manager said it hadn't worked in years.

Next door was a nail salon, No. 1 Pretty Nails. Mac saw a camera out front. It might be good. Inside, the smell of rubbing alcohol and nail polish cleared his sinuses. A long row of women tended to toes. He asked one for the manager. She guided him to a back room, where the elderly manager sat behind a desk. Mac showed her his badge. He explained he was investigating an allegation of police misconduct for the City of New York, and he needed to see the surveillance system. She didn't know where it was. They walked back to the front room to ask if anyone else knew. A pedicurist pointed to the ceiling.

The manager found a ladder, which Mac wedged against the salon wall. He climbed toward the square-paneled ceiling, pushing open a panel and craning his head into the darkness. Four feet away, he could see the faint blinking lights of a long-forgotten computer. As he wiped the dust from the monitor, the computer lit up—it worked. The monitor displayed a live feed of the street outside. Mac inserted a USB flash drive and downloaded the video. Five minutes later, he clambered down, a thick dust coating his jacket sleeves. He was starting to love this job.

Fieldwork was much more than evidence extraction. It seemed the best way to truly understand a case was to stand at the center of the incident location. From there, an investigator could visualize each CV's statement in motion, as if the incident were unfolding all over again. Our incidents could happen anywhere. Even places where the public wasn't allowed. And although not every fieldwork adventure yielded evidence, sometimes we hit the jackpot.

Phase 3: Closure

There were four categories of misconduct in our jurisdiction: Force, Abuse of Authority, Discourtesy, and Offensive Language. There were also four possible outcomes of an investigation: "Unfounded" meant that whatever was alleged *did not* happen. Sometimes the CV was lying; other times, just mistaken. "Exonerated" meant that whatever was alleged *did* happen, but that the officers' actions were legal.* "Unsubstantiated" meant that we were *unable to determine* whether an officer took an action, or, if they did, whether it was legal.† "Substantiated" meant that we determined that the officer's actions *happened* and were *unlawful*, and the agency would recommend discipline.

So, after the civilians' interviews, evidence gathering, fieldwork, and yet more interviews, investigators would end the investigation by writing a closing report and submitting it to the CCRB's board. The board would either send our recommendations to the NYPD commissioner or, in the most egregious cases (about 25 percent of substantiations), forward the cases to the CCRB's Administrative Prosecution Unit.[21] In those cases, an officer would face an administrative trial inside NYPD headquarters. No matter the bureaucratic path, the commissioner could, and often would, ignore our recommendations altogether.[22] By law, the only person who could discipline a member of the NYPD was the NYPD commissioner. It had been that way since 1873.[23]

Discipline came in many forms. At minimum, an officer could receive a verbal warning. In extraordinary cases, they could be fired. But most times, officers were disciplined by having their vacation

---

* In late 2022, the CCRB changed this disposition title from "Exonerated" to "Within NYPD Guidelines."

† In late 2022, the CCRB changed this disposition title from "Unsubstantiated" to "Unable to Determine."

days docked.[24] As little as one hour of vacation, as many as thirty days.* It was strange to be part of a system where violence might be punished in such a seemingly trivial way. Choke a man out, and the family trip to Aruba gets canceled.

The PBA could argue that paid vacation days hold cash value, and that for an officer, each docked day was worth somewhere between $200 and $700. But officers could accrue more vacation by working overtime. In 2022, NYPD officers made $762 million in overtime between cash payments and vacation accruals.[25] So, although an officer might lose a vacation day because they cursed on camera or kicked a guy in the groin, all it took was working a seven-hour overtime shift, and it could be as if nothing ever happened. Family trip to Aruba's back on.

And how could an officer pick up a seven-hour overtime shift? All they had to do was make an arrest! Of course, it'd have to be right before their tour ended. But seven hours of paperwork later, voilà. A common adage we heard, which remains unverified, was that around 80 percent of arrests in New York City were made in the last two hours of an officer's shift, morning, noon, or night. The practice of arresting people to make money on overtime was a well-known formula, sometimes referred to as "collars for dollars."[26] Bleak? Yes. But it was a system of people responding to incentives.

Like most organizations, the NYPD revealed its priorities through its disciplinary decisions. From 2014 to 2018, IAB substantiated exactly zero allegations of racial profiling by any member of the department. There were at least 2,495 complaints. From 2010 to 2017, the CCRB gave the NYPD solid evidence that eighty-one

---

* In some rare cases, officers received more than thirty days. But usually, this happened when an officer was found to have committed more than one act of misconduct.

officers provided false official statements. Each false statement was a fireable offense, but IAB substantiated only two.[27*]

Early on, Paul would tell Greg that his job wasn't really about justice. It wasn't even about police accountability. The officers on the street were being punished for the policy decisions of the NYPD executives—"the brass"—the inspectors and chiefs who were making millions upon millions in taxpayer dollars. The brass didn't lose vacation days when their policies—arrest quotas, stop-and-frisk mandates—led to the death of yet another Black man. If anyone was going to take the blame, it would be the officer who pulled the trigger, not the people who put him there.

Instead of justice, Paul sought preservation. To him, our job was to preserve people's memories—to ensure that this sad moment in American policing, in American history, would never be forgotten. It seemed we were the only ones memorializing these incidents. And although our records were hidden from the public, one day, maybe, that just might change.

---

* "In 2019, New Yorkers voted to add False Official Statements to the CCRB's jurisdiction."

2

Exonerated

"I frisk civilians when I fear for my safety."

"And when do you fear for your safety?"

"All of the time."

—NYPD OFFICER DURING CCRB INTERVIEW

Spring 2016. Mac's second week on the job. He sat at his new desk reading chapter 6 of the Investigative Manual: "Drafting Allegations—Pleading Language and Applicable Patrol Guide Procedure." Ever since middle school, he'd wanted to work in Oakland's city government. But he suspected that New York would offer him a unique insight into the criminal-justice system.

Mac put down the manual, grabbed a blank piece of paper, and wrote, "Lessons for Oakland" at the top. Not yet knowing what those lessons were, he looked out over the open-office floor, eyeing the tops of heads bowed down toward computer monitors.

Under the Bloomberg administration from 2002 to 2013, the mayor had made it a point to create open-office floor plans, with bosses working at the center.[1] This layout was designed to show every employee that their supervisors were working as hard as they were. But in the de Blasio administration, executives rebuilt their offices, while the open floor plans remained. Bloomberg had intended to create a horizontal workplace for every city worker. But the new offices at the CCRB made it more like a panopticon, with the mid- and low-level workers on the open floor and executives watching them through the blinds on their glass-walled offices.*

"Investigator Muir," said a voice from over Mac's shoulder. He turned around and saw a manager with a harried look on their face.

"Come here. Right now."

Mac asked what was going on.

"Just grab a notepad and a pen and come with me."

The manager about-faced and began to walk away. Mac nabbed a pen and pad, dashing to catch up. They pushed past a heavy steel door, marched down a twisting hallway, and stopped in front of a white door with a small glass viewing panel. An interview room.

From outside Mac could see Meaghan, a tenured investigator with curly black hair, angular glasses, and a piercing gaze that disguised the fact that she was only in her late twenties. Next to her was an empty chair.

Across the table from Meaghan sat a corporate-looking attorney holding a bulging case file. Next to him was a young woman in equally formal attire. She spoke as if holding back tears.

"Go in and sit down," the manager said. "This will be a great experience."

As Mac cracked open the door, Meaghan shot him a glare as if to say, "What the fuck are you doing here?" Behind him, the manager shot them both a thumbs-up, turned around, and walked away. With a touch of exasperation, Meaghan motioned toward the empty seat next to her.

Just like that, he was in his first CCRB interview.

---

* Michael Bloomberg was New York's mayor 2002–2013, and Bill de Blasio 2014–2021.

"Also joining from the CCRB," said Meaghan, gesturing toward the audio recorder.

"Mac Muir. Investigator." This was the first time Mac had ever spoken his name into the record.

The young woman launched into her story. She was at home in her Bronx apartment at 5:30 a.m. when her pit bull, Spike, started barking at the front door. She walked to the door in her pajamas, cracking it open. All she could see were two NYPD officers. Spike slipped out through the crack, tail wagging. One officer instantly drew his gun from its holster, backing away nervously. Spike followed him, tail wagging. The officer took two steps down the stairwell behind him and pointed his gun at Spike's head. The officer's partner stood behind Spike, frozen in shock. The young woman yelled out, "He's friendly! He's friendly!" The officer pulled the trigger one time, a shot rang out, and Spike collapsed to the ground.

Blood pooled across the tiled landing. Everyone stared in disbelief. The young woman stumbled forward, yelling, "What did you do?" She collapsed on top of Spike's body, cradling him in her arms. Stunned neighbors poured into the hallway, and the officers slowly backed away.

Inside the CCRB interview room, the woman spoke softly. She thought of Spike as her child, but as more officers arrived on the scene, none of them apologized. Without explanation, they bundled Spike's body into a tarp and placed him into the trunk of a patrol car. A month later, when this interview occurred, she was still battling with the NYPD to recover Spike's ashes. Her attorney had given Meaghan a thumb drive with surveillance footage from the hallway. The video corroborated everything.

A section of our training was dedicated to dog shootings. We'd watched video after video of police officers shooting dogs. In each one, an officer would see a dog off leash, approach it with gun drawn, and fire if the dog didn't back away.

The takeaway? Shooting a dog was legal. *Very* legal.[2] At the time, the CCRB even categorized Spike's shooting as "Abuse of Authority—Property Damage," as if the officer had knocked over a lamp in someone's home.

The day after the interview, Spike's case was on the front page of the *New York Daily News* under the headline, "Why did he kill my dog? Quick-trigger cop shoots pet in botched call: lawsuit." On the *Daily News* website, a shortened version of the surveillance footage showed fragments of the incident but not the fatal shot itself.[3] The article noted the NYPD's full statement, "The incident is being reviewed by our Force Investigation Division and the findings will be subject to a firearms discharge review board."

In July 2015, a year after the high-profile killings of Michael Brown and Eric Garner, the NYPD founded the Force Investigation Division (FID).[4] It wasn't part of Internal Affairs, and it was marketed as an elite unit to conduct investigations into NYPD shootings and deaths in custody. The press covered FID like it was an extraordinary accountability mechanism. Investigators jokingly called the FID the exoneration machine. Not only did FID appear to be a rubber stamp for most shootings, but that unit was notorious for withholding critical evidence, like BWC footage, from the CCRB. In all our years at the agency, we had never heard of FID substantiating a single allegation. Not one. And it's hard to know whether they did because they rarely, if ever, publicly released the results of their investigations.

Around the office, it seemed that everyone assumed Spike's shooting would be exonerated. The Director of Investigations had played the video of Spike's demise during training as an example of a clear-cut case.

"It's simple. He's charging."

One classmate raised her hand. "He's wagging his tail! How is that charging?"

Confidently, the trainer replied, "It doesn't matter if he's wagging his tail. He's still charging."

"But how can you call that charging?" she asked. "He's just walking forward."

"Exactly! That's charging. Walking forward is charging."

"So if the dog moves toward him in any way, it's charging?"

Smiling, the trainer raised his hands as if to signal that the discussion was over.

"Yes. And it's a split-second decision. If the officer fears for his safety, that's it."

The class sat in stunned silence. Over the next few weeks, 156,000 people would sign an online petition for the officer's dismissal.

Meaghan faced a dilemma. Legally, the officer could only have shot Spike as a "last resort," and if Spike was "too dangerous to control" or "posed an imminent threat of physical injury." That wasn't what the video showed. It showed an officer getting spooked and shooting a friendly dog. But a few months later, when Meaghan interviewed the officer, he said he feared for his safety. Spike was dangerous, he said. Shooting Spike was his last resort.

Meaghan thought about it carefully. She could see that the video didn't match up with the officer's story. Over the coming months, she spent hours and hours writing and rewriting a summary of everything she'd learned, working with a team of lawyers to build an airtight legal analysis of the officer's actions. And to the surprise of many, they came to one conclusion: Substantiated.

Meaghan's analysis was presented to a standard panel of three CCRB board members. One from the mayor's office. One from the city council. And one from the NYPD. At first, the board was unanimous: Substantiated. But their recommended penalty was Formalized Training, the second-lowest discipline possible. The recommendation was delivered to NYPD headquarters.

Nine months later, the NYPD's Department Advocate's Office intervened, requesting that the CCRB board reconsider their decision. In this written request, DAO noted that the partner of the officer who shot Spike believed that Spike was a dangerous dog, which was credible because he "loves dogs and can usually sense the spirit of a dog."

DAO's reconsideration request acknowledged that Spike did not fit the legal definition of a dangerous dog. But they argued that there was no reason the officer who shot him should have known this. He was a cop, not a lawyer. How could he know a legal definition? Therefore, DAO reasoned, he should be exonerated.

Meanwhile, the Force Investigation Division had completed their investigation: Exonerated. They ruled that Spike's death was justified because he charged at the officer, just like the CCRB trainer had predicted. As far as we know, the results of their investigation were hidden from the public.

In August 2017, the CCRB board reviewed DAO's reconsideration request, reconvened, and voted again. This time, the vote was not unanimous. The mayoral and city council representatives still voted to give the officer the second-lowest discipline possible. The NYPD-appointed board member, however, voted to exonerate. Despite the NYPD appointee's change of heart, the final vote of 2–1 meant that the case was officially substantiated. The final CCRB recommendation was hand-delivered to NYPD headquarters, and nearly a year and a half after the incident occurred, it carried a single message on behalf of the civilian population of New York City: retrain that officer.

As mandated by New York State law, then NYPD Commissioner James O'Neill held the final word on whether the officer who shot Spike would be disciplined and retrained. The word was "No." O'Neill declined to impose any penalty.

In September 2017, the woman's lawsuit settled for $35,000.

Years later, we found out that the NYPD had retrained the officer who shot Spike. In fact, they'd retrained him a month after the incident. It appeared that they didn't tell anyone at the time. After all, they didn't have to.

FROM 2019 TO 2021, exonerations were the CCRB's most common disposition.[5] In New York, a car stop was legal if there was an air freshener dangling from the rearview mirror. That was "driving with an obstructed view."[6] A vehicle search was legal if officers smelled marijuana, or if someone reached into the glove box too quickly and officers suspected they had a gun. If someone refused to provide their driver's license, even for a brief moment, officers could legally wrench them from the car and arrest them for "obstruction of governmental administration." If they fought back, that was another charge, "resisting arrest." If there was an unusual bulge in someone's pocket, officers could hop out of their unmarked vehicle to conduct a stop-and-frisk.[7] In public housing, officers could legally stop anyone they wanted and ask why they were there.[8] If officers had "reasonable suspicion" that someone was hiding drugs, they could strip them naked in the stationhouse. If an officer feared "death or serious physical injury," they could shoot. And they were exclusively trained to shoot to kill.

Many of these rules were in the NYPD Patrol Guide, the two-thousand-plus-page "bible," as officers called it. More rules were in the New York State Penal Law. And other rules lay between the lines of state and federal court rulings over the twentieth and twenty-first centuries.

A perhaps-surprising feature of the CCRB, as with civilian oversight agencies in almost every American city, was that our cases weren't about right and wrong. They were simply about whether officers were following their own rules—whether their conduct was technically legal. We were trained to be referees, and for almost every CCRB allegation, from stop-and-frisks to strip searches and shootings, there were circumstances under which the officer's actions could be considered legal.

Often, the laws around policing had been written with worst-case scenarios in mind. "What if they have a gun?" "What if they try to run the officer over?" "What if a riot breaks out?" As a consequence, decades of law-making had given officers the power to treat every single interaction like it might end in a shoot-out. Combining this entrenched legal power with the modern doctrine of "proactive policing" meant that officers could force themselves into situations that caused them to fear for their safety. And when an officer fears for their safety, the law gives them a wide berth.

Nationwide, officers are trained to view the world through this lens of threat assessment. "I feared for my safety" is a common refrain in a CCRB interview, conveniently blending a subjective feeling with an objective legal justification. Even Daniel Pantaleo's attorney claimed that he choked Eric Garner because he feared that Garner would rise up and throw him through the glass window next to them. The officer who needlessly killed Philando Castile told a state investigator, "I thought I was gonna die," before shooting Castile dead in front of his girlfriend and daughter in the face of no apparent danger. He'd taken fifty-six hours of "fear-based training" prior to the shooting, in which officers were encouraged to shoot first and worry about liability and lawsuits later. In a 2023 investigation by the New Jersey Comptroller into the private police-training industry, one speaker's slide advised, "Be the calmest person in the room but have a plan to kill everyone."[9]

Of course, CCRB investigators had a naturally skewed perspective. As of December 2024, out of approximately 34,000 sworn NYPD officers, 37 percent had never been the subject of a CCRB complaint. About 71 percent of officers had two complaints or fewer.[10] We rarely had cases where officers talked someone off a ledge, rescued baby ducklings, or hosted ice cream socials. But we imagined that being repeatedly trained to view work through the lens of fear, always being told to expect something cataclysmic, must have changed officers' outlooks on the world around them. As an officer once told Greg, "You know a cop's been on the job for at least five years when they always sit in a restaurant with their back to the wall. Full view of all entrances and exits." It seemed that an officer's life vacillated between wielding immense power and managing fear that bordered on paranoia. As then NYPD detective Edward Conlon wrote in his memoir, "The fact of the matter is that most cops lead double lives of some kind, of high contrast if not outright contradiction."[11]

THE VAST MAJORITY OF CCRB cases did not attract press coverage. Over the years, Mac and Greg would both have cases that garnered media attention, but none of them got as far as gracing the cover of the *Daily News*. Spike's death was an example of a CCRB case in the public domain and had the force of public outrage propelling it forward. But the stories we knew best played out in private.

On the other end of the media spectrum was a type of case so common that one or two could be found on almost any investigator's docket.

Imagine you're at home, asleep in your bed. It's about 6:00 a.m. If you have children, they're asleep in their beds, too, or maybe they're getting ready for school. Suddenly, you awake to a loud *BANG*! Your front door flies open, shattered by a battering ram. Eight police officers rush through the front door. They're wearing bulletproof vests. Some have assault rifles. Some have ballistic shields.

"NYPD! Get the fuck on the ground!"

Officers burst into your son's bedroom. One points his assault rifle at the bed and screams, "NYPD! Get the fuck on the ground!"

Officers burst into your daughter's bedroom. Another points his assault rifle at the bed and yells, "NYPD! Get the fuck on the ground!"

Yet more officers step into your bedroom and call, "NYPD! Get the fuck on the ground!"

You hit the ground, lying on your stomach. The officers stand you up. If you're not dressed, they watch you dress. The officers take you and your handcuffed children to the living room. They sit you down on the couch. If you ask any questions, you get no answers. You listen to the sound of officers flipping your mattress over. You hear glasses crashing, furniture tumbling. They upturn the entire house, and you have no idea what they're looking for. You wonder about your family heirlooms.

"Sarge!" an officer yells for their supervisor from your son's bedroom. A few minutes later, the sergeant stands in front of you holding a half-smoked marijuana cigarette. "So, whose is this?" Your son says it's his. You're lucky because, if he hadn't, there's a chance everyone else would have been arrested, too.

Officers escort your son outside, stepping over any debris that's been strewn across the living room. He'll be issued a summons at the stationhouse. The sergeant tells you that it's a crime to have drugs in the house with a minor around. He may have to call child services. They may take your son away.

You ask to see a warrant. The sergeant shows you a piece of paper. It has your name and address typed above a judge's signature. It says that someone reported there were guns and narcotics in your son's bedroom. The officers continue searching through your belongings, but they don't find guns or other narcotics. They uncuff you and your family, tell you to pick your son up at the stationhouse, and begin to leave.

The house is torn to pieces, as if a tornado had blown through. You ask the sergeant what you're supposed to do. He replies that your only option is to sue the city. He leaves. It's 8:00 a.m.

This incident would have been exonerated from start to finish. Officers are *supposed* to break down the door when they execute a search warrant. They're *supposed* to point their guns and tell everyone to get on the ground. They're *supposed* to watch you dress. They're often instructed to search everywhere, inside of everything, turning your house upside down in the process. And they're certainly allowed to curse during a "stressful situation."[12] And whether or not they find any contraband, your only obvious recourse is suing the city, a convoluted and time-consuming journey upon which many are reluctant to embark.

Search warrant cases were the bread and butter of a CCRB investigator's docket. The Fourth Amendment of the US Constitution prohibits the government from engaging in "unreasonable searches and seizures." This means that the government, police officers included, is not allowed in private homes—under most circumstances. A search warrant allows police officers to legally break into someone's home to search for evidence of a crime. An NYPD officer can obtain a search warrant using a simple five-step formula.*

Step 1: Find a confidential informant (CI). This could be practically anyone.

Step 2: Get the CI to tell you where to find guns or drugs. Offer something if they help you—cash payments, leniency in other arrests, whatever works.

Step 3: Submit sworn statement in criminal court saying the CI told you where guns or drugs are.

Step 4: A judge reviews the sworn statement and approves the search warrant, required to be executed within ten days.[13]

Step 5: Gather officers, break into location, seize guns or drugs, make arrests.

It was a reliable formula.

In 2020 alone, the NYPD executed more than 1,800 "no-knock" search warrants. Although officers found 792 firearms and 667 "quantities of drugs," the search warrant story was prettier on

---

* There were many paths to probable cause and a judge-signed warrant. But this was the road most traveled.

paper than in practice.[15] Around our office, tenured investigators swapped stories of the cover-your-ass desperation that embodied their search warrant cases. Officers would break down the door, and if they didn't immediately find what they were looking for, they would scramble for anything, *anything*, that could lead to "positive results," even if it had no relationship to what they'd been searching for in the first place.

A joint in your bedside table? Positive results.

Kept your expired credit cards filed away? That could be evidence of criminal possession of a forged instrument. Positive results.

Prescribed methadone?* That could be evidence of possession of narcotics. Positive results.

In fall 2016, about six months into his tenure, Greg sat in on a CV interview with a tall, thin man in his fifties. He'd struggled to find a stable home but finally found one in the basement of a two-story building in Jamaica, Queens. Early one morning, officers broke down his front door. They were there to search for cocaine, as their search warrant specified.

They handcuffed the man on his bedroom floor. An officer said, "Is there anything I should know about?" There wasn't any cocaine. But the man told the officer that he had a little weed buried at the bottom of an ashtray. He didn't think it was a big deal. The officers took him to the stationhouse and placed him into a cell. After a short while, he was charged with criminal possession of marijuana and released with a summons to appear in court. He had no idea why officers had broken into his home.

Over the next few weeks, Greg learned the search warrant had targeted a previous tenant who'd moved out the month before. To the CCRB, that didn't matter. A judge signed the search warrant.

---

* Methadone is a synthetic prescription drug used to treat morphine and heroin addiction.

A judge said there was probable cause to break into the apartment. And it didn't matter if the search warrant was based off bad information. To the CCRB, that was the judge's problem. And the officers? They were just following the judge's orders. In the end, the NYPD had another successful search warrant with "positive results."

The man called and withdrew his complaint because he didn't want his statement used against him in court. The case was closed as "Complaint Withdrawn."

A few months after the man withdrew his complaint, the lead investigator was working at his desk. Greg sat nearby, watching as a manager walked over and told him that the man who'd withdrawn his complaint was dead. He'd jumped off a building in Lower Manhattan, not far from our office.

"You know it's not your fault," said the manager.

"I know," whispered the investigator.

He turned back to his desk and put his head in his hands.

Eyes welling with tears, he looked up and saw Greg.

"Did I do anything wrong?" he mouthed.

Greg shook his head.

The investigator rested his forehead on his desk, sighed deeply, and stayed that way for a long time.

EARLY ON, when Mac was first meeting CCRB staff, he spoke with a tenured manager from another squad. He told her his plan for success: stay late every night. If he couldn't be better than his peers, he'd work harder.

"Oh no," she laughed, "You can't do that. You're only allowed to work thirty-five hours per week. No overtime for now."

That was fine, he replied. He would work whatever hours it took. He'd work without the extra pay.

"You're not understanding. It wouldn't be fair to the others if you got to work more than they did. If you work more hours, then how can we evaluate your work equally?"

On some level, what the old-timer said made sense. Everyone should be evaluated for their work on an even playing field. And on another, it foreshadowed a bleak reality. Our work, like policing itself, was a fun house of counterintuitive rules. Our jobs were to be public servants, but we were prohibited from going above and beyond.

If you wanted something from bureaucracy, one truth prevailed. It was always a matter of ease.

It was *easier* for an officer to make an arrest in the last two hours of their shift because overtime was easy money, and so many others did the same.

It was *easier* for IAB to randomly deny CCRB requests and let surveillance footage expire because there was no one to stop them from doing it because it meant less work.

It was *easier* for the NYPD to exonerate a dog's shooting and hide that they'd retrained the officer because admitting guilt would have meant the extra work of disciplining the officer and may have risked causing the woman's lawsuit to settle for much more than $35,000.

It was *easier* for the NYPD to announce, "There's an open investigation," because then they didn't have to explain what happened, and the press rarely followed up.

It was *easier* for officers to say they feared for their safety and to train them to fear for their safety in every possible moment because the term "I feared for my safety" was so often the perfect legal defense.

And almost always, it was *easier* to have a series of temporary solutions, even if they were expensive and inhumane, than to fix a complex, broken system.

Understanding ease was key to understanding a bureaucracy's incentives. Because in a bureaucracy, incentives don't simply tell people what to do. They tell people, especially people under pressure, to do what's easy.

In early 2019, a friend connected Mac with a former NYPD officer who'd left the job to work in police oversight. Describing his time working in the South Bronx, he said that a central problem in policing was that there were a million ways to have quotas without calling them quotas. Sergeants and lieutenants could demand "activity," and officers generally knew that if you didn't have an arrest every three months or so, you could find yourself on the path to getting fired.

As an officer, if he didn't bump into anyone to arrest, he had to be on the lookout. He needed to arrest *someone* every once in a while. And who was he going to arrest in the South Bronx? It wasn't going to be a white kid in a fancy car. That could be an important person's kid. And that important person might call their city councilperson, who might call the precinct, which might lead to him, the arresting officer, getting screamed at by his sergeant, or even the precinct commander. Arresting the wrong person could be a huge headache.

So, when officers looked for someone to arrest, they were all incentivized to look for someone who would cause the least friction. Someone who would make it *easy*. In the South Bronx, that meant finding someone who looked like they didn't know people, who perhaps looked like they didn't know how to hire an attorney. It meant arresting people who were poor. And in the South Bronx, the poor people were Black and brown. He hated this system. It's what led him to quit. But he knew that every single day, all across the city, the same set of incentives were leading thousands of officers to disproportionately police Black people.

It was easier that way, and so long as officers were pressured to summons and arrest a minimum number of people, it seemed like the system was pointing them in the direction of the most vulnerable: people of color, people who were poor, and people experiencing mental illness. Firing individual bad officers was a good idea, he said, but until the underlying incentives changed, the gears would continue to turn as they always had.

Back at his desk, Mac looked down at his paper titled "Lessons for Oakland."

Lesson #1: Officers are allowed to do far more than the public knows.

Suddenly remembering a prescient piece of advice he'd received years before, he jotted down another.

Lesson #2: Remember the golden formula of bureaucracy:
It's easier to say "No" than to say "Yes."
By default, a bureaucracy says "No."
If you make it easier to say "Yes" than "No," then the bureaucracy says "Yes."
Bureaucracy is a matter of *ease*.

That second lesson would stand the test of time.

3

Discourtesies and Offensive Language

You know, Officer, these two investigators are not total
pieces of shit. They merely sit in a valley of shit, surrounded
by mountains of shit on all sides.

—PBA ATTORNEY

Sometimes, I feel like we're just the word police.

—CCRB BOARD MEMBER

There's a concept in government called Regulatory Capture,
which happens when an agency charged with acting in
the public interest instead acts in ways that benefit the
industry it is supposed to be scrutinizing.[1]

However, when one group regulates the behavior of another
group, the regulators are usually less powerful, personally and politically. Over time, the regulators tend to mimic the behavior of the
people they're observing. It makes them feel more powerful.

This leads to a subcategory of Regulatory Capture called "cogni-
tive" or "cultural" capture.[2] It's the phenomenon of a regulated entity
having a powerful psychological impact on its regulators. As a study
from the *Harvard Journal of Law and Public Policy* put it, "This idea

emphasizes interest-group capture of the administrative process through the creeping colonization of ideas. Thus, an industry can somehow convince regulators to think like it."[3] At the CCRB, we had to step into our officers' shoes to do our jobs well. But for some employees, this exercise bled into the office, where simple interactions devolved into petty displays of dominance.

In summer 2017, three years to the day since Officer Darren Wilson killed Michael Brown in Ferguson, one of the CCRB's few Black investigators sat at his desk. He didn't have any interviews scheduled. He wasn't going to be meeting with the public that day. So, he attached a small black-and-white pin to the left side of his shirt that read, *Black Lives Matter*. He walked into the kitchen to make coffee.

"Good morning," said the investigator, waving to a higher-up, a white man.

The higher-up stopped in his tracks, stared at the pin, then walked past without a word. A few minutes later, the investigator was summoned into an interview room. He was told to take the pin off, so he did.

Not long after, Mac watched a manager call out to an investigator. "You have a new case."

The investigator wore headphones, so he couldn't hear. In full view of his colleagues, the manager walked over to the investigator's desk, placed the new case file on the investigator's head, and tipped it over. The file and its contents spilled onto the investigator's lap. He froze, gathered the loose papers, and quietly reviewed his new case.

There were the men at the CCRB, and everyone knew who they were, who'd earned reputations as serial harassers. "If they come to our desks, we just have to ignore them," more than a few women told us.

"Why don't they fire him?" Mac asked about the most notorious of the bunch.

A veteran investigator laughed. "Everyone knows if you sue the city enough, gain enough civil service titles, you become *unfireable*."

That was strange, Mac thought, because "unfireable" was a word usually reserved for the police.

With every new class of investigators, we watched as they too learned these bleak lessons. We'd see a Muslim investigator assigned to a manager who everyone knew held anti-Islamic views. We'd see young women assigned to a manager who was under investigation for sexual harassment. We'd see Black men have their impartiality questioned at every turn.

"Are you sure, given your experiences, that you can be impartial?"

Within a few years, many of them would leave with bitter tastes in their mouths, replaced with a new class of hopeful trainees who were searching for something called "police accountability."

"WHEN YOU ALL GOT HIRED, you knew you were gonna investigate racial slurs," a manager in her thirties told her squad, "and if you're not willing to say them to an officer's face, I don't know why you're even here."

As new investigators acclimated to their strange workplace, many wondered, how do we investigate an officer for allegedly using offensive language?

First, we had to define "offensive language." The NYPD Patrol Guide defined it as "discourteous or disrespectful remarks regarding another person's ethnicity, race, religion, gender, gender identity/ expression, sexual orientation, or disability."[4]

After identifying the accused officer, we had to directly ask them if they said the phrase. And if we didn't say the slur out loud, the threat of discipline loomed.

This made for a uniquely uncomfortable experience.

In spring 2018, a white officer allegedly barraged a subway rider with a series of slurs. A few months later, Mac leaned toward his partner, a Black male officer, and asked, "For the record, did your partner call Mr. Higgins a 'fucking fairy fa—t'?"

The officer froze. His attorney glanced over with a raised eyebrow, as if wondering what he'd say next.

"No. No. No."

The interview went on as normal, but when Mac stood up to leave, the officer blurted out, "Investigator, Jerry wouldn't say those things."

His lips quivered.

"I mean, Jerry might be a weird guy. He's older, yeah. He still lives with his mom. Some people might take him the wrong way . . ."

The officer's eyes misted over.

"But Jerry, Jerry would never talk to someone like that."

A tear ran down his face, and he looked at Mac with what felt like real anguish.

"Jerry's a good guy. He wouldn't do that."

The officer lowered his head, and his attorney placed a consoling hand on his shoulder.

"Have a good one," said the attorney.

"You, too, guys," said Mac. He walked out of the room.

Eventually, the allegation was closed as Unsubstantiated. There was just no way to know.

SOMETIMES AN OFFICER'S FOUL LANGUAGE could be a precursor to something more. In 2003, a Queens man told the CCRB that Police Officer Robert Smith called him a "crack baby," and a "fucking n—r." In 2010, another man complained that Smith told him, "Get the fuck out of here, n—r." In both 2003 and 2010, the civilians withdrew their complaints, and the cases were closed without investigation.[5]

The pattern would continue. In 2011, a Queens woman called 9-1-1 to report a sexual assault. Officers responded, including Officer Smith. The woman asked Smith for his supervisor's phone number, but he wouldn't give it to her. "That motherfucking bitch," Smith was overheard saying, "I don't know who she thinks she is." In this case, the CCRB obtained a sworn statement from the woman, and proceeded with a full investigation. In 2013, based on corroborating statements, an investigator substantiated one allegation against Officer Smith: "Offensive Language—Gender." The CCRB board recommended "Charges and Specifications," meaning that Smith would face a disciplinary trial. If found guilty, he might've been suspended, or even fired.

In 2014, while Smith was awaiting his disciplinary trial, another man filed a complaint. He alleged that while he'd been driving in Queens, Officer Smith had pulled alongside him and allegedly said, "How are you doing? You look like you're sitting on a cock. Go suck a cock. You are an animal. You are a dog. And a monkey." Without concrete evidence, the CCRB unsubstantiated these allegations.

But in 2016, before any disciplinary trial took place, Commissioner William Bratton wrote the CCRB a letter. He was retaining Smith's case "in the interests of justice," and imposing a discipline of his own choosing: "Formalized Training."

After his retirement in 2020, Smith wrote in a text message, "Bro I point my gun out the window now at nighers [sic] and watch their reaction and drive away. Hilarious." In a text to another former officer, he wrote, "I want to see mass nypd suicide and deaths. Those fake bitches." In another communication, he wrote, "Now the real [S]mith will shine. I even shaved my head. Klan."[6] By 2022, Officer Smith was in federal prison after pleading guilty to bribery and drug-transportation charges.[7] He is due to be released in 2025.

Smith's story shows how a lack of accountability emboldened one officer's racism, sexism, and willingness to break the law. But it also reflects an ongoing policy—in the NYPD, the vast majority of officers who use Discourtesies and Offensive Language remain employed, retiring with little fanfare.

Take Sergeant Lesly Charles, for example. "I'll take my gun and put it up your ass and then I'll call your mother afterwards . . . Your pretty face—I like it very much. My dick will go in your mouth and come out your ear. Don't fuck with me. All right?"

In 2012, Sergeant Charles was caught on tape during this unforgettable tirade.[8] Disgraced in the press, he faced the prospect of an administrative trial, where a CCRB prosecutor was scheduled to interrogate him on the witness stand.* But Sergeant Charles took a plea deal, agreeing to forfeit ten vacation days.[9] Shortly thereafter, the NYPD transferred him to IAB. As of 2025, he was still there, serving as a supervisor.[10]

OCCASIONALLY, THE COARSE LANGUAGE bled from our evidence to our interview rooms.

Summer 2021. Two investigators, both women in their early twenties, interviewed a Latino officer over Microsoft Teams. They were still working remotely because of COVID.

"And then I looked at the guy," the officer recounted, "and I said, 'What the fuck? Shut the fuck up.'"

The investigators stared at their screens.

"Dude, if you're gonna do that," he continued, "wait for us to fucking leave. What's the matter with you?"

"And then what happened?" asked one investigator.

"I told them to go to housing court, or some neighbor bullshit."

His union attorney piped up. "Now when you said, 'fuck,' how many years have you been on the force? Where are you from?"

"I'm from Queens," said the officer.

---

* The CCRB's administrative trials have, as far as we know, always been open to the public. These trials offered glimpses into the underworld of CCRB investigations, including public presentation of case evidence, but it was a rare occasion when a member of the press showed up.

The attorney looked directly into the camera and smiled. "He's a product of his environment."

When the interview was complete, everyone's webcams were still on.

"Have a nice day," said an investigator.

"Okay, bye," said the officer.

Thinking the call had been disconnected, the officer turned to his attorney.

"*Cunts . . . Fuck* this."

The officer glanced back at the computer. Realizing that the two stunned investigators hadn't yet hung up, he laughed.

"I love you guys," he said, pointing at the camera. "Have a good weekend."

He disconnected the call.

Shortly after the interview, the investigators asked the higher-ups what they could do about the officer calling them "cunts."

"Well," said one, with an air of finality. "You could file a CCRB complaint."

MOST INVESTIGATIVE POLICE-OVERSIGHT AGENCIES focus on holding officers accountable for breaking their own rules—the letter of the law.[11] But at the CCRB, there wasn't much law to differentiate between discourtesy and "talking like a New Yorker," so the agency seemed to make up the rules as it went.

Investigators once spent months debating whether an officer telling a family of tourists to "go back to Ohio" should be pleaded as a discourtesy, offensive language, or nothing at all. Board members spent years debating whether "bitch" was a discourtesy or offensive language, and they never seemed to settle on either. The agency also had an informal policy of letting off officers who mirrored a civilian's words.

In one case, a white lieutenant was trying to arrest a man in front of a bodega.

"Fuck you, n—a," said the man.

"Don't call me a n—a," replied the white lieutenant. Because the lieutenant was "mirroring," the CCRB never investigated this racial slur.

In contrast, once an officer was caught on audio consoling a young man after officers had burst into his home. "I'm really sorry, man," the officer said. "But you'll get through this shit." The CCRB substantiated a discourtesy allegation, and the officer faced discipline.

IT MIGHT SEEM INTUITIVE that police-oversight agencies focus on the law. If an officer does something unconstitutional, that's usually grounds for discipline. Further, most oversight agencies were molded by the minds of lawyers, who tend to view problems and their solutions through a legal lens. But with each investigation, we saw more clearly that the law provided too narrow a framework to improve policing.

According to a 2015 Yale Law School study in the *Journal of Criminal Law and Criminology*, most people don't care so much about the law when it comes to the police.[12] What they care about is *fairness*. The study polled citizens from fifteen major American cities, finding that when someone considered filing a complaint against the police, it was fairness, much more than lawfulness, that informed their decision to complain. Researchers also presented respondents with thirty-second videos of officers at work. The respondents were asked to evaluate each video. Again it was fairness, much more than lawfulness, that shaped their impressions of whether the officer had done right or wrong.

At the CCRB, CVs often came to us with only a faint idea of whether an officer's actions were legal, but they "just wanted to do the right thing" by filing a complaint. They believed an officer had done something *wrong*. But wrong could mean unlawful, unfair, unkind, or something else. The CCRB, however, concerned itself with legality and compliance with NYPD policy, whether or not it was fair.

As we progressed through the investigative ranks, the stakes of our cases rose. And while the racial slurs, broken bones, and deaths began to tally up, it seemed police oversight was designed to react to these incidents with only a cold calculation—lawful or unlawful—even if the public was searching for something more.

4

Abuse of Authority

Show me the man, and I'll show you the crime.

—CCRB MANAGER, QUOTING LAVRENTIY BERIA
(SOVIET MINISTER OF INTERNAL AFFAIRS)

In the United States, approximately 1 in 20 people live with severe mental illness.[1] This group represents around 5 percent of the total US population, but it is involved in one-tenth of all police service calls, occupies nearly one-fifth of the beds in jails and prisons, and constitutes one-fourth of the people killed by police.[2] The mentally ill are also disproportionately involved in CCRB investigations.[3] Most CCRB investigators were never trained to handle the medley of unique circumstances that came with serving people with severe mental illness. Often, it seemed the same was true for the officers in our cases.

Winter 2018. A uniformed officer walked down the aisle in the middle of Sunday Mass. He was looking for someone. An organ moaned, and its melody echoed between white marble pillars. He approached the altar, scanning the packed pews. He spotted his target sitting near the very front. She was white and in her mid-fifties with a puffy blue jacket. Leaning in, the officer whispered, "Don't make a scene." She stared forward, unflinching. The officer grabbed her forearm, lifting her upright. She screamed, "Blasphemy!"

Hundreds of heads turned as she tried to twist from the officer's grasp.

"Blasphemy! Get him off the altah!"

A priest stood at the altar, motionless.

"He's not helpin' the poor! And he's covering it up!"

The officer wrenched the woman down the aisle as the congregation gawked. The organ played on, and the woman continued to scream.

"He's a Pharisee! He's not fit to serve the church!"

She twisted her face in disgust. The officer yanked her through the front doors of the church, into the glare of midday on the Upper East Side.

"How dare you?" the woman exclaimed. The officer opened his squad car door and sat her inside. She squinted at his nameplate.

"That's a Spanish name. I can tell you're Catholic. Aren't you concerned with what the church is doing?"

The officer closed the squad car door and turned to his partner. His partner laughed. "That was, like, top ten. She's an EDP, right?"

"Oh yeah."

These types of cases, "Abuse of Authority—Forcible Removal to the Hospital," were nearly as common as search warrant cases. Almost every investigator had one or two on their docket. Sometimes, the CVs in these cases were particularly difficult to reach, as they were liable to live at the nexus of the criminal-justice system, the health-care system, and poverty. Their phone numbers might change on a regular basis, and they'd often move from jail to shelter to hospital with little to no warning. So occasionally, we had to go to them.

Little known to most New Yorkers, it seemed, was the fact that police officers could take custody—essentially arrest, handcuffs and all—of anyone who they considered "a threat to themselves or others" and deposit them at the nearest psych ward. The NYPD categorized these people as "emotionally disturbed persons" or "EDPs."[4]

EDP was both a verb and a noun. Its verb form, "We're gonna EDP him," meant that officers were going to take a person to the hospital for a psychological evaluation. "She's an EDP" meant something more nebulous. To call someone an EDP was to say at once that a person was mentally unstable, that they had been or could be removed to the hospital at will, and that they were fundamentally unreliable. In officer parlance, an EDP was a person who was not to be taken seriously, unless they were a threat. An EDP could be someone having a schizophrenic episode, someone drunkenly berating a bouncer, or someone who said something particularly offensive to the wrong officer on the wrong day. "EDPing," or removing someone to the hospital, was a sort of legal loophole where officers could make someone go away without enduring the legal formality of an arrest and a court proceeding.

These removals could look very different from case to case. Some people went voluntarily, calmly walking into the back of an ambulance. Others resisted, lashing out as officers wrestled them into handcuffs. Some kept resisting even after they were cuffed and had shackles placed around their legs. Rarely, officers would use a heavy white restraining blanket, informally known as "the burrito bag," and wrap a person inside.[5] If the person spit, their shirts might be pulled up over their faces, or officers might put a mesh "spit guard" around their mouths.

Officers *really* did not want to get spit on. Getting spit on meant more than an insult. And it meant more than charging the spitter with assault, as often happened. It meant a medical emergency. When someone spit on an officer's face, that officer took what was colloquially known as "the cocktail," a combination of heavy-duty antiviral drugs.[6]* The cocktail was uniquely unpleasant. Taking it

---

* Taking the cocktail was technically not required, but was "strongly encouraged."

could force an officer out sick for up to a month, hampered by nausea, vomit, and diarrhea. Said one CCRB manager, "I'd beat the hell out of anyone who spit on me. And I don't even have to take the cocktail. If someone spits at an officer, I'd say their response is pretty much always an exon."

Getting "EDPed," or being deemed an EDP by the NYPD, could have life-altering consequences.[7] Mac had a case with someone who was feeling suicidal and told the wrong person. Officers dragged them out of their home, and they were held at a psych ward for a week. They lost their job, and their life spiraled from there. In another case, a parent called 9-1-1 because their child was threatening them with a knife. Officers responded, and when they couldn't find a knife, they EDPed the parent because the child said their parent was crazy. The parent lost custody of their other child. Then they lost their job. Then they lost their work visa and were deported.

Many people trace the rise in homelessness among those with mental health issues to the slashing of social services in the 1970s and '80s. As governor of California in the 1970s, Ronald Reagan had slashed the state budget as a cost-saving measure, and as a consequence, people living in halfway houses or mental health facilities were cast out onto the street. This trend was replicated nationwide, and homelessness skyrocketed. These services had been most notably taken from veterans of the Vietnam War and people with such severe mental illnesses that they could not otherwise function in society. America never refunded its mental health-care system, and it became much more normal for people who needed help to be either living on the street or incarcerated.[8]

The less-told story was that these people still demanded the attention of their government. And over the years, the burden of care fell not on doctors and social workers, but on the police. At the CCRB, we saw this story as it continued to unfold in real time.

Across the office, they were known as "chronics"—people who filed complaints so regularly that we all knew them by name. The term was inherited from decades before, when the CCRB had been part of the NYPD.

There was Ms. Hardy, presumptively a Black woman who wore thick white makeup and insisted that she was not only white but brimming with white pride. "As two white people, I think it's best we discuss my case in private," she said to Mac, glaring at the horrified receptionist, who was also Black.

There was Ms. Beckett, who had a habit of barricading herself in public restrooms, causing entire precincts to grind to a standstill. After dozens of officers had arrived, a hostage negotiator would plead for her to open up, hoping that she wasn't armed or dangerous. She never was.*

There was Mr. Locke, a middle-aged man in South Brooklyn who hadn't left his home in years. An extreme agoraphobe, he would call 9-1-1 to complain about his neighbors. Inevitably, the responding officers would EDP him. "When the officers yell at me, I regress to the moment of my formative trauma. I become preverbal. An infant." He called Greg at least once a week.

When a chronic was removed to the hospital, extraordinary resources were dedicated to the process. There were the officers, of course. They often spent hours of a shift dragging someone into an ambulance, escorting them to a psychiatric unit, and making sure all the appropriate paperwork was filled out. If an officer was injured in the struggle, they might have to take days off to recover.

There were the EMTs, the nurses, the social workers, and the doctors. If a chronic was arrested, there would be an assigned public defender, a prosecutor, and a judge. There would be correction officers and the cost that came with housing and feeding someone

---

* She had, however, been arrested in the '80s for robbing a john in Times Square. "Honestly," mused one CCRB manager, "if you lived in the hood in the eighties and you didn't catch a charge in Times Square, you weren't there."

at Rikers Island. By 2023, that cost was up to $507,000 per person each year.[9]

If a complaint was filed, hundreds if not thousands of hours would be dedicated to requesting documents, interviewing officers, reviewing video footage, and compiling a report. For a chronic complainant, this might be a regular affair. Some might be EDPed or arrested a dozen times over the course of a single year. It was a bizarre cycle, with seemingly no restorative goal. A cycle that could, it seemed, drive a sane person mad.

Perhaps it was easier for the government to keep people suffering with mental health issues in an endless loop of hospitals and jails. It was, after all, much easier to convince a politician to fund a police department than an expanded mental health system.

In a more perfect world, perhaps the time, energy, and taxpayer dollars would have at least been better spent on homicide investigations. Or beds in mental health treatment centers. Or both. But in our imperfect world, the criminal-justice system is asked to bear a weight that it cannot carry. Despite its status as America's largest mental health service provider, the criminal-justice system was not designed to provide health care.[10] It is designed to incarcerate people, so that is what it does.

WINTER 2018. Greg's phone rang. "Finch, you have a walk-in," sighed Martillo, the mercurial receptionist who seemed to smirk through his tinny Brooklyn accent. "Lucky you."

Greg threw on the blazer hanging from the back of his chair, grabbed a handful of forms, and walked through the maze of cubicles and down a hallway to the front desk. Martillo looked at Greg, then glanced knowingly toward a man in his early thirties who sat with his hands clasped across his lap, eyes trained on the white paneled ceiling. He wore a stylish black hoodie, black jeans, and black-rimmed designer glasses. Greg walked over and extended his hand.

"Just so you know off the bat, I'm a federal agent. Homeland Security," the man said.

Greg scanned the man's eyes, trying to tell whether he was joking. "Okay, sir. Could you please fill out these forms? Then we can discuss your incident." Greg handed him a few intake papers and a pen. "Thank you so much. Please let the receptionist know when you're done and I'll be right back." He turned back toward Martillo, who raised an eyebrow sarcastically and mouthed, "FBI?" Greg walked back to his desk and picked up his phone.

"You're gonna want to second-seat this one," Greg said to Mac.

"Why? What's the case?" By this time, we'd been working together more frequently.

"I don't even know. But the CV says he's a federal agent."

Greg and Mac walked into an interview room and sat across from the CV. "So, you're a federal agent?" Mac asked.

"Yes, sir," the man said, beaming. "But I'm off the clock right now."

He slid a tidy stack of documents across the table. Greg and Mac combed through them. There was a typed statement, several pages long. "I prepared that for you." There was a handwritten note that he'd scribbled immediately afterward. "My contemporaneous notes." Photographs of the incident location. "I drove back when it was light out." And photographs of his driver's license and badge.

"What agency are you from again?" Mac asked.

"Immigration and Customs Enforcement," he replied. "Field agent."

Two days earlier, the man had been driving through the suburbs of eastern Queens, where the far edge of New York City juts up against greater Long Island. He was alone, wearing a black hooded

---

* Queens and Brooklyn are on Long Island. But colloquially, only the towns east of Queens are referred to as "Long Island."

sweatshirt and driving in a black sedan. But this wasn't an ordinary sedan. It was an ICE agent's sedan. Every window was so tinted that you could barely see inside, and the license plates had reflective covers to make them harder to read. Given the car's discreet appearance, the car might not have even been noticed by the average person as it passed by. But to a police officer, the same car, especially one driven by a Black man in a hooded sweatshirt, stood out like a sore thumb.

The man turned down a two-way street. From there, he could see two police vehicles that had pulled over another driver. Their blue-and-red lights swirled across the front lawns and landings. As he drove past this traffic stop, the four officers on scene turned their heads and froze at the sight of a car with fully tinted windows and license plate covers, none of which were legal in New York City. It was a summons bonanza. Instantly, the officers sprinted back to their vehicles, abandoning the first traffic stop altogether to pursue their new target. Lights and sirens.

The man pulled over. He turned on all the interior lights and wound down all the windows. Holding his federal ID, he rested his hands at the top of the steering wheel. He faced forward calmly. A raid jacket was draped over his back seat, and the reflective letters that spelled out ICE shone bright from the officers' headlights. An officer pulled out her flashlight and tapped it against the rear windshield. The man jerked his head to the right, toward the sound of metal on glass. Another officer appeared in the front driver's side window, shining his light to see inside.

"Let me see your ID," said the officer. The man handed over his ID and his badge. "So, you're a federal agent? Do you have a firearm?"

The man nodded. "Yes, I do."

The officer said he needed to step out of the vehicle.

"Why? I'm a federal agent. I have permits for these tints, and I'm supposed to carry my service weapon at all times."

The officer repeated himself. "I need you to step out of the vehicle. Now."

The officers patted the man down as he protested. "Are you kidding me? I'm a federal agent!"

An officer lifted the man's gun out of its holster. "Wait here." The officers walked back to their cars and huddled together. The man stood alone in the street.

"You think it's legit?" one officer asked another.

"I dunno. Looks legit."

The officers spent ten minutes trying to verify that the man was who he said he was. But they didn't know how. They called friends and supervisors with the faint hope that someone would know how to verify a federal agent's ID.

"Didn't you have a buddy at ICE?"

The officer shook his head. "No, DEA. I'll give him a try."

The officer pulled out his phone and made a call on FaceTime. "Hey, man," he said, holding his phone up to the man's ID. "Does this look legit to you?"

Although they weren't able to verify whether the man's ID was real, they returned his gun and badge.

"Sorry, man. We're just doing our jobs."

Afterward, one officer turned to the other and said, "It just didn't feel right, you know?"

The man hadn't come to the CCRB because he wanted the officers to be disciplined. Rather, he was astonished that the officers didn't know how to verify that his ID was real, and he wanted to fix their system. "Do you know how many federal agencies have agents operating in New York City? Thirty? Forty? I'm going to meet with NYPD leadership. It's crazy that their officers don't have a system for this." He also knew, as a federal agent, that one of the keys to bureaucratic survival was to document everything. "I file a complaint with the CCRB, then there's an official record of the incident. I file a lawsuit, the city settles the lawsuit. I go home with tens of thousands of dollars, and hopefully everyone knows to never do this again."

Over the following month, Greg transcribed the interview, ordered documents, and searched for witnesses. He was juggling about twenty other cases at the same time. While looking over the federal agent's case file, Greg found a handful of potential subject officers. Two officers in Sector A. Two officers in Sector C. A roaming traffic unit. It could have been any of them. "It would really speed this up if we did a photo array," Greg thought. That meant that Greg would create a lineup of potential subject officers, and the federal agent could come in and point out who had stopped him.

"I can come in again on Tuesday, during my lunch break," he told Greg over the phone.

That Tuesday, Greg walked into the waiting room and saw the man, this time outfitted with a bulletproof vest and the words *"FEDERAL AGENT"* emblazoned across the chest. There was no mistaking him.

"It happened again," the man said without his previous enthusiasm.

"What happened?" Greg asked.

"They stopped me again. They put a gun to my head."

Greg conducted a photo array for the first case, and the man picked out the officers who had pulled him over. Then, while the man sat in the waiting room, Greg walked around the office looking for someone to help out with the impromptu second interview. Every investigator, with a few rare exceptions, was required to have a second investigator, or "second-seat," in each of their interviews. Unfortunately, every investigator was also stretched to their outer limits by a never-ending workload, so whenever you needed a second-seat, you had to convince someone to step away from their work, stretching them even further. But the first investigator he asked pounced at the odd opportunity to interview a federal agent.

Back in an interview room, Greg's second-seat was beside him, poised with a spiral notebook and ballpoint pen. Across from them, the man sat solemnly in his bulletproof vest and dove into his new story.

He'd been in Queens again. Driving the same car, window tints and all, headed to the subway station. Behind him, lights and sirens. They pulled him over next to a bus stop on a four-lane street. The first officer was a white male. The second a Black female.

"I'm a federal agent," he told them, flashing his badge.

"Oh yeah? You have a gun on you?" the first officer asked.

He said yes. But this time, rather than taking his gun, they took his ID and went back to their car.

"There was that string of impersonations," the second officer whispered to the first.

"Yeah? Can you look this guy up?"

For the next five minutes, she clicked through the database on their dashboard. She paused. "Oh my god. It's him. It's him," she said pointing toward her screen. "He was arrested for impersonation."

The first officer took a sharp inhale. His breath shortened. He almost yelled into the radio, "I'm gonna need a couple more cars." He grabbed the microphone for the PA system, and his voice echoed across the street. "Get your hands out of the car. Right now."

In the car, the man shot upright and threw his hands out of the open window. "Are you being serious right now?"

The officer boomed, "I'm being dead serious. Get out of the car."

The man opened the car door and stepped out. Another police vehicle pulled up to the unfolding incident. "He's got a gun!" screamed the first officer, warning the newcomers.

With his hands above his head, the man yelled, "I gave you my ID! I told you I'm a federal agent!"

"Get on your knees and don't go for the gun," the first officer yelled back.

"Get on my knees?" He froze, looking down the long stretch of concrete before him. For a moment he paused, as if to consider whether to kneel or again demand that he be treated with the deference he felt he deserved.

"Get the *fuck* on the ground," one of the newcomers, a white male officer in his late forties, yelled into the man's left ear.

The man turned and found himself looking down the barrel of an NYPD officer's Glock 19. Three other officers pointed their guns at him and each screamed, "Get on the ground!"

The man got down to his knees. Leaning forward, he placed his chest against the concrete. The first officer walked up, pulled the man's arms behind his back and locked his wrists in a pair of steel handcuffs. The first officer took the man's gun, then his badge.

A lieutenant arrived. He was a heavyset Black male in his late fifties. Within five minutes, he figured out that the man was, in fact, an ICE agent. He had never been arrested for impersonation. Rather, someone had been arrested for impersonating him. In their panic, the first two officers had misread the search results.

The lieutenant pulled the man to the side and apologized. "This is embarrassing. You shouldn't have to go through this."

On the other side of the median, traffic whirred past. Blue-and-red lights swirled on the streets and sidewalks. Officers milled around the man's vehicle, asking one another what had happened.

The lieutenant looked the man in the eyes. "Listen, there's a lot of white cops out here that are trigger-happy, trying to shoot somebody. You gotta be careful. Maybe you should get a less conspicuous car. You're Black. Some of these guys are jealous. They just can't believe you're a federal agent. You bump into one of these white officers who don't know how to handle this situation, and you might get shot. Really, man, I don't want to have to speak at your funeral."

The lieutenant handed the man his gun and his badge, adding, "Have a good night, sir," before walking away.

Back in the interview room, the man seemed exhausted. "How was I supposed to know that it wasn't gonna go any further, that he wasn't gonna shoot me?"

The interview concluded, and Greg turned off the audio recorder. Then he asked, "Were you ever able to meet with the NYPD about this?" During their first interview, the man had seemed confident that, at the very least, he could get the NYPD to create a policy for verifying federal agents' IDs. It would have been a simple solution that seemingly benefited everyone.

"Yeah. I met with them." In a meeting with NYPD higher-ups, he'd explained his situation. "They said they weren't going to change anything." When he demanded an explanation, they ended the meeting. It had been easier for the bureaucracy to say no.

The man was a federal agent, with a gun, a badge, and the power of the United States government legitimizing his every action. In this way, he was among the most powerful CVs that Greg or Mac had ever had. Yet throughout this saga, NYPD officers scarcely believed a word he said. He was treated not like a fellow member of law enforcement, but like a Black man with a gripe about policing. Perhaps a criminal. But through cold professional eyes, this case boiled down to a simple set of allegations, beginning with "Abuse of Authority—Vehicle Stop." In the end, one officer had a few vacation days docked for pointing his gun. The second officer was instructed not to make the same mistake again.

UNDER THE NEW YORK CITY CHARTER, the CCRB had the authority to investigate four categories of misconduct: Force, Abuse of Authority, Discourtesy, and Offensive Language. Bribery, blackmail, and other versions of corruption were all kept outside the CCRB's jurisdiction. Those cases had always been referred to IAB. Abuse of Authority was an outlier because, while Force, Discourtesy, and Offensive Language were fairly obvious in meaning, the term

"Abuse of Authority" was so expansive that it could mean almost anything to a civilian. But in our world, this term had a very narrow legal meaning.

Per CCRB rules, Abuse of Authority was mostly limited to specific Fourth Amendment violations (home entries, stop-and-frisks, vehicle stops and searches, etc.), threats (of arrest, or of use of force, or of forcible removal to the hospital), failures to provide identifying information (name, shield number, a copy of the search warrant), and a handful of miscellaneous offenses, like failing to obtain a language interpreter.*†

The boundaries of the CCRB's jurisdiction were up in the air from 1992 to 1994, when the NYPD was embroiled in a landmark corruption scandal. Officers had been engaged in widespread brutality and narcotics trafficking, which led to sweeping reforms, including overhauls of both the CCRB and Internal Affairs, as it was then known.

The Mollen Commission, a mayoral panel tasked to independently investigate the corruption, was comprehensive and stinging in its final report. Its lead counsels wrote in a 1993 *New York Times* op-ed that "today's corruption is characterized by brutality, theft, abuse of authority and active police criminality." In 1992, it seemed likely the Mollen Commission would recommend that the CCRB take over many of IAB's responsibilities. Chief Charles Campisi, who ran IAB from 1996 to 2014, wrote in his memoir that the NYPD had reformed Internal Affairs in 1992 specifically to prevent civilian oversight from taking root, adding:

---

* The allegation of threat of force could be particularly tricky. Conspicuously putting a hand on a holstered gun was clearly threatening and could feel like an abuse of authority, but it wasn't technically considered a threat of force or abuse of authority until the gun was lifted out of the holster.

† In 2018, the CCRB added Sexual Misconduct to its jurisdiction.[11]

The Department wanted no part of that, and with good reason. Civilians are not cops, they can never truly understand police work, they're not trained investigators, and thus they can never effectively understand and combat police corruption. Despite its troubled history with corruption, the Department was determined to prove that it could police itself.[12]

The NYPD created a new and improved Internal Affairs, adding the word "Bureau" at the end and tripling the number of officers in its ranks.[13] By touting IAB as "new and improved," the NYPD was able to prevent the CCRB from impartially investigating police corruption. Instead, the CCRB was left to investigate Force, a limited interpretation of Abuse of Authority, and Discourtesies and Offensive Language. All of which, of course, the NYPD could ignore.

While the CCRB's version of Abuse of Authority was narrow in scope, we still received thousands of such allegations every year, between 7,231 and 8,064 each year from 2014 to 2018.[14] Between the car stops, home entries, refusals to provide shield numbers, and more, Abuse of Authority cases always seemed to offer a new insight into the incentives of policing.

IT OFTEN SEEMED THAT POLICING was a strange dance of safety, deference, and being in the know. Officers saw the law through a different lens than civilians, and if you demonstrated that you could see through their eyes, they might treat you like one of their own.

Take, for example, a PBA card. "They're like get-out-of-jail-free cards for cops," a supervisor told Mac one day in mid-2016, referring to the ID-sized plastic courtesy cards that the union gave to officers to pass on to their families and friends. PBA cards weren't a major part of a CCRB investigator's caseload, but one was liable to show up every few months or so when a CV whipped one out during a traffic stop and it didn't work. These cases were like Easter eggs for tenured investigators or the start of a history lesson for new ones.[15]

"They don't actually get you out of jail," another supervisor told Greg. "But they might get you out of trouble."

When a PBA card worked, an officer's friend or family member would escape a minor infraction, like a broken taillight or double-parking.* Rather than receiving an expensive summons, they'd be let off with a simple verbal warning.

In 2018, the *New York Post* reported that the PBA, with its nearly 24,000 members, had slashed the annual number of courtesy cards issued from thirty to twenty per police officer. An anonymous NYPD retiree was quoted as saying, "They are treating active members like shit, and retired members even worse than shit," adding, "All the cops I spoke to were . . . very disappointed they couldn't hand them out as Christmas gifts."[16]

This practice wasn't regulated. The nearly half a million cards printed each year by the PBA were part of a legal Wild West. But it didn't stop there. The DEA (Detectives' Endowment Association), SBA (Sergeants Benevolent Association), LBA (Lieutenants Benevolent Association), and CEA (Captains Endowment Association) all had their own so-called get-out-of-jail-free cards. And anyone could purchase these cards online, as they were often resold on secondary markets like eBay. There was even said to be a CCRB manager who had an LBA card and a DEA card tucked into his own wallet.

This phenomenon was not unique to New York City. Police unions issued similar cards "for decades in most police departments across the country."[17] It's unclear exactly when this practice

---

* The subtext of a PBA card was that one officer was telling another, "If you fuck with this person, I will fuck with you."

started, as official documentation is scarce.[18] But in 1927, the *Los Angeles Times* reported that a city councilman was trying to stamp out the practice of police officers issuing courtesy cards. He said the cards had been issued in "untold numbers," and that "holders of the cards are often reckless and indifferent toward observing the laws and that therefore the cards are often the direct cause of accidents." The councilman proposed legislative reform, but his bill didn't pass.[19]

In New York and New Jersey, newspapers in the early twentieth century frequently reported on a widespread practice in which public officials, from governors to mayors to police officers, would issue courtesy cards as part of elaborate favor-trading schemes.[20] In the twenty-first century, these cards were no longer tools for overt bribery, but the tradition of bestowing them to friends and family members remained.[21]

In a nation just beginning to reconcile with the overpolicing and mass incarceration of Black and brown people, these courtesy cards highlight a sharp contrast. While Black and brown people are arrested, jailed, and sometimes killed for what seem to be the slightest transgressions, or no transgression at all, officers, their family members, and their friends are often a little less accountable to the law than everyone else.

5

Stop-and-Frisk

It is simply fantastic to urge that [a frisk] performed in public by a policeman while the citizen stands helpless, perhaps facing a wall with his hands raised, is a "petty indignity."

—TERRY V. OHIO (1968)[1]

A Black boy runs down a South Brooklyn street on a hot summer Sunday. He's just turned thirteen.[2]* In one hand, he's grasping a small bundle of envelopes his mother just gave him. The other hand is empty. He runs with his arms outstretched as if he were a small airplane, tilting left, then right. "Brrrrrrrrrrrr," he hums to himself, imitating the engine. His legs pump faster and faster as he nears the post office.

He arrives, winded. He rests his hands on his knees and takes a few deep breaths. The post office is closed, so he slips the envelopes through the mail slot. He holds his hands over his eyes and peers through the front glass, studying the strange booths and dim fluorescent lights. Harbingers of adult life. He turns around to head home. But as he faces the street, he sees that an unmarked black sedan has parked right next to him. A white

---

* Studies suggest that Black children are seen as more adult-like than White children, a phenomenon known as adultification, and thus, less innocent and more culpable.

man in a hooded sweatshirt and jeans steps out of the front driver's side
door and pulls out a gun.

"Freeze."

The officer stands with his gun pointed at the ground. "Don't move."
Two more officers step out of the vehicle. None of them are in uniform.
The boy stands frozen in place. One officer walks up to him and grabs his
belt, feeling around his waistband. "What did you put in that mailbox?"

The boy blurts out, "The mail?"

The officer runs his hands up and down the boy's thighs. "Why were
you running?" Another officer looks inside the mail slot.

"I like running," the boy says apologetically.

"Did you have a gun? Did you put a gun in here?" asks one officer,
pointing at the mailbox.

"What? No. Why would you think that?" He's on the verge of tears.
An officer runs their hands up his rib cage and across his arms.

"How old are you?" asks one officer.

"Thirteen."

"You look like you could be seventeen. You can't be running down the
street like that," the officer tells the boy. "Somebody's gonna think you're
doing something bad."

The boy insists that he didn't do anything. "They were just envelopes."

After a while, the officers say he can go. "Just stop running. Don't run,
man. It's not safe."

The boy walks the four blocks to his house. When he arrives, he finds his
mother. Seeing that he's upset, she holds him in her arms.

THE BOY'S MOTHER FILED A complaint with the CCRB. A month
later, after making the long subway ride from South Brooklyn to
Lower Manhattan, she sat in an interview room across from Mac.

"What the hell are they saying my boy can't run?"

The officers hadn't recorded this stop-and-frisk, neither in their
memo books nor in a required stop report. But over the next few

months, Mac tracked them down by using the AVL (Automatic Vehicle Location) system, which, when the CCRB still had access, showed a GPS record of the officers' vehicle in front of the post office at the incident time.* Both the boy and his mother asked to mediate their complaint. Eventually, they met with the officers behind closed doors, came to a resolution, and the case was sealed from public view.

It is undisputed that stop-and-frisks rarely result in summonses, arrests, or any meaningful progress in a police investigation.[3] In a study of 685,724 stops conducted in 2011, only 2 percent led to officers recovering contraband.[4] Despite the empty-handed nature of this practice, from 2004 to 2012, the NYPD reported conducting 4.4 million stops.[5] More than half these stops included frisks, and about 20 percent featured the use of force. In the words of Nicholas Peart describing the trauma of being stopped and frisked by NYPD officers in a 2011 op-ed for the *New York Times*: "Essentially, I incorporated into my daily life the sense that I might find myself up against a wall or on the ground with an officer's gun at my head. For a black man in his 20s like me, it's just a fact of life in New York."[6]

In 2013, a federal court ruled that the NYPD was "liable for a pattern and practice of racial profiling and unconstitutional stops."[7] This ruling was widely misinterpreted as a ban on stop-and-frisk. But stop-and-frisk was never banned.[8] Rather, NYPD's practice was curtailed and subject to federal monitoring, and still the tactic of stopping and frisking young men, Black and Latino men in particular, would continue to be a normal and legal part of American policing well past the publication of this book.

---

* The AVL system allowed NYPD supervisors to view officers' locations via a digital map with a live display of where each police vehicle was. In 2019, IAB stopped giving the CCRB critical AVL data because, according to them, the system was too unreliable. It sure seemed reliable to us. Mac spent years campaigning for the CCRB to get direct AVL access, to no avail.

In 2014, the *American Journal of Public Health* published a study about the impact of stop-and-frisk on young men in New York City.[9] The results were damning. Those who had been stopped by the police were significantly more likely to experience anxiety and PTSD. Further, the more physically intrusive the search, the more likely the traumatic impact. Words like "stop" and "frisk" lose meaning in the press. But as in the cases of Nicholas Peart and the boy at the post office, the real-life experiences of stop-and-frisk were often those of strangers' hands groping innocent bodies.

The impact of even one traumatic incident in a person's life can have multigenerational consequences. A bad breakup in one relationship can lead to domestic violence in another. A family's car accident can lead to a divorce. Such incidents inevitably butterfly outward, impacting friends, families, and coworkers. From this perspective, to imagine the collective psychological damage done to overpoliced communities is truly beyond human comprehension. The public health and economic consequences are simply too seismic, the stories too many to boil down to statistics alone.

Because the fallout has been so difficult to measure, scholars and academics haven often drifted toward documenting individual accounts of police violence rather than analyzing its greater harm to public health. In 2009, *Urban Affairs Review* published a study of police encounters in St. Louis, Missouri, concluding that stops of young Black men were characterized by violence, humiliation, and threats, whereas police were more deferential to young white men.[10] The study included a wide body of startling firsthand testimony, including this harrowing story: "We was [sitting] in the car; we was just sittin' in there. [Police] got us out the car, check[ed] us and said he found some drugs in the car. And [the officers] said, 'One of y'all goin' with us.' [To decide] they said, 'Eeny, meeny, miny, moe, catch a n---a by his throat,' and locked up my friend because he was the oldest."

This study is a stark reminder: policing at its worst inflicts extraordinary degradation upon its citizens—funded, in all likelihood, by you, dear reader. But even the intrusions that were not so explosive, like the stop-and-frisks that the NYPD deployed so liberally, had measurable consequences.

In 2019, Harvard University and Columbia University jointly published a first-of-its-kind study focused on 250,000 children in New York City, aged nine to fifteen, during the height of stop-and-frisk. They found that exposure to stops and frisks had lowered school attendance and significantly reduced test scores for Black boys from ages thirteen to fifteen. The study also determined that lowered educational performance for these Black boys had long-term implications, impacting child development, economic mobility, and racial inequality.

We think it's fair to say that, across the political spectrum, Americans in 2025 are aware that people of color, particularly Black people, are treated differently by the police. The hard evidence is there: startling arrest rates and extraordinary incarceration rates. But more palpably, it's a reality that bleeds into popular culture, dramatized in television and film, endlessly reported by news media. These inequities are an ongoing tragedy, yet a bitter consequence of it being front and center in the public consciousness is that this narrative is normalized, becoming fodder for social media chatter and newsroom commentary that trivializes the human cost—the pain, suffering, and despair—it leaves in its wake.

The Harvard-Columbia study warned that there is "evidence that the consequences of policing extend into key domains of social life, with implications for the educational trajectories of minority youth and social inequality more broadly."[11] Yet today, this type of policing, the invasive stop-and-frisk, remains a staple of a CCRB investigator's docket.

. . .

SPRING 2020. SOUTH BRONX. "WHAT you touchin' my dick for, bro?" asked a Black man in his late teens. A vehicle stop for double-parking had spiraled into something even less pleasant.

"Relax," droned the officer as he slid his hands up the man's thighs toward his groin. Officers were trained to interchangeably yell, "Relax," or "Stop resisting," whenever a civilian wasn't fully cooperating.

"Just relax," said another officer.

"Nah, bro," said the man. "He just touched my dick. What you mean, 'Relax'? You want your dick to be touched? You gonna relax, bro? You buggin' out, bro."

Because the officers smelled marijuana, they could legally frisk and search everyone in the car. It was all exonerated.*

SUMMER 2019. Mac sat in a CCRB interview room across from a Black man in his late twenties. He'd been pulled over for a broken taillight in Jamaica, Queens. "They search my genital area, and they search my . . . cleavage. I had shorts on. I felt I was violated."

His voice lowered. "I felt like I was violated and I was sexually assaulted. That's how I really feel inside." He continued, "I was very embarrassed. Taking me out the car. Searched my trunk and in the glove compartment. They didn't find anything. And they told us to go on our way."

THAT SAME SUMMER, another vehicle stop in Jamaica, Queens. "She grabbed right in between when she was searching me," a young

---

* Following New York's legalization of marijuana in 2021, officers were no longer allowed to search vehicles solely based upon the smell of marijuana coming from a vehicle.

Black man told Greg. "So, I said, 'You're digging me up. You're pulling my pants down.'"

He had a cell phone video of the incident but said it was too painful to watch.

"I want to react to this, but I can't react to·this. And then I'm looking at her, and I'm looking at him." His voice wavered. "It's just—in that moment—because it's an upsetting moment, it kind of messes with my head. You know what I mean? Because I'm getting upset, and I'm not trying to react in an upset manner. But it's frustrating that I'm being touched in my genitals." His voice was very quiet, almost whispering. "Whether it's through the clothes, you know what I mean, or whatever. You're groping me. That's how I feel. And then you're digging in my pockets, and you're pulling my pants down. And I have to stand still for this. And I don't even feel like you should be touching me in the first place. Because I didn't tell you to touch me. And I don't understand what the reason is."

At the CCRB, an allegation was considered a "frisk" whenever an officer felt over a CV's clothes, often in search of weapons or drugs.* Officers could legally frisk someone whenever they had a "reasonable suspicion that the person has committed, is committing, or is about to commit a crime" and a "reasonable belief" that the person might be "armed and presently dangerous."[12]

The two of us worked on hundreds of frisk cases. It was normal to receive complaints about officers jostling men's genitals, but it was extraordinarily rare for an officer to be disciplined because their frisk was too rough. Frisks, no matter how physically or emotionally invasive, were allowed so long as the officers had a legal justification.

---

* Sometimes referred to as a "pat-down search" or a "Terry stop," a reference to the 1968 US Supreme Court case "Terry v. Ohio."

IN NOVEMBER 2014, during an interview with *Meet the Press*, former mayor Rudy Giuliani defended the disproportionate influx of white officers policing Black communities. "Ninety-three percent of blacks are killed by other blacks," he stated, adding, "I would like to see the attention paid to that that you are paying to this," and "White police officers wouldn't be there [in black neighborhoods] if you weren't killing each other."[13]

Despite the racial overtones of Giuliani's lecture, it's important to examine his logic. Murders, he says, are higher in poor, predominantly Black neighborhoods. By his reckoning, police are supposed to prevent murders. Therefore, goes the former mayor's reasoning, police need to be in poor, predominantly Black neighborhoods to save lives. It's why Giuliani crassly declared in 2016, "I believe I saved a lot more black lives than Black Lives Matter."[14]

Former New York City mayor Michael Bloomberg, in a February 2015 speech at the Aspen Institute, defended his rationale for the expansion of stop-and-frisk under his administration: "Ninety-five percent of your murders—murderers and murder victims—fit one M.O. You can just take the description, Xerox it and pass it out to all the cops. They are male minorities, 16 to 25. That's true in New York. That's true in virtually every city."[15] As Bloomberg described it, the solution couldn't be more obvious. In 2015 in New York City, 94 percent of suspected murderers and murder victims were minorities.[16] And the vast majority of suspected murderers were male.[17] So why not stop as many male minorities as possible? Isn't that what the police are supposed to do?

The roots of Bloomberg's ideology, the one that led to the mass expansion of stop-and-frisk, trace back to an argument between Mayor Giuliani and an NYPD deputy early in the 1990s.

In New York City, crime in the '70s, '80s, and '90s was stunningly high. In 1990 alone, there were 2,262 murders, compared to 391 in

2023.[18] This fueled a constant media frenzy. Shortly after taking office in 1994, Giuliani appointed outsiders to run the NYPD. They radically transformed the Department, and crime rates took a nosedive.

But one day, Giuliani read a newspaper article about another city that had been making many more gun arrests than the NYPD.[19] This made him mad. He'd campaigned on a "tough on crime" platform, and he believed he was getting shown up. He called a deputy commissioner into his office and furiously asked, "Why are the cops over there arresting more people for guns than the cops here?" The deputy commissioner told him that, actually, this was good news. The NYPD was making fewer arrests because they had reduced gun crime, and there were simply fewer people to arrest. Their lower arrest rates were a sign of success.

Giuliani disagreed.

"Crime goes down, arrests go up!" he said to the deputy commissioner.

"No, crime goes down, arrests go down," the deputy commissioner replied.

"No, crime goes down, arrests go up!" Giuliani insisted.[20]

Shortly thereafter, Giuliani had his way. He forced out key members of the NYPD, including the deputy commissioner who'd stood up to him. He replaced that NYPD commissioner with the former fire chief, his loyal friend who had "no experience in a municipal police force."[21] And from that point on, if crime went down, arrests would have to go up. In New York City, there would be more police and more policing, no matter what was happening on the streets.

AT THEIR RESPECTIVE CORES, STOP-AND-FRISK, Broken Windows—the idea that low-level crime leads to more serious crime, which rose to prominence in the '80s and '90s when it seemed New York was on the brink of collapse—and "proactive" policing were all framed as attempts to control perhaps the most fundamental challenge in local government: murder. When you boil it down, New York's politicians and police leaders essentially said, "We can either police the hell out of Black and brown communities, or every year hundreds of Black and brown people are going to be murdered." It's a framework that would continue to be replicated, in one way or another, in many American cities. But as recent studies suggest, framing these draconian policies as either-or choices has not produced the outcomes their advocates predicted.

In 2016, a *Washington Post* analysis of those studies noted that in 1990, several years before Giuliani took office, crime in New York City had already begun its steep decline. The murder rate would plunge from 30.7 murders per 100,000 residents in 1990 to 8.9 in 1998, and thereafter steadily declined to a low of 3.4 in 2017.[22] Violent crime followed a similar trend. Weighing the rates of murders and violent crimes against the number of stops and frisks, the *Post* concluded that "simply put, there's almost no correlation" between more stop-and-frisk and New York's crime decline.[23]

Despite the dubious results of stop-and-frisk as a crime-reduction tool, let alone its human costs, in 2013, when a federal judge ruled that the NYPD's stop-and-frisk policy was illegally targeting minorities, police and political leaders nevertheless declared that ending it would trigger a crime wave.

"No question about it, violent crime will go up," NYPD commissioner Ray Kelly warned in a *Meet the Press* interview shortly after the ruling came down. "And this case has to be appealed, in my judgment, because it will be taken as a template and have significant impact in policing throughout America."[24]

In a press conference, Mayor Bloomberg lodged a sharper complaint:

> This is a dangerous decision made by a judge who I think does not understand how policing works and what is compli-ant with the U.S. Constitution as determined by the Supreme

Court. I worry for my kids, and I worry for your kids. I worry for you and I worry for me. Crime can come back any time the criminals think they can get away with things. We just cannot let that happen.[25]

Bloomberg played a well-worn political trick. On one hand, he correctly claimed that crime was higher in poor Black and brown communities. On the other hand, he attempted to justify a draconian policy by falsely claiming that white families like his needed to fear those same crimes.

Bloomberg bound himself to this narrative. In a radio interview that same year, he said, "I think we disproportionately stop whites too much and minorities too little. It's exactly the reverse of what they say."[26] A three-term mayor, Bloomberg enjoyed remarkably high approval ratings throughout most of his tenure in office.

Bloomberg insisted that stop-and-frisk had in fact saved the city and that its end would trigger a descent into chaos. Yet, from 2011 to 2020, arrests for violent felonies in New York City barely changed at all. In 2012, the NYPD made 23,494 such arrests. In 2020, they made 22,128. In the years between, the number never went higher or lower.[27] Over time, Bloomberg and his allies' claims began to look less like victory speeches and more like the empty words of those American generals who for years insisted that the Vietnam War had been a success.

By 2020, Bloomberg, then running for the Democratic Party presidential nomination, had changed his tune. He stood on a national debate stage in Nevada and said, "If I go back and look at my time in office, the one thing that I'm really worried about, embarrassed about, was how it turned out with stop-and-frisk . . . It got out of control," adding, "We cannot go out and stop people indiscriminately, and that was what was happening."[28] Nonetheless, in 2019, the NYPD reported 13,459 stops, and 88 percent were of Black or Latino people.[29]

In retrospect, stop-and-frisk proved to be a disastrous policy, arguably ineffective and unquestionably harmful. But with the benefit of hindsight, it's important to remember the political pressure that shaped stop-and-frisk and policies like it.

"The Perpetual Crime Wave Crests, and a City Shudders," read the *New York Times* in August 1990.[30] "Crime-ravaged City cries out for help: DAVE, DO SOMETHING!" belted a *New York Post* headline in September 1990, referring to then mayor David Dinkins. "Crime-ravaged City cries out for help: BILL, DO SOMETHING!" echoed a *New York Post* headline in July 2020, referring to then mayor Bill de Blasio.[31] Politicians are under tremendous pressure to act boldly in the face of calls to action. They need to do *something*. And afterward, they must declare that *something* worked.

From Giuliani to Kelly to Bloomberg, political leaders repeatedly decided to sacrifice the mental and physical health of hundreds of thousands of Black and brown men in pursuit of a lower murder rate. And no matter the intent, it was a stark example of ambitious white men participating in an age-old American tradition: disregarding the lives and experiences of Black people.

One might assume that throughout the stop-and-frisk era, police officers themselves were supporting stop-and-frisk. After all, the NYPD's overtime budget rose, and crime indeed appeared to decline.[32] But that's where this story takes an abrupt left turn. In fact, from its very beginnings, while the politicians and executives who controlled the NYPD were pressuring their officers to conduct more stops and more frisks, perhaps the most formidable forces in law enforcement, the unions, were sounding the alarm that these policies were primed to lead America down a very dark path.

In 2019, after Michael Bloomberg first apologized for stop-and-frisk, PBA president Patrick Lynch issued a press release: "Mayor Bloomberg could have saved himself this apology if he had just listened to the police officers on the street. We said in the early

2000s that the quota-driven emphasis on street stops was polluting the relationship between cops and our communities."[33]

And sure enough, Lynch's press releases from the early 2000s, throughout the ascent and decline of stop-and-frisk, are smattered with pleas for reform.[34] The department, he repeatedly claimed, was forcing quotas on the officers, who were then forced to summons, stop, and frisk citizens against their will. In 2012, he wrote that these quotas had "become ineffective in fighting crime and serve as a tremendous source of friction with the communities that our members are sworn to protect."[35] Lynch's statements were only the tip of the iceberg. Throughout the lower ranks of the NYPD, countless more officers were beating the same drum.[36]

IT TAKES YEARS OF EXPERIENCE in the criminal-justice system to begin to understand the relationships between police officers, police unions, and police departments. If there's anything we learned at the CCRB, it's that these three groups are extraordinarily different, rendering the term "the police" as broad and unwieldy as "the Middle East."

Rank-and-file officers are at the bottom level of the policing hierarchy. They're usually represented by unions. The people who control police departments, the brass, are not low-level officers, but high-ranking, highly paid chiefs. All three groups—the rank and file, the unions, and the brass—have profoundly different incentives.

Rank-and-file officers quickly acquire, as former NYPD detective Edward Conlon wrote, the "general understanding that the less said the better."[37] So usually their only public voice is their union. The public, however, often views police unions as bad-faith actors because they're liable to defend even the most flagrant abuses of authority and because they seem to rally against accountability at every turn. Consequently, a police union's calls for reform can easily get lost in the fray or be simply disregarded as self-serving ploys.

In almost every city, politicians appoint the police chief ("the Commissioner" for NYPD purposes), who appoints leadership, or "brass."[38] Consequently, the chief and the brass are often beholden to the whims of politicians. In New York City, the brass are either not unionized or are represented by smaller unions than rank-and-file officers. In either case, the brass influence negotiations with unions over pay, treatment, and policy for the rank-and-file officers.

The brass are not incentivized to reverse destructive policy decisions, particularly if those policies lead to larger budgets. The brass are typically in the later years of their careers, anticipating quiet retirements with substantial pensions, benefits, and the prospect of lucrative opportunities in the private sector. It's in their best interests to avoid rocking the boat.

To avoid rocking the boat may require embracing or at least tolerating harmful policies. But the brass can fend off damaging publicity through their press office spokespeople, cite questionable crime statistics, and silence those officers who dare speak out against abusive practices like stop-and-frisk.[39] It's a cycle lacking in accountability, because when America talks about police accountability, they talk about officers like Derek Chauvin. But behind every Derek Chauvin, there's a brass who guided him to George Floyd's neck.

6

Policing in HD

Every solution creates new problems.

—CCRB MANAGER

P aul slammed his fist on his desk and put his forehead in his hands. "Fuck."

Greg looked over. "What's up?"

Paul groaned. "They fucked it up." He pointed at his computer monitor and waved Greg over. "Look at this shit." Greg pulled beside him.

Over the previous six months, Paul had kept a close eye on the political battle over the rules that would soon govern body-worn cameras: when officers were required to record, how the data was stored, who had access, and the discipline for those who failed to adhere to those rules. For Paul, it was a question of wiggle room. Could officers claim ignorance about the policy because it was too complicated? Would the CCRB have access to their footage? Would the public see any of it? And would there be consequences for bad actors? The NYPD had published their final draft.

Paul placed his hand on the computer screen, palming the wall of text.

"They can do whatever they want."

IN SPRING 2017, THE NYPD finally began phase one of a plan to roll out BWCs to every uniformed officer in the department. Body-worn cameras, or BWCs, as we called them, are attached to the fronts of officers' uniforms. To turn one on, the officer need only reach to the center of their chest and press a small button. Initially, BWCs were issued only to uniformed officers in a few scattered precincts, and of the department's more than thirty-five thousand members of service, only thirteen hundred were given BWCs.

Every officer equipped with a BWC was required to record most of their encounters with the people of New York. They didn't always follow this rule. To turn their BWC off, an officer could press the same button at the center of their chest. At the end of an officer's tour, they would return to their stationhouse and place their BWC in a small black charging port. File by file, they would label each recording and upload them to the NYPD cloud. Officers were permitted to view their own footage, but not other officers'. We did not have direct access to these files. Neither did the public.

When the BWC rollout first began, the two of us had hoped to get lucky and stumble upon one of these videos. But as summer turned to fall, neither of us had a single case with said footage. Then Mac, now a Level II investigator, received a complaint about an incident in the 71st Precinct.

"Hot damn!" he exclaimed, looking over his newest complaint.

"What's up?" asked Alicia, a woman in her early twenties only a few months out of college. Mac was Alicia's new mentor.

"Seventy-first Precinct. They've got BWCs. Let's request the footage."

Mac printed out a long piece of paper. Eight and a half by fourteen inches, the standard for document requests.

Date and Time of Occurrence: August 15, 2017. 1:30 a.m.

Officers: Unknown white male officer.

Incident Type and Outcome: Officer pushed civilian away
from crime scene. Crime unknown.

Related Paperwork: Unknown.

Civilians: Black female individual.

Location: Ebbets Field Housing Complex.

Mac gave the document request to Oliver. Oliver would email
a scanned copy of the request to IAB. IAB would send it to the
NYPD Legal Bureau. And over there, we could only hope that an
NYPD attorney would fish through an ocean of files to raise our
incident from the depths. But you had to wonder, whose idea was it
to have NYPD attorneys decide which footage to give us? It seemed
like they'd be the last ones to give over evidence of NYPD misconduct. Each case meant more liability.

Over the years, we would send thousands of requests for BWC
footage, and the responses would vary dramatically. Sometimes,
NYPD legal gave us everything. Sometimes, footage was redacted.
Other times, videos were conspicuously missing. Success or not, the
process was consistently frustrating.

A few weeks after Mac turned in his request, Oliver called out
from over his cubicle wall.

"Hey, Mac, you got footage. Fifteen files! Let me know what's
in there."

As Mac scrolled through the files on his desktop, he wondered
why some officers had more than one recording. Over time, we'd
learn that officers were prone to turning their cameras on and off
throughout a given incident. Thus, multiple recordings.

• • •

SOME CITIES USED BWCs THAT automatically recorded whenever an officer activated their siren, discharged their Taser, or drew
their firearm.[1] The NYPD could have purchased these features, but
they chose not to.[2] For example, in 2020, the department's Legal
Bureau claimed that they would not purchase GPS tracking for
BWCs because "New York City's density and topography present unique challenges for GPS that may hinder its accuracy."[3] You
had to hand it to them, NYPD Legal could make a bullshit excuse
sound all too reasonable.

Mac clicked the first file. The video showed a man lying on the
ground with a bullet in his neck. It ended abruptly. Mac leaned back
in his chair, glancing through the tenth-floor window. The midday
sun reflected off the World Trade Center.

"Bro. Oh my god," said Alicia, who'd been watching over his
shoulder, "Did that guy live?"

Mac turned to her, "I don't know." Mac quickly searched for the
incident on Google.

"Yeah, he lived."

Mac clicked the second file.

THE OFFICER IS ON A *dark residential street. He jogs, then sprints. He
turns under a steel scaffolding. Bright construction lights flood a long,
straight path ahead. His sprint continues. The camera bounces up and
down. Lights swirl. It looks like there's a figure ahead. The audio kicks
in, capturing only the officer's heavy breath and his quickening footsteps.*

Thud. Thud. Thud.

The figure in the distance draws closer.

"Hey!" yells the officer.

*The figure turns a corner. The officer dashes out from under the scaf-
folding and into the dark night. He runs around a flower bed, turns one
corner, then another, then emerges onto a sidewalk.*

A group of plainclothes officers are piled on top of a man in his early twenties.

"He dropped a gun," shouts one officer, withdrawing his flashlight and walking into a cluster of bushes. After a few moments, the light glimmers.

"Gun's right here, guys."

The man on the ground is silent. From a window in the projects above, someone hurls an angry insult. A uniformed Hispanic male officer looks up toward the voice and mockingly yells, "Wahhhh!" Turning back to the plainclothes officers, he points at one, then waves toward the man on the ground. "Come get your boy. Come get your dude. Your chase, your dude."

Off camera, Mac hears his CV's voice.

"What's going on? That's my brother."

"Get back," says an officer. "Police incident."

She'd alleged that at this moment, an officer had pushed her in the chest. But neither she nor that officer were ever captured on camera. All Mac had was the mournful sound of her voice.

Mac swiveled away from his desk. It was the first time he'd viewed BWC footage for one of his own cases. In only a few minutes, he'd witnessed more than ever before. But this made him wonder.

In each of Mac's past cases, a movie had been seared into his mind: a choreography of movement, an imprint of every interview, a reel that held every scrap of evidence. Where everyone stood. What actions they took. Who said what. That movie was "the preponderance of the evidence," ready to be replayed at a moment's notice. He prided himself in his mental archive of incidents. Would his cases from the past have looked different on BWC? What had he been missing? There was no way to know.

And would every new video be this dramatic? A shooting? A wild foot chase? The answer was a resounding "No." This case was an anomaly, a scene from *COPS* in a sea of videos that would usually be much calmer, and sometimes far stranger.

ON THE OTHER SIDE OF the office, Greg had a new manager.

"Oh God," she said, "Greg, you've got your first BWCs. Can you look at them?" She sounded concerned. Most managers who rose through the CCRB ranks had either mastered pain avoidance, had a masochistic streak, or perhaps a mix of both. A new variable was often unwelcome. A source of anxiety. An opportunity to screw up.

Greg opened the first of four files and peered into the unknown:

LATE AT NIGHT, a white male officer chases a man in his mid-forties down a driveway in north Brooklyn. Near the front door, the officer catches him, pinning him against a wall of white siding. The audio kicks in.

"You're under arrest," the officer says.

"I live here," the man says.

"I'm arresting you for the weed. Not because you live here."

The officer grabs the man's arms and wraps handcuffs around his wrists.

Click. Click.

He turns to his left. A woman stands fifteen feet away, centered in the driveway floodlights. "Let go of my brother."

"Ma'am, back up or I'll arrest you for trespassing."

"I live here," she says.

"Ma'am. I said back up. You're being recorded."

The woman silently stares into the camera.

"Ma'am. Everything you do is being recorded."

She sways back and forth, as if intoxicated, and calmly steps toward the officer, who still has the man pinned against the wall.

"Ma'am. I will arrest you for trespassing. Step back."

She steps closer. "I live here."

"Ma'am. What the fuck are you doing?"

Spellbound, it seems, she steps even closer.

In one swift motion, the woman reaches directly toward the BWC and rips it from the officer's chest. She places it on her own chest and sprints to the end of the driveway. She turns around, revealing that the officer is racing toward her.

Suddenly, the camera points toward the sky, freezes there for a moment, then in a blur comes crashing to the ground. She's spiked the BWC in a touchdown celebration. The audio crackles like an old radio. The video ends.

GREG LEANED BACK, ASTONISHED. PAUL cackled. "You know how much those cameras cost?" Greg had no idea. "Four hundred and fifty dollars," he said, laughing. "One for every officer."

He pointed his thumb toward the screen like he was in an "I'm With Stupid" T-shirt.

"Well, two for this guy."

With more than thirty-five thousand uniformed members in the NYPD, there was a lot of expensive equipment. "Man, all these videos are just gonna be used to speed up prosecutions. Now prosecutors don't even have to witness-prep officers. They can just play this video, and that lady gets hit with a felony for criminal mischief." Like most NYPD equipment, BWCs would be used to expand police power, not restrict it.[4] Paul turned back to his desk. "Probably not what the activists had in mind."

In Greg's case, the woman and her brother didn't answer his calls. Because he couldn't get a sworn statement from a witness, the case was closed without investigation. In this case if he hadn't seen the BWC footage, all he would have had was the text of the initial complaint— "An officer hit my brother"—and the brief narratives on each arrest report. With every BWC video, we were getting a crash course on policing like never before, and with every passing day, our work began to feel like watching a livestream from behind the blue wall. A brief glimpse of policing in high definition.

Over the years, we watched countless hours of BWC footage. Each video was a movie unto its own. And behind each of these movies, an officer was the executive producer, director, narrator, and main character. Officers decided where the camera pointed, when it recorded, and when it turned off. But BWC footage, like all evidence, was only a fragment of a bigger story. And the public could access only a sliver. Critically, the wide array of videos in our cases would show us how often officers find themselves in perplexing situations, many of which would require vast professional knowledge, extraordinary communication skills, and a depth of empathy that overlap in very few human beings. We saw firsthand how policing asks officers, who are first and foremost required to put people into cages, to do the impossible: make everybody happy.

7

Notorious

I bet Bullethead's been here fifty times. I bet he's like, "Fuck
it. I'll just tell them what happened." What's the worst that
could happen? He gets another promotion?

—CCRB INVESTIGATOR

CRB investigators have their own unique style of folklore. Because their jobs are filled with drama, from police
shootings to showdowns with union attorneys to emotional CV interviews, it takes a truly monumental story to stand
out from the pack. But every tenured investigator had their greatest hits. And if you passed their desk late at night, they just might
regale you with one.

There was the time, a few years before we started, when a man
showed up in the waiting room wearing a chicken costume. The
chicken submitted a ludicrous complaint against an imaginary officer. Only after the fact did the investigators realize that the chicken
had been wearing a hidden camera, and that he had, in fact, been an
officer in disguise.

There were the times when an investigator might flip through
an officer's memo book entry and find a penis drawn on a random
page—an endemic problem of NYPD officers "cocking" each other.
And there was the desk sergeant at the 42nd Precinct who would

document the precinct's comings and goings in mesmerizing Old English calligraphy. There was the time an inspector stopped a man on the Coney Island boardwalk for carrying an open container of alcohol and proceeded to kick off the man's prosthetic leg. Or the time an older man had an affair with a young woman, not knowing that she was the daughter of an NYPD higher-up. Safe to say that, in the end, the man was in cuffs.

But office folklore was more than just the wild stories. There were certain individuals who were recurring characters, and sometimes, they became so notorious that we couldn't help but talk about them in hushed tones.

"You don't know about Terrell?" whispered Oliver in fall 2016. "Man, that guy's not playing around."

A tenured investigator, a woman in her thirties, piped up from over a cubicle wall. "Terrell?" She laughed. "He's a frequent flier. That man's flying business class." She had a new complaint—one of over thirty-five in Terrell's storied career.[1]

"Everybody," said Oliver, waving his five investigators over, "check this out." They gathered around a computer monitor to watch a video of Detective Terrell, a tall, Black, muscle-bound officer in his early forties, playing dice on a sidewalk with a group of young men. Behind them, a young man was handcuffed in the back of a squad car.

If you ace out, you gotta let him go," one of the young men says. "All right. Bet," Terrell says, blowing the dice. He rolls, and the crowd erupts into cheers.

"A detective gambling for another man's freedom," Oliver said. "Only in the Bronx."

"And look," another investigator said. "He lost and doesn't even let the guy go!" Mac watched as Terrell drove away without releasing his detainee.

"They asked for community policing," quipped Castor. "Guess this is what it looks like."

Back at his computer, Mac watched an NBC News report about the dice-game arrest. The reporters interviewed the man who'd been handcuffed in Terrell's car. "He doesn't find any money, he doesn't find anything, he just decides to try to just, take me. Puts me in the car. No reason at all." The newswoman asked him what he would want to say to the police commissioner. "Terrell is really a bad, bad cop, and he does things the wrong way," the man replied. "He doesn't follow the rules, he doesn't follow the law, he doesn't care about the law. He thinks he's the law."[2]

Mac turned to Oliver. "Why don't they fire guys like this?"

Oliver shook his head. "The guys who rack up these many CCRB complaints? They usually get promoted. It's a sign they're really in the streets, making arrests. Any cop will tell you that. The more you police, the more people complain you're policing."

He shrugged.

"On the other hand, if the department didn't like Terrell? They'd sure as hell use the CCRB as an excuse to get him fired. They'd put him on IAB monitoring, ding him on little things. They wouldn't fire him for gambling with someone's freedom. But if they decided to go after him, they'd build a record, maybe fire him for losing his memo book a few years down the road. That way, it'd all be in their control, and the CCRB wouldn't get any credit."

Oliver looked down at a closing report he'd covered with edits. Red ink seemed to flood the page. Mac asked, "Shouldn't they at least fire guys who are literally gambling with people?"

Oliver laughed. "If they fire Terrell, he sues the department, the union sues the department, he appeals to the state board, years of litigation, he probably gets his job back, everyone spends a lot of time, energy, and money . . ." Oliver threw up his hands. "It's really just easier to keep him around."

As of November 2024, Detective Terrell had been the subject of thirty-eight CCRB complaints and ninety-eight individual allegations during his twenty-two-year career. Only three officers in the department had been the subject of more allegations.[3] The City of New York had settled twenty-seven lawsuits against Detective Terrell to the tune of at least $876,500.[4] Unsurprisingly, some settlements were hidden from the public.

From 2011 to 2019, the average NYPD officer made about 5 to 8 arrests per year.[5*] As of November 2024, over the course of his career, Detective Terrell had made 607 misdemeanor arrests, 206 felony arrests, 80 arrests for violations, and 3 arrests for unknown infractions: 40.7 arrests per year.[6]

THE LATE-NIGHT FOLKLORE fashioned "frequent fliers"—the officers who were in our interview rooms most often—as urban legends. These were the frequent fliers, who seemed to be back at the CCRB every other month. Terrell was a prime example. Bullethead was another.

"You know why they call him Bullethead, right?" a manager asked Mac. It was spring 2016, when Mac was still in training.

"Did he shoot somebody?" Mac asked.

"No, no," said another investigator. "His head looks like a bullet." Mac frowned.

"No, really," the investigator said. "Google him. He's basically a celebrity."

Mac found a *Daily News* article from 2013 with Grieco front and center. Then an Anti-Crime officer in Brooklyn's infamous 75th Precinct, Grieco had allegedly entered an apartment without a warrant, found drugs in the closet, and staged them on a coffee table to make it look like they'd been lying in plain sight. That way,

---

* We made several attempts to calculate this data more precisely. However, given differences between sets of NYPD arrest data and the total number of NYPD officers changed ever-so-slightly every year, this was the best estimate we could come to. We acknowledge that the average number of arrests per year is weighed down by officers with administrative roles, and welcome future study in this arena.

he wouldn't have needed a warrant. Grieco arrested the four men inside, but the criminal cases came under scrutiny. One defendant reported that Grieco had offered them their freedom in exchange for a gun: "[Grieco] was saying, 'Look, guys, I got 150 guns off the streets last year. If I can get more this year, I'll get promoted and can transfer closer to home. Just get me a gun.'"[7]

"Do *we* call him Bullethead?" Mac asked.

"No," Oliver said. "*The streets* call him Bullethead." He paused. "I mean, *we* call him Bullethead, too. He knows that's his nickname." At the time, Sergeant Grieco had the most complaints of any officer Mac had heard of. And by 2024, he'd tallied up forty-one CCRB complaints and one hundred and one individual allegations during his nineteen-year career.[8]

Years later Mac received a complaint from a mother in Brooklyn. One of her two sons had been murdered by a gang member, and when detectives hadn't been able to identify his killer, a good Samaritan resolved to crack the case. Eventually, they tracked down her son's murderer and he was caught, tried, and sentenced.

But then, according to the mother, a friend of her son's murderer falsely reported to the police that her surviving son had hidden guns and narcotics in their family's home. Revenge.

The police, not knowing the report was false, used it to obtain a search warrant. And so, on one early morning, at about 6:00 a.m., officers from the Intelligence Bureau and the local precinct drove to her home. Inside, the mother heard strange men's voices at the front door. Then, a loud slam. She wondered if this was it. Had the friends of her son's killer finally come to retaliate against her family? Would they try to kill her surviving son? Would they try to kill her?

She walked to the front hallway in her pajamas. Her daughter's head poked out of a bedroom door.

"Mommy, someone's breaking in."

A buzz saw whirred against the front door's lock.

The mother walked toward the front door. "Who is it?"

"It's the police. Step away from the fucking door! Search warrant!"

The mother was relieved. "All you had to do was knock," she said. "I'll open the door." She reached for the front door handle.

An officer screamed, "Don't touch the door! Don't touch the fucking door!"

The door caved in. Ten to fifteen officers in raid jackets flooded the apartment hallway. An officer looked at the mother. "Hit the floor."

"I'm not hitting the floor." She sat down in a chair in the living room.

A white sergeant with khaki shorts, multicolored tattoos, and an unusually round head presented her with a paper warrant that read *NO KNOCK*. "We're looking for firearms, cocaine, and crack. Who's in the apartment?"

There was her daughter, her surviving son, and an old friend who'd been sleeping on the couch, there to keep her company as she grieved. The mother told the sergeant that she would have called the police if her child had a gun. "I'm that kind of mother."

The sergeant told the mother that he had a credible source—a CI—who reported that on a specific date, inside the apartment, her surviving son had showed him firearms and a pile of drugs. The mother replied that this was impossible. That was the date of her deceased son's birthday. The whole family had spent the entire day in the apartment to celebrate her son's life. Only the family had been present. She'd been set up.

But that couldn't matter to the sergeant in the khaki shorts. His team was still required to search the apartment from top to bottom. Officers walked into the deceased son's bedroom, where the surviving son had been sleeping. The bedroom had been left almost untouched since the murder. But the officers pulled the surviving son out of his brother's bed and began to tear the room apart.

The mattress was flipped, the shelves were broken, the bed frame was cracked. The deceased son's belongings were strewn across the floor. And hidden in the back of the bedroom closet, the officers found a small container of marijuana.

Positive results.

They handcuffed everyone, took them to the stationhouse, and held them all until midafternoon.

Then the sergeant in the khaki shorts appeared. "You can go." The officer removed each of their handcuffs and handed her son a summons for possession of marijuana.

The family returned to the apartment, photographed as much as they could, and began to reassemble their home.

Back in the office, Mac described the sergeant to a more tenured investigator.

"That's *definitely* Bullethead," they said. "I'm surprised you've never had a case with him. Tattoos? Khaki shorts? Round head?"

A few months later, Mac was back in an interview room. Across from him sat a high-ranking director in the sergeants' union and Sergeant Grieco himself. Over the course of the interview, the sergeant explained that while he didn't remember precisely what happened, it sounded like it was completely normal.

"And did you make the decision to take everyone to the precinct?" Mac asked.

"Yeah, probably," the sergeant said.

He seemed to answer every question directly when he had every opportunity to deny, forget, or pin the blame on someone else. Although he couldn't remember the finer details, he described the layout of the apartment, took responsibility for what happened, and explained every procedure that led him to make each decision. He was forthcoming to a degree we rarely experienced.

"Is there anything that I haven't asked you about that you'd like to add to the record?"

"No."

"This interview is now concluded. The time is now 10:15 a.m."

Mac turned off the recorder.

"This was a normal search warrant," the sergeant said with the slightest tone of irritation, as if he wasn't sure why anyone would have filed a complaint. "Our conversation was very respectful."

Mac substantiated four allegations against Sergeant Grieco: one for each family member he'd improperly detained at the stationhouse. Legally, he could have taken only the son because he was sleeping in the bedroom where the marijuana was found and admitted it was his. The sergeant didn't have any reason to think the marijuana belonged to anyone else. The NYPD agreed with Mac's conclusion, and as punishment, the NYPD told the CCRB that Sergeant Grieco would be formally retrained.

By 2024, over the course of his nineteen-year career, Sergeant Grieco had made 266 felony arrests, 166 misdemeanor arrests, 27 arrests for violations, 2 arrests for unknown infractions, and 1 arrest categorized as "Other."[9] That's 24.3 arrests per year compared to the department average of 5 to 8, and he'd supervised countless more, as was true in Mac's case. Now that was a man who made the gears turn.[*]

SPRING 2019. Greg sat on the carpet in the lobby of the records department on the third floor of the United States District Court for the Southern District of New York. The courthouse itself was at the nexus of many worlds, tucked between the southern end of Chinatown, the court where *Law & Order* was filmed, and the federal jail where, a few years later, Jeffrey Epstein would spend his final days.

---

[*] In March 2022, the *Daily News* reported that Sergeant Grieco had crossed a rare threshold. The city had settled more than $1,000,000 in lawsuits against him. According to the article, the NYPD press office retorted that Grieco "keeps New Yorkers safe by taking guns off the street and 'has made and supervised hundreds of arrests that did not lead to any civil litigation.'"

Before him loomed a metal cart carrying eight dark brown folders—case files, thousands of black-and-white pages. He was looking for Assman.

Specifically, Greg was looking for courtroom testimony by Detective Jeremiah Williams about his nickname, Assman. At first glance, the case files appeared to be well-kept, but in fact, it took half an hour just to get the pages in order.

Indictments. Press releases. Photographs of narcotics. After another hour, Greg landed on a courtroom transcript with the name Williams typed at the top.

Q: As you said, you wore plain clothes, right?

A: Yes.

Q: So that you can blend into the community unnoticed, right?

A: Yes.

Q: In a vehicle that everybody in the community knows as a police vehicle, right?

A: That is correct.

Q: Everybody recognizes you in the community, right?

A: That is correct.

Q: Because you have done a lot of arrests in that area, right?

A: Way over 200, yes.

Q: So they got to know you?

A: Yes.

Q: In fact, they have a nickname for you, right?

A: I believe they do.

Q: That nickname is Assman, right?

A: Yes.

Q: Because when you pull over guys who are arrested, you wear gloves, you tell them to drop your pants, and you stick your hands into their ass, right?

A: That is incorrect.[10]

ASSMAN WAS ASSIGNED TO THE 47th Precinct in the North Bronx. He'd been there for a long time.

The first record we found of the detective's notorious moniker was in a 2007 lawsuit. In that case, a man alleged that Assman and his partner stopped him on the street, strip-searched him on the side of the road, and that one of them put their hand into his anus. When he resisted, they arrested him and transported him to the stationhouse. There, while he was handcuffed and allegedly being beaten by two other officers, either Detective Williams or his partner allegedly placed a latex-gloved finger inside of the man's anus multiple times, causing "excruciating pain."[11]

Section 208-05 of the NYPD Patrol Guide stated in all caps, "UNDER NO CONDITIONS SHALL A BODY CAVITY SEARCH BE CONDUCTED BY ANY MEMBER OF THE SERVICE." If officers needed to obtain drugs from a person's anus, which happened more often than one might imagine, they needed to notify their supervisor, obtain a search warrant, and "seek the assistance of a medical professional."[12]

Court records show that officers did in fact recover cocaine from the man's anus. Despite this, the Bronx DA's office dismissed the charges, and the criminal case was sealed. The City of New York settled the lawsuit for $2,750.[13]

The CCRB knew Assman well. There were several separate and apparently unrelated instances in which he either referred to himself as Assman, allegedly introduced himself to civilians as Assman, or allegedly took actions that pertained to this nickname. Those references took place over a span of several years, in different locations in the Bronx, with different civilians of various ages and backgrounds.

In 2020, the CCRB found that Detective Williams had conducted an unlawful strip search. Nearly five years later, his administrative trial was still pending.

As of May 2022, over the course of his twenty-two-year career, Detective Williams had made 232 felony arrests, 681 misdemeanor arrests, 3 arrests for violations, and 1 arrest categorized as "Other," averaging 41.7 arrests per year as compared to the average of 5 to 8.[14]

As of January 2025, Detective Williams has been the subject of twenty-two CCRB complaints and sixty-one individual allegations.* As of January 2025, the NYPD had not imposed any discipline for that case, but the City of New York had publicly settled sixteen lawsuits in which Detective Williams had been named to the tune of over $294,000.[15] Six additional lawsuits were pending. From 2008 to 2018, Detective Williams received thirteen raises, was promoted to detective, and was assigned to a plainclothes unit.[16]

It was hard to believe the NYPD kept Assman around. Even if the dozens of allegations against him were somehow false, he seemed more boogeyman than protector of his Bronx neighborhood. We wondered if any other workplace in America would reward this truly spectacular notoriety. But the NYPD wasn't like most workplaces.

New York City agencies were driven by the Bloomberg-era city-management craze of datafication. Echoes of that era still reverberated through our own office, fostering a work culture that

---

* Six allegations were substantiated, two from the 2019 case.

incentivized investigators to avoid scrutiny by making their data look good. At times it seemed we were all being managed via one key metric—the average amount of time it took to close a case. Of course, the quality of an investigation is essential. But quality is difficult to quantify, so often, a measurable statistic prevails.

The NYPD, however, prioritized the metric of arrests. The more arrests officers tallied, the more convincingly the brass could claim they were doing *something*. As a consequence, the quality of arrests was subject to far less scrutiny than the quantity.

Some might see Detective Williams as a man who committed heinous acts, terrorizing citizens he was sworn to protect and serve. But through a bureaucratic lens, his arrest numbers translated into dollar signs. In turn his boogeyman status was overlooked. Detective Williams was a moneymaker. Should the NYPD have fired him, or even had this pattern of allegations investigated more thoroughly? The bureaucracy said no.

There's a cost to creating metrics that are simply designed to show you're doing something. Because metrics create incentives, and incentives create culture. And some cultures avoid holding bad actors accountable if it impacts the bottom line.

8

The Black Hole

This isn't what I thought it would be. I spend half my time
chasing cases that go nowhere.

—CCRB INVESTIGATOR

*December 2016. Six weeks after the election of Donald Trump,
a man sits at a bus stop at the intersection of West 125th Street
and Amsterdam Avenue in West Harlem. It's late at night. He
reads from a copy of* People *magazine, focusing on the featured cover article, "The Obamas Say Goodbye." After nearly two hours waiting for his bus,
he realizes that service stopped at midnight, and he begins to walk home.*

*Seemingly out of nowhere, he hears a man yell, "Get the fuck off my
block."*

Another man yells, "Get the fuck out of here."

*He turns around and sees two police officers sitting in a marked
NYPD SUV. They pull alongside the curb.*

The driver calls out, "Yeah, you. I'm talking to you."

The man freezes on the empty sidewalk.

*The officer in the passenger seat bellows, "Get the— Get the fuck out
of my office."*

*The man runs away from the officers, hiding in a nearby emergency
room. At the front desk, he asks to use the phone and frantically calls 9-1-1.
He tells the operator that he's scared to walk home and that the officers are*

circling the block looking for him. Following procedure, the 9-1-1 operator offers to send more officers to his location. The man replies that he doesn't want any more police. He says he's scared to be a Black man. The operator transfers him to a detective from IAB, and then disconnects the line.

IAB WOULD REPORT THAT THEY lost the audio recording of their conversation with the man. It would never be recovered. The detective who spoke with the man never got his name or any of his contact information. The callback number from the 9-1-1 call led to the front desk of the emergency room, where there were no records of the man ever having walked in.

The case was forwarded to the CCRB. After weeks of searching, there was no way to find the man, so the case was closed with the disposition Complaint Unavailable, and a full investigation was never conducted.

WHEN SOMEONE FILED A COMPLAINT against the NYPD, they rarely knew that we'd have to find them and obtain more information. According to New York City rules, an officer couldn't be disciplined as a result of a CCRB investigation unless a witness provided a sworn, notarized statement.* But finding even one CV could be a tall order. Some CVs didn't have homes and were very difficult to track down. Others may have been put off by the invasiveness of an investigator's contact attempts—we'd call, email, and send letters to just about any point of contact that showed up in a public records search.

If we found them, a complainant first had to give a statement over the phone and confirm their name and contact information.†

---

* There were exceptions to this rule, but they were few and far between.

† If a civilian went through with their complaint, their name would inevitably be provided to the officers they complained about.

They'd be asked to turn over whatever evidence they had—photos, videos, audio recordings, etc.—along with the names and contact information of any witnesses. Then they'd have to travel to our office in Lower Manhattan, usually during business hours, and spend an hour or two filling out forms and providing an audio-recorded sworn statement. Sometimes we would ask them to come in several times, to provide more evidence or pick from a photo array of potential subject officers. Most complainants were poor. Many couldn't afford to take time off work to come to our office. Between travel expenses, childcare, lost wages, and the simple cost of time and energy, the process wasn't just a pain in the ass, it was a barrier to entry.

On an individual level, CVs rarely benefited from filing CCRB complaints. By filing a complaint, you were formally announcing to the government, whose officers had just upset you enough to file a complaint, that you had a problem with the government. This was a nerve-racking contradiction, especially for poor Black and brown people who were rightfully skeptical that we could do anything to help.

No anonymous complaints allowed. And while it was rare for an officer to overtly retaliate against someone for filing a complaint, even the threat of retaliation could keep someone up at night. In the impossibly complicated business of policing, it was never a good idea to be on a cop's bad side. Your city was their office. And this was not customer service. If you complained to the manager, your service was not primed to improve.

Perhaps most important, any statement provided to the CCRB risked being used against a CV in criminal court. Defense attorneys would sometimes advise their clients not to provide sworn statements. In turn around 7 to 11 percent of CCRB cases were "Closed—Pending Litigation."[2] Although each of these cases could technically be reopened after a months- or yearslong criminal case concluded, they rarely were.

The CCRB didn't steer CVs toward financial compensation, either.* Money only came if you filed a lawsuit, a separate process where the city might give you a cash settlement but would rarely admit wrongdoing. Most CVs didn't know how to get an attorney or were afraid that getting one would be too expensive. Among the cases we worked, lawsuits were rare.†

Rather than money, many CCRB complainants simply wanted to sound the alarm that something wrong had happened. For them, filing a complaint was a moral decision. It just seemed like the right thing to do. And when something happens that feels wrong, people usually want to know why.

In one case, a woman in her twenties was maced by police near the scene of a shooting at a Bronx housing project. A year later, she was still calling to ask what happened: "I did nothing wrong. No one deserves that . . . It's extremely hard. Every day going out, thinking that they're after you. And I know that someone who hasn't been in a situation like this, they might not be able to understand, but it's a real thing in my mind. You know? I want to know what happened."

From 2016 to 2023, the CCRB received about 35,000 complaints. Around 50 percent of those cases, approximately 17,400 were closed without any investigation because, after filing the complaint, the CV withdrew their statement, we couldn't find them, or they just plain told us to leave them alone.[3]

To the two of us, it made sense when people backed out of their complaints against the NYPD. But each time they backed out, no matter how alarming their allegations were, our hands were tied

---

* We have no evidence that a substantiated allegation led to a higher lawsuit payout. If there was any clear benefit, it was that the CCRB would usually identify the officers in question.

† And if you waited too long to file a notice of claim—basically, a heads-up that your lawsuit is coming—you were generally barred from bringing one later.

from digging deeper.[4]* Their story was lost to what we called the Black Hole.

Mac had a case with a woman who called IAB and reported that an officer had smacked a cigarette out of her mouth and punched her in the shoulder. When Mac first called her, she sounded scared. She said that after she filed her complaint, IAB detectives showed up at her house unannounced. When she asked to watch surveillance footage of what happened, one detective replied, "There's probably not any cameras there, anyway, but if there were, then basically, like, you would be destroying this officer's life, his family, his children, his everything." Over the phone, she told Mac, "At this point, I don't want to deal with it anymore. I don't want to think about it anymore, you know?" She went on, "I was telling him, like, the way you're talking to me, it's like you're making me feel like I lied, like I'm gonna go to jail for something. He just kept, like, sucking his teeth and rolling his eyes. Like, really making me feel uncomfortable."

The tactic had its desired effect: "They told me that I had the choice to withdraw, and I did it. I walked away from them because it was too uncomfortable for me."

Mac told her IAB was wrong. The officer's life was not going to be ruined, and it was her right to file a complaint. She asked to think it over. She'd call back another time. But over the next few weeks, when Mac called and sent her emails, she didn't pick up or write him back. The case was closed as Complainant Uncooperative.

Given that IAB allegedly pressured the woman to withdraw her complaint, Mac generated a new case. Ironically, procedure required that the case be transferred back to IAB, and we never heard about it again.

---

* Many amendments have been made since we started, most significantly "self-initiating complaints" usually based on media coverage.

Occasionally, IAB detectives might bully someone into withdrawing their complaint. But there were other ways they could jam up our intake process. For example, IAB was prone to sending us complaints with incorrect or missing contact information, like when they reported that a civilian's name was spelled Zalerie Bappipfe. Not a real name. It wasn't even close.

The misdirection wasn't limited to absurd spelling errors. In 2017, for almost four months, IAB stopped forwarding cases to the CCRB. Then, without warning, they sent us a backlog of several hundred cases. In many, surveillance footage of serious allegations had already expired. And at least a few CVs, offended that the CCRB had taken so long to contact them, refused to participate in any investigation at all.*

Sometimes, IAB conducted separate investigations into the same incidents the CCRB was already investigating. But where a CCRB interview might last an hour or more, an IAB interview might last five to ten minutes. Where CCRB investigators tended to ask neutral probing questions, IAB's desire for an officer to be exonerated was frequently laid bare in CV and officer interviews alike, where leading questions prevailed.

"So officer, did you fear for your safety?"

It seemed that IAB used their own investigations to undermine the CCRB process, exonerating or lightly disciplining officers before the CCRB investigation had even concluded.

Later, if an officer had already faced light discipline from IAB, the NYPD might use this as the basis to dismiss more serious CCRB charges.

In light of IAB's procedural antics, it was clear that their bureaucracy was not designed to meaningfully pursue police

---

* Although the 2017 IAB stoppage was an especially protracted period of obstruction, there were regular delays in getting case referrals from IAB, meaning footage often expired and CVs often lost patience while their complaints wound their way through the maze of middlemen to us.

accountability. Rather, IAB could be best understood as the NYPD's brand-management team. When an officer did something particularly sensational like molest a child or hire a hit man to kill their spouse, this was very bad for the brand, so IAB would be all over it, and the officer would be promptly arrested.[5] Sometimes the same was true for money laundering, bribery, and other overt corruption. IAB could be incredibly thorough when the brand was on the line, with elaborate undercover units to run stings on officers alleged to have stolen as little as twenty dollars.[6]

But because the NYPD brand did not benefit when a person had their constitutional rights violated (e.g., freedom from unreasonable search and seizure), IAB could bury these issues with sham investigations even when the facts were served up to them on a silver platter.

Through brand-motivated investigations, a CV's resistance or intransigence could be exaggerated, an officer could have words put into their mouth to make it appear as though their decisions were more reasonable than they were, and what might have initially appeared to be a violation of the Fourth Amendment could quietly disappear into the Black Hole. When potential constitutional violations were quietly exonerated, these actions could then be chalked up to officers trying to do something, which was inevitably good for the brand. Knock someone over the head? Maybe they deserved it. Frisk someone walking home? Maybe they should have known better than to walk around in a high-crime area. Killed a suspect in a shoot-out? Cops arrest criminals, right? Sometimes they have to shoot them, right? IAB rarely answered the question that an air crash investigator might ask—why did this happen, and how can we prevent it from happening again? Rather, IAB usually answered the question—what outcome is most favorable to the NYPD brand?

And for anyone who disagreed with this logic? They could be directed to the bottom line, as NYPD merchandise grossed millions of dollars every year.[7] The fact is that IAB protected one of the most recognizable brands in the world. And an objective, fact-driven investigation after every incident? Not great for the brand.

Our investigative work was further complicated by another unit within the CCRB. The mediation unit, run by about five administrators, arranged informal conciliation as an alternative to investigation.[8] A mediation itself was a confidential meeting between a professional conflict negotiator, a CV, and the officer they filed a complaint against. It was voluntary, so either the CV or the officer could back out at any time.

For the most part, mediations worked well. The sessions we personally witnessed were heartfelt conversations where CVs and officers found common ground. According to the CCRB, around 90 percent of attempted mediations were resolved amicably, with the parties agreeing to proverbially shake hands and move on.[9] However, when a case was resolved through mediation, there was no investigation into what really happened. It didn't matter if evidence revealed clear misconduct. If the case was mediated, records of the incident would be effectively sealed. From 2015 to 2019, an average of 431 cases went to mediation each year.[10] That was about 10 percent of CCRB cases, and they headed in one direction—straight into the Black Hole.

Reformers tried to pull stories back from the Black Hole. In 2015, international tennis star James Blake was tackled by a plainclothes NYPD officer in a dumbfounding case, in which Blake was mistaken for a suspect in a credit-card-fraud ring. Blake started the process of suing the city. Over the course of prolonged negotiations, a combination of city officials and police-reform activists convinced Blake that there was a problem with policing only he had the power to solve. So in late 2017, instead of going after a standard cash settlement, Blake himself helped to create the James Blake CCRB Fellowship. This fellowship would pay for one CCRB employee with a single responsibility: figuring out why the CCRB was so bad at tracking down CVs. They would identify which CVs we'd lost track of, go find them, and obtain sworn statements that investigators otherwise wouldn't have. It seemed like Blake had been told that this was among the most pressing issues in police oversight.[*] The fellowship's creation was celebrated from the *New York Times* to ABC News as a step forward in police reform, but the coverage ended there.

From 2018 to 2020, the Blake fellow joined our office and studied the life of a CCRB investigator. They frequented community-board meetings, spoke with members of the most heavily policed neighborhoods, and had unprecedented access to every member of the CCRB staff. The fellow spent hundreds of hours interviewing investigators about the process of finding CVs, trying to get to the root of the problem, and traveling the five boroughs in search of the people we hadn't found. Agencywide, a staggering amount of staff time was dedicated to the Blake fellow's research, usually at the expense of casework.

In November 2020, the Blake fellow publicly reported their findings. There was no press. It all boiled down to two basic recommendations. First, investigators needed to be nice. Second, the agency needed more investigators. After all that time and energy, the Blake fellow reported what every tenured investigator already knew: that we had to be cordial and that we needed more help. And bizarrely, although the fellow had worked relentlessly to track down

---

[*] As incomplete a picture as it provided, the poorly named truncation rate (as if it were the CCRB's choice that CVs fell off the map) served as an oft-repeated statistic—used by the CCRB and reformers alike to shape agency policy. And how straightforward and ready at hand a number it was. How many people's complaints is the CCRB not even bothering to investigate? "Fifty-eight percent," an outsider might bemoan. But unfortunately, the truncation rate oversimplified a complex problem to the point that the statistic was rendered completely useless.

our missing CVs, the agency's rate of finding them had fallen.[11] The Black Hole seemed to be expanding.

Absent from the report was any acknowledgment of the incentives influencing the people involved. Perhaps victims of police misconduct might not be incentivized to talk to the government. Perhaps investigators were poorly incentivized, as well. Blake's attempt at reform was well-meaning, but in the end precious energy had been poured into restating the obvious, and nothing much had changed.[12*]

This saga reflects a common problem in the criminal-justice system. Oftentimes there are calls for more studies and research when there is already enough data available to understand the problems and their potential solutions. What was needed was not another study, but action.

The final line of the Blake fellow's report read: "I would like to meet with IAB to discuss the items mentioned above and ways IAB and CCRB can collaborate more efficiently to provide optimal service to the complainants/victims of police misconduct." If our investigative intuition had taught us anything, IAB would not be our source for best practices. They seemed to like the Black Hole exactly how it was. And they weren't the only ones.

While the Blake fellow had worked on one side of the office, struggling to wrench cases from the Black Hole, on the other side, investigators celebrated each time another case was sucked in.

---

* We really cannot stress enough how much this was largely a waste of everyone's time and energy. Perhaps most significantly, this review highlighted the reality that other oversight agencies do not formally track a truncation rate, nor do they adversely categorize cases in which complaints do not move forward with the investigatory process. It turned out that the metric of truncations was unique to the CCRB. By 2021, after all that effort, the term "truncation" had been phased out of CCRB annual reports altogether.

One squad had a big gold bell. Every time a CV withdrew their complaint, when the lucky investigator hung up the phone, they would stand up, grab the squad bell, and ring it as if they were closing the New York Stock Exchange. Their squad mates would briefly cheer, they'd all exchange high fives, and only then would they get back to work. The bell was intended to improve morale, and in some small way, it probably did.

Every investigator was stretched thin. At any given time, each one of us might have been personally managing fifteen to thirty-five active investigations. A single case could have ten victims and fifteen officers to interview, with several dozen hours of video to review. And for every case, we needed to gather the evidence, memorize all the facts, conduct the interviews, and write a thorough legal analysis to present to our board. If we did anything wrong, we might be disciplined. And if we did everything right, nobody cared. Then, like a drumbeat, every two weeks or so, the queue of incoming cases would come back around.[13*] Another three cases would land on our desks in manila folders, bearing the weight of something much heavier than paper. Catching cases was a setback in any investigator's week, a wave splashing into a sinking boat.

INVESTIGATORS WANTED TO MAKE THEIR mark by improving the criminal justice system. But when each of them was dropped into this bureaucracy, they began swimming in a sea of incentives. And slowly but surely, as the current pulled them farther from shore, their behavior started to change.

With some time at the CCRB, one could become professionally proficient, even excellent, at investigating police misconduct.

---

* In *Blue Blood*, Edward Conlon describes the NYPD detectives' parallel system as "the catching order."

But there was a personal cost to being in that workplace. Hope could devolve into cynicism, ambition into apathy, skepticism into paranoia. The tools for survival were not for the faint of heart. As a tipsy boss once confided to Greg at a holiday party, "Just so you know, everyone above you here has stabbed each other in the back." At times, the CCRB culture fed off petty bureaucratic vengeance, and it was no coincidence that it was founded as a branch of the NYPD.

At a certain point, despite their lofty academic credentials, many investigators would find themselves doing the absolute bare minimum. The work would become less about public service and more about psychological survival.* And as we spent each day interviewing officers, we began to see that their world of perverse incentives looked a lot like ours.

Meanwhile, from just 2016 to 2023, over twenty thousand CCRB cases were closed without full investigations.[14] And those were incidents where someone had gone through with filing a complaint; we had no way to know how many others had gone unreported. To conduct a complete investigation into an allegation of police misconduct was to examine a single tree in a remote forest. Yet, with each incident that made the long journey from someone else's memory to our own, patterns began to emerge. One pattern stood out among victims and witnesses alike: They didn't want the same thing to happen to anyone else, whether or not what the officer had done was technically legal.

On paper, every allegation was determined by a preponderance of the evidence. This essentially meant that, based on the evidence, there was a 51 percent likelihood that misconduct had taken place, or not. Was it likelier or not that the officer had broken the law? That they had violated the Patrol Guide? That a CV had fabricated

---

* Managers rarely had supervisory experience. They had investigatory experience. So it tended to feel like their employees were under investigation.

their complaint entirely? These questions and their answers would determine whether an allegation was unfounded, exonerated, unsubstantiated, or substantiated. But in practice, we all knew that the board held our substantiations to a higher standard than 51 percent.

Whenever an investigator submitted a closing report, it was sent to the board for a final vote. There, substantiated allegations were bound to be closely scrutinized. The board was liable to flip an allegation from substantiated to unsubstantiated or exonerated, especially if one of the more vocal NYPD-appointed board members disagreed with the investigator's conclusion.

"When I ran a precinct, I told my men to do exactly what this officer did," the board member might say. "That's just normal policing." According to an internal memo leaked in spring 2021, half of the CCRB's dozen or so board members voted to uphold substantiated recommendations on a regular basis, at least 92 percent of the time. But in stark contrast, two NYPD appointees flipped our substantiations with alarming regularity.

From 2016 to 2020, Salvatore Carcaterra, a former deputy chief who organized the NYPD's response to threats of terrorism following the 9/11 attacks on the World Trade Center and who also managed CompStat for a time, voted to uphold a mere 45 percent of investigators' substantiated allegations, by far the lowest number on the CCRB board.[15,16] Frank Dwyer, a Harvard graduate and former deputy inspector who'd also run CompStat for a time, agreed with only 57 percent of our substantiations.[17]

If the board flipped an allegation, it reflected poorly on the investigator and their manager. And if an investigator developed a reputation for substantiating too many "borderline" allegations, then they'd be taken less seriously or were seen as biased. Then even their most egregious cases would beg the question: Were they twisting the facts?

In 2017, Greg had a case in which he'd worked for months to prove that an officer was at the scene of an arrest. After he'd proved it, he interviewed the officer, and she lied to his face. He closed the case and recommended a false official statement. "Hey," Greg called out to his manager, "did you see that Sal's voting on my case?" The manager stood up, walked over to Greg's desk, and put their hand on his shoulder. "Well," the manager said. "The case had a good run." Sometimes, the Black Hole wasn't just a place, like IAB or DAO—sometimes it was a person, somebody who could make sure good cases never saw the light of day.

Because the NYPD board members were so prone to flip a borderline case, every tenured investigator knew to save their ammo for the battles that mattered most. Substantiate the most serious, slam-dunk allegations and be conservative with the cases that risked attracting Sal's watchful eye. He was known to demand that investigators be reprimanded, and from time to time, he'd direct his own investigation, insisting that the policy unit analyze an investigator's past cases to see whether they had been substantiating more allegations than their peers.

In 2019, a CCRB higher-up pulled Mac into his office to tell him a board member was complaining his closing reports were too long. We both knew which board member. "How do I fit thirty allegations into less than twenty pages?" Mac asked. "If I'd shortened that report, they wouldn't have had any idea what was going on. This is a complicated case."

He leaned back in his chair and laughed. "I'm just passing along the message. But make them shorter."

LATE INTO THE NIGHT, EVERY night, it seemed, Reilly sat working at his desk. He was a tall, burly man, with long black hair and piercing blue eyes. No one seemed to know precisely what he did, but it was common knowledge that whatever it was, it was very important. He'd been at the agency longer than any of us, and he seemed to be called into every significant meeting. His desk was adorned with the nameplates of his former coworkers, all of whom had resigned or been fired. Some nights, Reilly would roam the agency floor, looking to amuse himself with a new investigator.

"How do these motivational posters make you feel?" Reilly might ask, pointing toward the office wall. "They don't make me feel very motivated." For a time, the walls were covered in framed posters that had affirmations like "Ordinary is not an option" underneath photographs of nature. "You know how much these cost? Three thousand dollars. I think we should do something," he'd say, having no intention of doing anything himself, "I think *you* should file a complaint."

YEARS EARLIER, REILLY STOOD BEFORE a long table covered in dozens of large glossy photographs. Each one displayed a different angle of an autopsy. A man's legs, covered in road rash. Hands, scraped and bloodied. A chest, naked and hairless. A face, peaceful but for a large gash above the left eye. A skull, sawed open. A brain, bloodred. Reilly had to choose which photographs would be entered into evidence.

IAB had exonerated an officer who killed a man. The District Attorney's Office had declined to prosecute the officer. But the CCRB had a newly formed Administrative Prosecution Unit, and in one week, they would put the officer on trial, recommending termination. But the day after Reilly stared at those photos, the CCRB received a letter from the NYPD.

It would be detrimental to the Police Department's disciplinary process to allow the CCRB to continue its prosecution ... based on the interests of justice the Police Commissioner has determined that the CCRB should not be allowed to continue its prosecution of [the officer]. Accordingly, please be advised that it is the Department's intention to dismiss the Charges/Specifications in this matter, and there will be no disciplinary action taken against [the officer].

How was this possible? "The CCRB has no teeth," the public complained.[18] Perhaps getting an officer fired for killing a man would begin to change that perception. But sure enough, buried in the fine print in section two of the Memorandum of Understanding (MOU), there it was:

> In those limited instances where the Police Commissioner determines that CCRB's prosecution of Charges and Specifications in a substantiated case would be detrimental to the Police Department's disciplinary process, the Police Commissioner shall so notify CCRB. Such instances shall be limited to such cases in which there are parallel or related criminal investigations, or when, in the case of an officer with no disciplinary history or prior substantiated CCRB complaints, based on such officer's record and disciplinary history the interests of justice would not be served.[19]

With that one paragraph, the NYPD had the power to unilaterally commandeer almost any case that the CCRB tried to prosecute. So that's exactly what they did.[20*]

Legally, the CCRB's operational relationship to the NYPD was tenuous, often relying on a series of MOUs that were signed by the leaders of both agencies.† The MOUs governed the fine print. What

---

* From 2012 to 2021, the NYPD retained at least ninety-five CCRB cases in "the interest of justice."

† More technically, the CCRB-NYPD relationship was governed by the overarching City Charter and CCRB rules, with MOUs to fill in the gaps of day-to-day operations and expanded CCRB powers like the Administrative Prosecution Unit.

cases would be prosecuted? What were the penalties for each allegation? What documents would be shared? Would we have BWC access? And so on.

The problem was that these MOUs were not law, and it appeared that the NYPD could cease to honor any of them at any time. So whenever Mac recommended a policy solution—"Why don't we sue them for taking so long to give us documents? The public would side with us."—a supervisor might reply, "The department could just back out of the MOUs, and we wouldn't have anything to investigate." Because the day-to-day work of our investigations relied on the NYPD's cooperation via sketchy agreements, the CCRB seemed to structurally resemble an HR company that the NYPD had contracted to conduct internal investigations, with the threat looming that they might cancel our contract at a moment's notice.

While this proverbial threat loomed, an investigator could work on a case for years, memorizing every detail and meeting everyone involved, only to have it suddenly disappear into the Black Hole. To continue their work, many would have to protect themselves with a cocoon of cynicism—ringing a bell to celebrate a complaint withdrawn, or plotting revenge against the motivational posters that adorned our walls—all to shield the hope that our work was leading to less misconduct, that things were not so bleak as they seemed.

Part II

BEHIND THE BLUE WALL

9

The Academy

Summer 2016. Early in the morning, a caravan of carpoolers carried bleary-eyed investigators to an off-limits section of College Point, Queens. By 7:00 a.m., we were staggering through a wide-open parking lot. The bright morning sunshine glistened against the soaring blue glass of the NYPD's new police academy. The building's architects described it as a "horizontal skyscraper," and we heard more than one officer warmly refer to it as the Death Star, but whatever you called it, it was a striking feat of architecture for a municipal building.[1]

Officially, our CCRB training was only two months long. Graduation had come and gone, and now, three months later, our class of investigators each had a full docket of cases. But we'd all been told there was one final lesson before training was really over: two days at the NYPD academy.

The investigators walked across the wide campus green and checked in at the visitors' booth. A uniformed officer greeted them with the warmth of a suspicious customs agent. "Go that way," he said, nodding toward the front entrance. Past the revolving doors, through the cavernous lobby, and up a flight of stairs, we trailed into a shiny new classroom shaped like an amphitheater.

"Good morning!" an NYPD sergeant boomed to the scattered audience. There were hundreds of seats but only twenty of us. Before him was our training class, already reduced from ten to seven, and another class that started a few months after us. A training instructor from the CCRB sat in the corner taking notes.

The sergeant explained that, over the next two days, we'd receive a highly condensed version of an NYPD cadet's training, which normally lasted six months. One at a time, NYPD instructors would enter the classroom to give us a taste of the Academy.

There was the Narcotics sergeant from the Bronx. "So, what do you guys know about narcotics?" Mac glanced over at another investigator, who'd proudly earned her reputation as class stoner. She covered her mouth, stifling a laugh.

"I mean Narcotics," said the sergeant, "the unit. Have you guys dealt with Narcotics?"

At this point, none of us had investigated a Narcotics officer. We learned that there were eight Narcotics units, one in every patrol borough. Bronx. Manhattan North. Manhattan South. Queens North. Queens South. Brooklyn North. Brooklyn South. Staten Island. Each was its own distinct unit, a department unto itself.

"Narcotics is a special command. And each command is different. If you learn anything today, it should be this: every division of the NYPD has its own culture." He looked at the investigators knowingly, but none of us seemed to catch his drift. "We even have our own culture here at the academy. Isn't that right?" He pivoted toward the corner, where his otherwise silent partner leaned against the wall and nodded. "Mm-hmm." The sergeant turned back to the class. "But you know, not all those cultures . . . get along."

The Narcotics sergeant pulled a fistful of Ziploc bags from his pocket. "You guys want to see some drugs?" He handed the bags to an investigator in the front row. "Come on now. Pass them around the classroom." One by one, the investigators passed the bags, forming a strange assembly line.

The sergeant chuckled. "In those bags are vials of crack cocaine and heroin."

Each of us handled the vials like rare museum artifacts, cautiously eyeing them in our outstretched hands.

"That's what we're out there for. To take this off the streets."

When the bags reached the back of the classroom, the sergeant walked up to the last investigator, who sat before a small mountain of paraphernalia. The sergeant grabbed the bags in one arm and cradled them to his chest. "This is all of them, right?" He winked and walked back to the front of the classroom.

Next there was the officer who ran Taser training. "You know a lot of people have misconceptions about Tasers. I can assure you that they're perfectly safe. To be a certified instructor at my level, I've been tased with a full charge over fifty times. And look at me now!" The officer pulled his Taser from its holster and lifted it for the class to see.

"Who wants to get tased?"

After a little prodding, a few brave investigators gathered in a circle at the front of the classroom. "Okay, so hold hands," the instructor said. "Now you hold this prong . . ." Every Taser had two barbs that shot out like harpoons. When the barbs latched into a person's skin, an electrical surge would paralyze the target for about five seconds. The instructor handed one barb each to the investigators beside him.

"Everyone ready?"

Zap.

Then there was the lieutenant from counterterrorism, a Black man in a sharp suit. He struck a serious tone. "You know," he said, pausing to look around the classroom. "You know what they say about you? Do you know what cops say?" The room was silent. Early on, we didn't know what other people at the CCRB said about us, let alone what cops said.

"For cops, the CCRB is a collection of stories. And in every stationhouse locker room, those stories get passed around whenever a new recruit arrives or someone gets called in for an interview." The lieutenant described a CCRB case where an officer had chased a man with a gun and wrestled him to the ground. In the struggle, the officer struck the man. According to the lieutenant, the CCRB substantiated a force allegation against that officer.

"And really, that officer saved the man's life because he could have shot him. And instead, he got CCRBed. Then he didn't get promoted to sergeant." The lieutenant began to barrage us with story after story of CCRB investigations in which he felt officers had been unfairly disciplined. After a while, Greg felt like the air had been sucked out of the room. What had he signed up for?

The lieutenant's gripes exemplified a contradiction that still echoes throughout the NYPD ranks. Officers and their unions would complain about the CCRB, and really any form of outside oversight, but they ignored that the NYPD itself was the only institution that decided whether they were disciplined. The CCRB's recommendations were exactly that: recommendations. And despite a 2019 audit that raised serious questions about continuing allegations of favoritism and inconsistency in the NYPD disciplinary process, the CCRB's boogeyman status among officers never seemed to fade.[2]

Then the lieutenant made a surprising pivot.

"Now you won't catch me saying it outside this room," he said, looking up and down the classroom. "But despite what they say, we need you. I need you. Because now that I supervise officers, I realize that there are questions you ask them that I can't. You're an important part of the policing equation. We need to hold bad officers accountable. And when I can't, someone else has to be there. And that's gonna be you guys."

On the second day, we heard from a Latino sergeant who'd designed the entire academy curriculum. As he flipped through PowerPoint slides, he got around to the academy's cultural-sensitivity training. It began with a screening of the 2005 Academy Award–winning movie *Crash*, in which a white police officer pulls over a Black man and sexually assaults his wife, only to be redeemed when he later saves her from a burning vehicle.[3] That officer's partner then kills a Black hitchhiker without facing any consequences.

Greg looked down at his paper copy of the syllabus. It seemed that *Crash* was the officers' entire training on cultural sensitivity. He raised his hand and asked, "Is there any more training after you watch the film?"

"Well, we have a forty-five-minute debrief where the cadets discuss the movie, how it made them feel, and what they would have done in those situations." The sergeant clasped his hands. "And that's the end of that!"

Another new investigator, a white woman in her early twenties, raised her hand.

"Do NYPD officers learn about Stonewall? Don't you think that's important for them to know?"

She was referring to the uprising at the Stonewall Inn, a pillar of Greenwich Village's gay community in the 1960s. In 1969, NYPD officers had infamously cracked down on anti-cross-dressing laws and a prohibition on selling alcoholic beverages to "homosexuals," beating and tear-gassing hundreds of protesters over several days. It was a seminal moment in the LGBTQ+ movement for civil rights, and in the history of New York City.[4]

"You know," the instructor said, "we tried to fit that in there, but we ran out of space."

As the class filed out around lunchtime, Mac stopped next to the Latino sergeant.

"How long has that been the training?" Mac asked. "Watching *Crash*?"

Mac suspected it'd been part of training since 2005 or so, when the movie first hit theaters, and that no one had taken the time to pick a more instructive film.

"We put *Crash* in just last year," the sergeant said enthusiastically. "It's a big step up." He paused and lowered his voice. "You should have seen what we had before. It was a big diagram of races, with tips for how to deal with them. Like, 'Russians are loud and boisterous,' and 'Chinese people are mercantile focused.' It took me years to get *Crash* in there."

Mac wondered what else was on that diagram.

Greg, who had overheard their conversation, chimed in, "You ever seen *The Wire*? You could use that instead."

The sergeant snapped his fingers. "I've been meaning to get around to that show. I've heard great things."

After lunch, there was our final training, hosted by the NYPD's lead use-of-force instructor for new cadets. He was a remarkably fit short white man in his late twenties or early thirties. For about twenty minutes, he described cadets' force training, demonstrating various jujitsu moves as he spoke.

"And in a situation like that, you gotta take him down like this," he said, gleefully flipping an imaginary opponent to the ground.

Later, he outlined various ways to make a home entry. "And in that case, you're gonna want to stand in the threshold of the door," he said. But when the CCRB's training instructor told him that he'd need a search warrant in that specific circumstance, things started to get weird.

Thus began an hour-long diatribe, in which the tactics instructor railed against the CCRB's attorneys, claimed that we—the investigators—might be criminals, and denounced the existence of police oversight itself. "No one should have to tell you how to do your job!" he bellowed over and over. It got to the point where the tactics instructor, chest heaving, had to be escorted out of the room by a lieutenant.

"Sorry about that," the lieutenant said, returning to the class-room. "This job is just stressful. Some guys take that stress out on anyone who makes their jobs harder."

The investigators exchanged bewildered glances. It felt like we'd been held hostage.

"He's stressed about the CCRB, but there are more stressful parts to this job. There are the moments where you have to hold someone's hand as they go into diabetic shock, when you have to watch someone die. I mean, being a cop is worth it. You really help people. But the most stressful part is the suicides. You see a guy one day and think he's totally fine, close to retirement, and the next day he blows his head off." The lieutenant lowered his head, and his eyes seemed to well up. "That's the real stress. That's the stuff you take home with you."

The room was silent.

"All right, everyone," said the CCRB instructor, cutting through the silence. "Our day is over, and that means you've completed your time at the academy. Congratulations!"

The investigators streamed out of the classroom.

Mac and Greg walked out through the main lobby, stopping only to stare at a platoon of new cadets who marched past in military formation. They wore only white T-shirts and white boxer shorts. A uniformed drill sergeant bellowed marching orders. In unison, the cadets dropped to the ground, beginning a sequence of push-ups on the glassy floor.

As they walked across the parking lot, Mac turned to Greg.

"What the fuck just happened?"

While our two days at the academy gave us a glimpse behind the blue wall of silence, they'd left us with many more questions than answers. Why did going to the NYPD academy feel like jour-neying to somewhere far away from modern-day New York City? Had policing always been like this? What we could sense about this place was that it hadn't been invented out of thin air. The NYPD culture appeared insular, secretive, and cynical. We knew it came from somewhere; it would just take years of research to pinpoint exactly where that was.

10

From Ireland to the NYPD

All the cops turned Irish, the Jewish cops, like Goldberg,
but also the Italian cops, the Latin cops, and the black cops.[1]

—TOM WOLFE, *The Bonfire of the Vanities*

While we learned to police the police, it was easy to lose perspective. But in the backs of our minds, we couldn't stop wondering—where did this all come from? We were deeper inside policing than we ever thought we'd be. When we thought of the police, we no longer pictured Chief Wiggum or Columbo. We were thinking of officers we'd personally met. Our experiences begged the question, what created all of this? Over our years of researching, we found different stories. There's the militarization of the police and the German influence in the early twentieth century. There's the expansion of surveillance that spawned from the American occupation of the Philippines. There's the influence of French colonization on the War on Drugs. But looming above this all, certainly in New York City, were two powerful stories, one about slave patrols that had shaped the national narrative, and a much longer history that shaped the officers themselves.

. . .

"THE SUN NEVER SETS ON the British Empire" was a common adage in the nineteenth and twentieth centuries, but British colonialism had a humble beginning. In the 1580s, when Russia had begun its expansion east of Moscow, the French had voyaged to Canada, the Portuguese had colonized Brazil, and the Spanish had established colonies throughout the Americas, all the English had were four failed settlements in Ireland.[2] But that was about to change.

The English escalated efforts to colonize the island of Ireland by force, and in doing so, they developed a blueprint for totalitarian control that would define geopolitics for centuries to come. The English conquest of Ireland began well before the 1580s, but this decade marked the beginning of the Plantation of Munster, when English settlers were first given seized Irish land en masse. Early on, English forces formed plantations where the Irish were expelled from their lands and English and Scottish settlers were empowered to form their own segregated communities. Tens of thousands of Protestant English settlers emigrated to displace the Catholic Irish, claiming hundreds of thousands of acres at a time. In turn, the settlers became dependent on the English monarchy to ward off those Irish who attempted to retake their homelands.

This was a powerful political maneuver, pitting poor settlers against a people whose land was being colonized. As anthropologist Conn Malachi Hallinan put it:

> For it was in Ireland that the colonial powers first saw the effectiveness of divide and conquer, of pitting religious and/ or ethnic groups against one another in a war that both could only lose. It is of no small importance today to examine the unfolding of that process in Ireland. With minor variations, it became a colonial blueprint for the rest of the world.[3]

In those early years, nearly half the Irish population was displaced or killed in wars for religious and political autonomy. In

1650, the population of Ireland was 1.5 million. In 1652, after the Cromwellian conquest, it was 850,000, of whom 150,000 were English and Scottish settlers. Almost overnight, Ireland had become "a nation of dispossessed people dominated by foreign landlords."[4]

Throughout this saga, the English made fervid attempts to "de-historiciz[e] and de-culturiz[e]" the Irish people, seeking an "erasure" of the "feral" Irish identity.[5] These attempts at cultural eradication climaxed in the "Penal Laws" enacted in 1695.[6] Under these laws, Catholics in Ireland could not vote, hold rank in the army, become professionally licensed, possess weaponry, study law or medicine, speak or read Gaelic, or play Irish music.[7] All Irish Catholics were required to pay taxes to support the Protestant Church.[8] The English limited inheritance laws so that, by 1703, Irish Catholics owned less than 10 percent of the land where they comprised 90 percent of the population. Only if an Irish Catholic son agreed to convert to Protestantism, he would be allowed inheritance rights.[9] Thus, Irish Catholics were often forced to choose between their land and their culture.

Over the next two centuries, the Irish people went from clans of independent herders and farmers to "a country of . . . landless peasants, locked into a bare subsistence economy."[10] Reduced to a source of rent capital for English landlords and cheap labor for English industry, the disenfranchised Irish lived in "material conditions . . . comparable to those of an American slave."[11*]

There were three formative eras of Irish immigration to America. The first era was from 1607 to 1775, in which several hundred thousand immigrants came from the north of Ireland and primarily settled in Pennsylvania, greater Appalachia, and Massachusetts.[12] In exchange for passage to the New World, many agreed to work as indentured servants for four to seven years. By the 1740s, nine out

---

* Of course, in any aspect other than "material conditions," the comparison loses credibility.

of ten indentured servants in Pennsylvania were Irish.[13] In the second era, from 1815 to 1845, one million Irish immigrants, half of them Catholic and half of them Protestant, emigrated and spread more broadly across the United States.[14] But the most consequential era was yet to come.

BY THE 1820S, in the heat of the Industrial Revolution, London's population had more than doubled in the past century, surpassing Beijing as the largest city in the world.[15] London's new landscape was "sprawling and disorderly," and each parish was responsible for hiring its own security force. For increasingly common cases of civil unrest, the army was called in.[16] In 1829, Sir Robert Peel, the British home secretary, disbanded the local security forces in London and formed the Metropolitan Police. It was the first modern police department, and unlike its predecessors across Europe, London's new police force was designed to serve the public, not the interests of monarchs or the private sector.[17] The department had nine founding principles. They boiled down to the following:

1. Policing exists to prevent crime.
2. Public approval is required for success.
3. To earn public approval, police must convince the public that the law is worth following.
4. The more force is used, the lower public approval.
5. Police earn public approval by following the law and enforcing it equally.
6. De-escalate before resorting to force.
7. The police and the public are equals.
8. Police must never break the law, or even appear to.

9.   The test of policing is the absence of crime, not the presence of police.[18]*

In 1845, the New York Police Department—one of America's first—was founded in the image of London's Metropolitan Police.[19] But in that same year, the demographics of New York City, and the United States as a whole, began to drastically change.

Due to the catastrophic potato famine of 1845, a mass migration of Irish Catholics to the overwhelmingly Protestant United States had begun.[20]† From January 1846 to December 1851, more than 410,000 Irish passengers arrived in New York, and from 1845 to 1855, up to 1.5 million Irish immigrants settled throughout America.[21] As many as 90 percent of these Irish immigrants were Catholic.[22] But when the Irish Catholics arrived in Protestant America, they found that the stereotypes engendered by the English had preceded their arrival. In England, "Protestant [had become] synonymous with privilege and Catholic with dispossessed," and only decades before, the United States had been 13 English colonies.[23] A storm was brewing.

Irish skin may have been white, but socially the Irish were often treated by Protestants on par with "free Negroes." "Most historians would agree that there was very strong prejudice [against the Irish]," explained James Barrett, author of *The Irish Way*. This led to various difficulties for Irish immigrants, particularly when it came to securing work.[24]

However, although they first struggled to find employment in American cities, unlike their Black contemporaries, the Irish were

---

* NYPD Commissioner William Bratton told the *New York Times* that he carried these principles with him at all times, "like the Bible."

† Because Irish Catholics had been forced onto smaller parcels of land, many could only grow potatoes to feed their families and livestock. But in 1845, the fungus known as blight spread across Ireland. By the end of 1845, one-third to one-half of the potato crop was ruined. In 1846, three-quarters of the harvest was lost. By 1850, three million people would leave Ireland, half by emigration and half by death.

permitted to accumulate power in two crucial arenas: politics and policing.

In 1851, the Boston Police Department hired the first Irish police officer in American history.[25] By 1855, 305 out of 1,149 members of the NYPD had been born in Ireland.[26] According to CUNY professor Edward O'Donnell, the total Irish contingent of the NYPD, including the members who had Irish-born parents, was probably closer to 50 percent.[27] In the early 1860s, contemporaries estimated the NYPD to be half Catholic.[28] An 1886 survey of 2,936 NYPD officers revealed 974 had been born in Ireland, and at least 1,745 had Irish parents.[29] Suddenly, in America's largest city, the Irish had become the new enforcers of American law, a direct descendant of the same English common law that had led to centuries of their own oppression in Ireland.[30]

By 1890, in a city with just over 1.5 million residents, 275,000 New Yorkers had been born in Ireland, and more than 600,000 were of Irish descent.[31] But given their history, the Irish hadn't held English law or bureaucracy itself in very high esteem. Even the word "bureaucracy" was first used in the English language by an Irish author who, in 1818, described it as "office tyranny, by which Ireland has been so long governed."[32]

London's Metropolitan Police had been founded in the image of public service, but the Irish had experienced only the most oppressive qualities of English common law, which were neither sacred nor just. The law they knew was a tool to accumulate power, written by a government that hated them. So, the Irish, finally wielding the power of the law in their own hands, used it the way the English had taught them: to accumulate power.

From the 1850s to the 1890s, the NYPD devolved into an unprecedented and sprawling corruption racket. Nearly every officer had to bribe their way into promotions, many extorted local businesses into protection schemes, and the department itself created an underworld of illegal gambling like America had never seen.[33] It all led to America's first sweeping civilian investigation into police misconduct, the Lexow Committee of 1894.[34]

William "Big Bill" Devery, whose Irish-Catholic parents had both escaped poverty and starvation in Ireland, was the baddest of the NYPD's bunch from the 1870s through the early 1900s.[35] Devery was notoriously corrupt, famously charming, and extraordinarily effective when it came to navigating bureaucracy. He was best known for his courtroom catchphrase, "Touchin' on and appertainin' to that matter, I disremember," a predecessor to the ubiquitous modern police response of "I don't recall."[36] As muckraking journalist Lincoln Steffens described Devery, "[He was] a disgrace, no more fit to be chief of police than the fish man is to be director of the Aquarium. But as a character, he was a work of art, a masterpiece."[37] Sure enough, in 1898 Devery became the NYPD's first chief of police.[38]

A half century later, in 1948, John Timoney was born in Dublin, Ireland. In the 1990s, he rose to become an NYPD deputy commissioner. He was an architect of CompStat, a tool used to track which crimes were being committed in each precinct, and he later ran the Miami and Philadelphia police departments. He wrote in a 2000 book review for *The New York Observer* that the "blue wall of silence" had origins in a centuries-old Irish culture, adding that the 1894 Lexow Committee's chief prosecutor told an Irish officer who refused to inform on his fellow officers, "That is your nature, a distinct feature of your race. The word informer carries a terrible significance there." Alluding to the English use of informers to quell Irish rebellion well into the twentieth century, Timoney added, "The Irish distaste for traitors runs deep and is imbued in every schoolboy, as I can attest from experience."[39]*

* In 1898, when Brooklyn, Queens, and Staten Island were incorporated into New York City, the previous NYPD title "Superintendent" was replaced with the new title "Chief of Police."

The Irish influence in the NYPD persisted through the twentieth and twenty-first centuries. In the 1960s, even after significant
efforts to recruit ethnic minorities, 42 percent in the NYPD ranks
were Irish-American.[40] The profession itself had come to be colloquially known as "Irish welfare."[41] In 1964, two social scientists
described the NYPD as the "classic stronghold" of the Irish.[42] That
same year, former NYPD commissioner Francis Adams remarked
in a televised statement, "If it weren't for the Irish, there would be
no police. And if it weren't for the Irish, there would be no need for
them."[43]

In New York, modern policing was shaped by an Irish history of
resistance and secrecy that aimed to preserve a culture that outsiders
sought to eradicate. And this culture was not limited to officers of
Irish descent. In the 1980s, Tom Wolfe embedded with the NYPD's
Bronx homicide squad before writing his critically acclaimed novel,
The Bonfire of the Vanities. In it Wolfe wrote, "All the cops turned
Irish, the Jewish cops, like Goldberg, but also the Italian cops, the
Latin cops, and the black cops."[44] Among lower-level officers and
detectives, this cultural drift still resonates today. But the Irish pres-
ence in the NYPD has been most pronounced in its highest ranks.
By our count, as of 2022, twenty-eight of the past forty-three NYPD
commissioners were of Irish descent, including all three commissioners under Mayor de Blasio.[45] Even in 2021, an article from *The
New Yorker* noted that some officers were still describing an informal
fraternity of powerful NYPD executives as the "Irish Mafia."[46]

So, how is all this relevant to American policing today?

In 1973, Professor Wilbur Zelinsky of Pennsylvania State
University formulated a profound historical theory called the
Doctrine of First Effective Settlement. He wrote, "The specific characteristics of the first group able to effect a viable, self-perpetuating
society are of crucial significance for the later social and cultural
geography of that area."[47] In 1989, David Hackett Fischer wrote
Albion's Seed: Four British Folkways in America. In it, he detailed

the ways in which various migrations of British settlers had shaped modern American life: Puritans had shaped the foundation for Massachusetts' educational culture, gentry from the south of England had shaped Virginia's plantation culture, Quakers had shaped Midwestern industrial culture, and the Scots-Irish had shaped ranching and agrarian culture in the West and South.

In his 2011 bestseller *American Nations: A History of the Eleven Rival Regional Cultures of America*, Colin Woodard expanded on Zelinsky's and Fischer's theories, highlighting that the modern-day culture of the American Southwest is defined by its original Spanish colonizers, that Quebec and New Orleans are defined by early French settlers, that Appalachian politics trace directly back to Northern Ireland, and that the Dutch values of commerce and multiculturalism persist in New York City even though the Dutch are long gone.[*]

Over the years, we began to suspect that the Doctrine of First Effective Settlement can apply not only to geographic regions, but to individual institutions and professions as well. Corporate culture largely revolves around the values and goals of a corporation's founders. Modern universities and colleges tend to teach through the frameworks designed by their founding members. Much of today's entertainment industry stems from the Hollywood studios that shaped American culture in the 1930s and 1940s. There are reasons that the terms "institutional knowledge" and "corporate culture" are ever present from the halls of Congress to Goldman Sachs to Disney. That's because, no matter the industry, traditions and strategies for professional success are passed down from generation to generation, forming an institutional timeline tracing back to an organization's initial successes and failures.

---

[*] The general concept continues to echo throughout modern politics. Just ask J. D. Vance, who in a 2021 interview mused that, "American history is a constant war between Northern Yankees and Southern Bourbons, where whichever side the hillbillies are on, wins."

The first Irish in New York didn't create the NYPD, but they quickly shaped its culture. They found strategies for survival in the face of scrutiny that would protect and strengthen their profession for generations to come. These strategies, from the now-familiar "I don't recall" and the blue wall of silence to blurring the line between public service and personal enrichment, remain tremendous barriers to meaningful police reform.

After Derek Chauvin murdered George Floyd in 2020, a common refrain on police reform was "We need to change the culture." But the institutions and cultures within American government were shaped by religious and cultural fault lines that are easy to overlook. In many ways, the NYPD's culture is rooted in an anti-colonial Irish tradition, a culture strengthened by its resistance to change.[48*] Today, the NYPD is the largest police department in America by a wide margin. Its influence on both national and international policing is unprecedented. When high-ranking officers retire, they often go to other police departments as consultants or chiefs, encouraging those departments to adopt the same rules and structures that make the NYPD appear so successful.

CompStat, invented by the NYPD in 1994, has now become "the norm in most major police departments."[49] As of 2018, NYPD detectives were stationed in Sydney, Singapore, Abu Dhabi, Tel Aviv, the Hague, London, Santo Domingo, Montreal, and more.[50] In many ways, the NYPD became to policing what the American military is to militaries abroad: the gold standard.

Although the racial demographics among NYPD officers have shifted over the years, changing the culture of an institution isn't as simple as changing the racial makeup of the people inside it. To change the culture of an institution, you need to change the incentives of the institution itself.

---

* From the 2015 *President's Task Force on 21st Century Policing Report*, "[Police] behavior is more likely to conform to culture than rules."

11

Tough on Crime

We are *terrible* at estimating our risk of crime—much worse
than we are at guessing the danger of other bad things.[1]

— MAGGIE KOERTH AND AMELIA
THOMSON-DEVEAUX, FIVETHIRTYEIGHT

*S*ummer 2018. A man walks into the 47th Precinct stationhouse.
Armed with surveillance footage that shows a woman leaving
his apartment with his very expensive coat, he's going to report
a robbery. But he doesn't trust the police. So, he turns on his cell phone's
audio recorder and puts the phone in his pocket. Two detectives escort him
into an interview room. They watch the footage together.

"You sleep with her?" the first detective asks.

The man denies sleeping with the woman.

"You paid for the pussy and didn't get nothing," says the second
detective.

The man denies paying for sex.

The second detective continues: "Come on, you brought a girl to your
room, and you're not gonna try to fuck her? You're fucking full of shit.
You're full of shit, man. You're full of shit, bro."

The man simply says, "No. No. No."

"So what? You're a good guy?" asks the first detective. "You're just
bringing girls off the street to your house?"

"There's a guy from Manhattan," says the second detective. "I have a case with him. He fucking brought a tr—y up there to watch TV, then that person caught him. And once the tr—y was going to get busy, he pulled a gun out on the tr—y and kicked the tr—y out. Because that's what you do if you fuck tr—ys."

"I'll tell you right now," says the second detective, now with a greater air of authority. "She probably was a tr—y. Your poor choices do not constitute a complaint."

The man said his coat was worth several thousand dollars. He wanted to file a complaint. If his coat had been worth less than one thousand dollars, New York State criminal law would have categorized the theft as petit larceny, a misdemeanor. But thefts of property worth more than one thousand were classified as grand larceny, a felony. Grand larceny, unlike petit larceny, is one of the seven index crimes that commanders have to explain at CompStat.

"Did you kiss her?" asks the second detective.

"No."

"So how do you know it's not a guy?"

"That's not a girl. That's a tr—y," says the first detective.

"Shame on you. Shame on you," says the second detective. "You lost. This ain't a crime, man. You lost."

"How's this not a crime?" the man asks.

"We hear this story every fucking day, bro. We're not investigating this. You lost, okay? We're not investigating that. We have a lot of serious shit going on here. We're not wasting our time with that."

The second detective cuts off the first. "We get her, we bring you and her to the Bronx district attorney, they ain't prosecuting this shit, man. This is a fucking waste of time. You got beat, and that's the end of it. So, we're done here."

The man stands up and begins to walk out of the room. He starts to cry, and he does not stop. The officers follow him downstairs and out of the stationhouse, and he gasps for air between slow, quiet exhales. Tears

stream down his face. As he walks out of the stationhouse doors, the first
detective calls out.

"My man. Stop. Those aren't real tears."

THE NEXT MORNING, the man filed a complaint with IAB and sent them the audio recording of his conversation with the detectives. More than three months later, a sergeant interviewed him. The sergeant listened to the audio, identified two officers, interviewed them both, and two months later, completed IAB's investigation: Failure to Take/Make Report—Exonerated. Their final report made no mention of anyone calling the woman a tr—y, or any of the degrading remarks the detectives made throughout the tape.

IAB forwarded this report to the CCRB. But there was a glaring issue. They'd identified the wrong officers.

While IAB had been exonerating the wrong officers, the CCRB had been conducting its own investigation and had quickly identified the two detectives—one of them had said his name on the audio recording. He turned out to be a first-grade detective, the highest rank for detectives in the NYPD.

During this detective's CCRB interview, the investigator asked what happened.

"He probably had somebody over where he picked up a he-she and the he-she told him to have a shower or something like that. The person came out from the house and left with stuff."

"And for the record, what do you mean by 'he-she'?"

"Male masking as a female."

The investigator substantiated three allegations against each detective: Discourtesy—word, Abuse of Authority—sexual misconduct (sexual humiliation), and Offensive Language—gender identity. The CCRB's board agreed with the investigator's recommendation that misconduct had occurred. The NYPD docked each detective between one and five vacation days. We never found out precisely how many. A year later, the first-grade detective retired.

OVER THE COURSE OF OUR TIME at the CCRB, we found that the NYPD was under immense pressure to keep crime low. The NYPD uses seven major felonies, known as index crimes, to track the crime rate in New York City.[2]* According to the department, from 1990 to 2009, crime declined by 77.75 percent.[3] In 2011, a New York University School of Law publication described the phenomenon as "a Guinness Book of World Record's crime drop."[4]†

From 2010 to 2021, however, New York City crime rates plateaued—in 2010, there were 105,115 index crimes reported. In 2021, there were 102,741. In the years between, the number of index crimes reported was never higher than 111,335 (in 2013) or lower than 95,593 (in 2020).[5]

These statistics seem important. But to derive real meaning from them requires examining the political rhetoric that ultimately made them so important to the NYPD story.

Used in its modern political context, the term "law and order" was first popularized by George Wallace, the former (and future) governor of Alabama, and former vice president Richard Nixon in their respective 1968 runs for the presidency. Wallace, a Democrat who ran on the American Independent Party ticket, campaigned on a platform of allowing states to resegregate.[6] For him, law and order meant keeping the peace by reverting back to the Jim Crow era. Nixon took a more nuanced approach. Asked to define the term "law and order" at a campaign event in September 1968, Nixon

---

* The seven NYPD index crimes are Murder, Rape, Robbery, Felony Assault, Burglary, Grand Larceny, and Grand Larceny Auto.

† We have found no evidence to support that this claim was made by Guinness World Records.

replied: "The greatness of America, with few exceptions, over the period of our history, is that we have had the combination of having a system in which we could have peaceful change, peaceful progress, with order. Now that's what I want for America."[7]

As president, however, Nixon would use the term "law and order" to sow discord among his political enemies. In doing so, he would profoundly shape the future of American policing.

In June 1971, President Nixon announced the beginning of what would become known as the War on Drugs, sending a $155 million funding request to Congress with $105 million dedicated to treatment and rehabilitation for addicts.[8] The proposal, however, gave states and cities a mandate to aggressively criminalize drug use, which Nixon believed was most prevalent among his most prominent detractors—Black and brown people and liberals.[9]

In 1980, after Ronald Reagan secured the Republican nomination for president, he spent a month traveling between Texas, California, and New York, with one notable exception, a campaign rally outside of Philadelphia, Mississippi.[10] Many knew this town for only one thing: It was where, in 1964, three civil rights volunteers had been lynched by the Ku Klux Klan. But a local official had informed the Reagan campaign that this would be an ideal venue for winning over "George Wallace inclined voters."[11] This strategy proved effective.

Throughout his presidency, Ronald Reagan used the phrase "law and order" to tremendous effect.[12] He won two terms, each in landslide victories, and he left office as one of the most popular presidents in American history. Reagan's coalition was comprised of three major groups: (1) conservatives who believed that states, not the federal government, should regulate American life; (2) "George Wallace inclined voters," who wanted to resegregate America in one way or another; and (3) "Reagan Democrats," who had switched allegiances from the Democratic Party.[13]

Democrats remained largely on the defensive through the late 1980s and early 1990s. Because the terms "law and order" and "tough on crime" had been so successful for Nixon and Reagan, Democrats began to adopt the terms themselves. In a televised statement in 1989, Senator Joseph R. Biden Jr. said, "I know it's hard to believe, but this very day, violent drug offenders will commit more than 100,000 crimes—on this day alone. And the sad part is that we have—we have no more police in the streets of our major cities than we had 10 years ago."[14] The subtext of his speech was clear: we aren't doing enough about crime. Since the police do *something*, we need more police. But the meaning of "something" was yet to be defined.

In March 1992, in the heat of the presidential primaries, then governor of Arkansas Bill Clinton gave a press conference at the Stone Mountain Correctional Institution in Stone Mountain, Georgia. Behind him stood a phalanx of mostly Black prisoners, later described by an editor of *The Nation* as "the iconic image of '92." Stone Mountain itself, home to a Confederate version of Mount Rushmore, was well-known as the site where, in 1915, the modern Ku Klux Klan was founded.[15]

When he accepted the Democratic nomination for president of the United States in July 1992, Clinton told his audience, "[President George H. W. Bush] talked a lot about drugs, but he hasn't helped people on the front line to wage that war on drugs and crime, but I will."[16]

In August 1994, Senator Biden stood on the Senate floor and said, "I think . . . for the first time, the American people are over what sort of got laid in stone during the Nixon era: The Democrats were soft on crime and Republicans were tough on crime." He continued, "Every time Richard Nixon, when he was running in 1972, would say 'law and order,' the Democratic match or response was 'law and order with justice,' whatever that meant. And I would say, 'Lock the SOBs up.'"[17]

Three weeks later, President Clinton successfully pressed Congress to pass the Violent Crime Control and Law Enforcement Act, commonly known as the 1994 Crime Bill. It was the largest bill of its kind in the history of the United States, funding 100,000 new police officers, $9.7 billion in funding for prisons, and $6.1 billion in funding for various crime prevention programs.[18] The bill called for $8.8 billion in grants to expand "community policing" but failed to define what that meant, except to say that it is "community-oriented policing."[19] For the next two decades, the Democrats' tough-on-crime rhetoric held steady.

The social value of the 1994 Crime Bill has been widely criticized. Vanita Gupta, who ran the Justice Department's Civil Rights Division under President Obama, said the bill "created and calcified massive incentives for local jurisdictions to engage in draconian criminal-justice practices that had a pretty significant impact in building up the national prison population."[20] In 2009, Gil Kerlikowske, director of the Office of National Drug Control Policy, announced that the term "war on drugs" would no longer be used because it was "counter-productive."[21]

Over the course of this saga, the definition of "law and order" held multiple conflicting meanings. Wallace evoked it to encourage white supremacy. Nixon spoke of these concepts, law and order, as basic principles of a functioning democratic society. And as the term evolved it became a slogan, still with multiple meanings: (1) there should be less crime, and/or (2) I support law enforcement, and/or (3) I support the ongoing criminalization of Black and brown people.

As the meanings of "law and order" overlapped, something very important was lost in the fray: when someone personally supported law enforcement, there evolved a baked-in assumption that this support contributed to a reduction in crime. It's the same premise that leads Americans to say, "Support our troops," in times of war. More support, it seems, increases morale. In war, higher morale brings us closer to victory, but in contrast, there is little evidence that public support for officers leads to less crime.[22*]

Policing is not war. It's a series of interlocking systems, a bureaucracy that runs on rules and laws that create incentives for its employees. You can win a war, and you can support the troops who fight the war, but there is no way to "win" policing. It isn't designed to end.

Yet in the American political discourse, from the Nixon administration in 1969 to the present day, the police became political avatars. Avatars who needed support to win impossible wars on drugs and crime. They were no longer people working in police bureaucracies, employees with job descriptions and incentives. They were simply "the police." And over the same political timeline, Americans stopped asking what a police officer actually does. All we knew is that they did *something*.

Just as in New York City, violent crime in America dropped, spectacularly, over the course of thirty years. According to the FBI, in 1991 there were 758.2 violent crimes per 100,000 members of the US population.[†] The violent-crime rate then dropped almost every year until 2014, reaching a low of 361.6, and remaining under 400 over the next five years.[23]

If that's surprising to you, you're not alone. Americans are barraged with news about crime. In his 2017 inaugural address, President Trump seemed to sum it up by declaring, "And the crime, and the gangs, and the drugs that have stolen too many lives and

---

* We are distinguishing public support from public confidence. Higher public confidence in police likely increases the likelihood that witnesses will come forward to solve alleged crimes. Higher public support, absent a basis for public confidence, is essentially meaningless.

† As per the FBI, violent crime includes the offenses of murder and nonnegligent manslaughter, rape, robbery, and aggravated assault.

robbed our country of so much unrealized potential. This American carnage stops right here and stops right now."[24]

Based on Trump's rhetoric, one might've assumed America was riding an unprecedented crime wave. Violent crime had, in fact, risen by 4.1 percent from 2015 to 2016.[25] But Trump wasn't capturing the big picture: from 2008 to 2015, violent crime in America had actually dropped by 19 percent.[26]

"If Chicago doesn't fix the horrible 'carnage' going on," Trump tweeted on his fifth day in office, "I will send in the Feds!" Yet even in Chicago, where Trump railed against a rising murder rate, violent crime in 2016 was in fact down more than 64 percent from a peak in 1991 and 8 percent lower than in 2008, when President Obama took office.[27]

Inflammatory rhetoric comes at a price. In 2019, when crime dropped to its lowest point in four years, 64 percent of Americans believed there was *more* crime nationwide than there had been in 2018. This misconception reflects a decades-long trend: according to Gallup, from 2003 to 2021, while crime was steadily declining, at least 60 percent of Americans believed that crime was actually on the rise.[28]

Why is this? Because most Americans don't learn about crime trends from personal experience, or even from the president. They learn about crime trends from the media, the industry whose mantra is "If it bleeds, it leads."

"Nationwide Crime Spike Has Law Enforcement Retooling Its Approach" read an NPR headline in July 2015.[29] The previous month, CNN asked, "Is a new crime wave on the horizon?" and a BBC News headline asked, "Why has the murder rate in some US cities suddenly spiked?"[30] That August, a *New York Times* headline declared, "Murder Rates Rising Sharply in Many U.S. Cities."[31]

In 2015, America had the *third-lowest* violent-crime rate since 1990. But because the two lower years were 2013 and 2014, the marginal increase was reported as a crime wave. And someone has to do *something* about a crime wave.

Simply by increasing crime coverage, the media can espouse fear that crime is rising. A 1981 study of newspapers in Chicago, San Francisco, and Philadelphia found that when local newspapers dedicated more space to crime stories, the residents of those cities feared crime more than their counterparts in cities with less crime coverage.[32] Simply put, more crime coverage means more fear of crime, whether or not that fear is warranted. Furthermore, crime coverage itself can be profoundly misleading.

As of early 2025, police departments across America are not required to report their crime statistics to an independent body.[33] Some departments voluntarily report their statistics to the FBI. But when they do, they do so differently. In Seattle, "violent crimes" include homicide, rape, robbery, and aggravated assault.[34] In Baltimore County, "violent crimes" also include human trafficking.[35] In Kansas City, Missouri, "violent crimes" are broken down into even more categories, including "strongarm robberies" and "non-fatal shootings."[36] Other police departments, like the NYPD, have gone long stretches without using the category "violent crime" at all.[37] There is no clear national standard.[38]

The result is that "crime is up" can mean something different in every American newspaper. For example, a headline in the *Topeka Capital-Journal* might say: "Robberies Up 50 Percent."

This could mean one of three things:

Weekly Format: If, from January 8 to 15, 2011, there were two robberies, and from January 8 to 15, 2012, there were three robberies, the *Capital-Journal* headline could read, "Robberies Up 50 Percent."[39]

Monthly Format: If, from March 1 to 31, 2011, there were ten robberies, and from March 1 to 31, 2012, there were fifteen robberies, the *Capital-Journal* headline could read, "Robberies Up 50 Percent."[40]

Annual (To Date) Format: If, from January 1 to July 1, 2011, there were one hundred robberies, and from January 1 to July 1,

2012, there were one hundred and fifty robberies, the *Capital-Journal* headline could read, "Robberies Up 50 Percent."[41]

Each of these identical headlines would have drastically different meanings. The weekly format would indicate that there had been one more robbery than usual, a statistical anomaly. But the annual (to date) format would mean that over six months, there had been fifty more robberies than usual, perhaps indicating that Topeka was besieged by a serial robber. As a Topekan glancing at the headline, however, there would be no way to know the difference.

And that's a major problem because most Americans read headlines far more often than they read the news: according to a 2014 study by the American Press Institute, 59 percent of Americans surveyed said that they hadn't read past a headline in the previous week.[42] Social media exacerbates this problem. A 2024 study published in Nature Human Behavior found that around 75 percent of links to news and public affairs information on Facebook were shared without the user having clicked to read beyond the headline.[43]

Given that a "crime is up" headline can mean so many things, it's no wonder we usually assume that crime is indeed up. Even though crime has declined sharply over the past thirty years, when crime was up on one particular week, month, or year, that's what we saw in the headlines.

But there's a clear reason why news outlets use the weekly, monthly, or annual formats. When police departments publish crime statistics, they almost always compare those statistics to the previous week, month, and year.[44] The headlines simply borrow from their format.

This comparative format, pioneered by the NYPD's CompStat, was initially intended for police executive, not public, consumption.[45]*

---

* The word "CompStat" has a double meaning: (1) it's the name of a weekly meeting, founded by the NYPD, that police departments hold to discuss crime statistics, and

Beginning in 1994, the NYPD used these statistics as a management tool to ensure that local precinct commanders were at least *aware* of the crimes in their precincts and could account for them in weekly meetings. In the NYPD's CompStat meetings police brass would ask precinct commanders not just *what* crime was taking place, and how much, but *why*. As CompStat's creator described the system, it was "a live audit of overall police performance."[46]

The invention of CompStat in 1994 marked the birth of data-driven policing. It was only then that crime tracking, data mapping, and forced collaboration between divisions of local police departments began to be standardized as crime-fighting strategies. CompStat was a solution to New York City's crime wave. But with this solution came another new problem.

While CompStat provided a forum for NYPD executives to interrogate precinct commanders about their work, many found the process humiliating. And precinct commanders, like most people, are willing to do a lot to avoid being humiliated.

At the CCRB, with every passing week, we began to see more ways that police officers, detectives, and their bosses could influence the crime statistics in their precincts. Because with every crime, there's a story, and the police have the final word on that story's arc.

A lot can happen from the moment a crime takes place to when a police officer writes a report, to the time that report is handed to a detective, and finally when the crime becomes a statistic in the local newspaper. First, an incident can go unreported, as many do. Second, police officers and detectives can decide whether or not a crime even occurred. If someone yells in the street, is it disorderly conduct or simply a "10-91 Non-Crime Corrected?" If someone

(2) it's the name of the NYPD computer program that holds police departments' crime statistics. In speech, CompStat usually refers to the meeting and sometimes refers to the computer program ("Do you have the CompStat numbers?" or, "I'm going to CompStat on Friday" or, "CompStat was terrible").

bumps into an officer, is it a mistake or assaulting a police officer? If a sex worker steals a client's expensive coat, is it tough luck or a robbery? The answer often comes down to the inclinations of officers, their bosses, and the incentives that guide them to do what's easiest.

At CompStat meetings, precinct commanders' careers were on the line.[47] Even marginal increases in crime were subject to extreme scrutiny. As Eli Silverman and former NYPD captain John Eterno wrote in their definitive book *The Crime Numbers Game*:

> Commanders presenting at [CompStat] meetings are exposed to, at times, what can best be described as bullying behavior by senior officers. This may involve yelling, berating, and even embarrassing the commanders who were chosen for their command positions by the same upper echelon who . . . sometimes abuse them.[48]

By the end of the 2000s, cities across America, from Los Angeles and Oakland to Chicago and New Orleans to Baltimore and Miami all adopted versions of the NYPD's CompStat model.[49] But these cities hadn't just adopted a computer program and a weekly meeting. They'd institutionalized a hazing ritual for their most ambitious police leaders, and this ritual had one overarching rule: if you wanted to avoid scrutiny, crime numbers *needed* to be down. Just like that, the crime rate dropped in every one of these cities.[50]

But while crime rates went down, and Americans believed that they were going up, something even more confusing was happening behind the blue wall. As police officer Robert Zink, recording secretary of New York City's own PBA, wrote in a 2004 article for *The PBA Magazine*:

> The department's middle managers will do anything to avoid being dragged onto the carpet at the weekly Compstat

meetings. They are, by nature, ambitious people who lust for promotions, and rising crime rates won't help anybody's career . . . Of course, when you finally get a real handle on crime, you eventually hit a wall where you can't push it down any more. Compstat does not recognize that wall so the com-manders have to get "creative" to keep their numbers going down.

So how do you get "creative"? Here are a few ideas: don't file reports, misclassify crimes from felonies to misdemeanors, or report a series of crimes as a single event. In the words of Robert Zink, "A particularly insidious way to fudge crime numbers is to make it difficult or impossible for people to report crimes—in other words, make the victims feel like criminals so they walk away just to spare themselves further pain and suffering."[51]

You see, the NYPD bureaucracy didn't need crime to be down in reality. But it did need crime to be down *in the data*.

12

Broken Bones and Stitches

You know, we see the same videos you do. And when we text them to one another and talk about them in the stationhouse— well, I won't comment on any specific video—but I will say that some of those officers? They're not one of us.

—NYPD FORCE INSTRUCTOR

S ummer 2016. A man sits on a bench inside the Staten Island Ferry. He's drunk and has fallen asleep. When the ferry docks in Manhattan, a group of officers approaches him.

"Buddy," says one. "You gotta get off."

"I'll get off the fucking boat when I wanna get off the fucking boat," slurs the man, staggering to his feet.

The officers grab him by the arms, walking him off the gangway. As they step onto land, the man takes off his baseball cap and tosses it at an officer's head. That officer swiftly punches him in the face, fracturing the man's nose and eye socket. He's knocked out cold.

A CCRB INVESTIGATOR TRACKED DOWN surveillance footage from the ferry terminal and substantiated one allegation: force— physical force. The case went to the CCRB prosecution unit, and the officer faced a trial. If found guilty, he stood to lose twenty vacation days. But on the witness stand, the officer told the court that he feared for his safety, thinking the man's hat "might have been filled with razor blades." The NYPD judge found him not guilty, and the case was dismissed and sealed.

SPRING 2018. We'd both been promoted to Level III investigators. Now we'd been assigned the most difficult cases. Force (with broken bones and stitches). Melees. Chokeholds. Shootings.

WINTER 2018. A middle-aged man emerges from his front door and into the brisk Manhattan morning. His young son sits on his shoulders, running his fingers through his father's hair. They're in Washington Heights, where wind streams between the brick buildings. Together, they walk to school.

As they cross the street, two uniformed officers emerge from around a corner. They're both white and in their late thirties. The father recognizes the officers. Four days before, they'd nearly arrested him for smoking a joint nearby. It was a harsh exchange. The officers threatened to deport him. He said he'd shoot them if they weren't cops. It ended when he ran away. But now the officers were back, and he couldn't escape.

"Sir, you're under arrest," says the first officer, gesturing toward the sidewalk. "Walk with us."

The son tugs the father's hair. They walk to the sidewalk's edge. Glancing up, the father pleads with the officers. "Let me bring my son back to the house. I'll call his mother."

"Stand still," commands the second officer.

"Can I put my son down?" asks the father.

"Stand still," the officer repeats, grabbing his forearm.

"Papi! Papi!" yells the son from above.

"Let me put him down," says the father.

"You're under arrest," says the first officer, planting his feet squarely on the ground.

Without warning, he yanks the father's forearm. The father, the son, and the two officers all fall forward. The son topples from his father's shoulders, careening headfirst toward the concrete.

The second officer catches the son midair, his tiny head dangling just a few feet from the sidewalk. The father spins around in shock. Wrapping his arms around his son, he pulls him away from the second officer's grasp. He holds his son close and huddles over him, as if to form a small cocoon.

The officers try to pry the son away, but they can't. Instead, they lift the father upright. With the son still wrapped in his father's embrace, the officers fling them both to the ground. The son's head bounces against the concrete. The officers push the son away, then wrestle the father into handcuffs.

"Papi! Papi!" shrieks the son, stamping his feet and flailing his arms. His head begins to swell.

The officers punch the father over and over. The son screams. A neighbor leans out from the fire escape above, recording the officers with his cell phone. "That's abuse!" he yells. "That's abuse!"

The second officer looks up. "Shut the fuck up."

THE FATHER WAS ARRESTED FOR endangering the welfare of a child, resisting arrest, obstructing government administration, and disorderly conduct. Shortly thereafter, the Manhattan DA dismissed the charges, and the arrest was sealed.[*]

---

[*] On one hand, officers would use charges like disorderly conduct, obstruction of governmental administration, and resisting arrest to paper over bad arrests and excessive force. These charges would also make it more difficult for an arrestee to successfully sue for damages. When officers are forced to choose between honestly describing their own poor decisions (bad for the brand) or exaggerating a civilian's resistance during an unlawful arrest (good for the brand), the choice is often easy.

In the hours following this incident, the officers' supervisor conducted an investigation. He knew that surveillance cameras had captured the altercation, but he didn't obtain the footage. He independently determined that there was "no apparent misconduct" and recommended "no further action" on the case.*

That afternoon, the father's sister called the CCRB, and the case was assigned to Greg.

The following Monday, upon Greg's request, the field team went to the incident location, and they quickly found the surveillance footage the NYPD had failed to seek. It captured everything.

A few weeks later, after the son had recovered from his head trauma and was back in school, Greg stood beside the father in Washington Heights. Together, they eyed the same sidewalk where officers had thrown him and his son to the ground.

"Can you walk me through what happened?" Greg asked.

Without missing a beat, the father dashed back into his apartment, returning with his son's stuffed doll. He placed it on his shoulders, grabbed it by the ankles, and began to pantomime losing his grasp.

"I thought my son was going to die," the father said. He lowered himself to the pavement, laying chest first along a wrought iron fence. "This is where they started punching me," he said. Alone on the pavement, the father twisted and flinched as if it was happening all over again, pointing to where his son hit the ground and narrating each subsequent blow.

Greg said he didn't have to lie there, but the father shot him a piercing look. "I need you to understand." He continued twisting.

Around the office, Greg's case became simply known as "kid-on-the-shoulders" case, and the surveillance footage capturing the incident became a sort of parenting Rorschach test.

---

* The officer's supervisor recommended that someone still attempt to retrieve the surveillance footage. As far as we know, no one from the NYPD ever did.

"That guy's a bad father," said one manager, a mother.

"Those officers are fucked up," said an investigator in her early twenties.

"I don't see why they couldn't let him walk the kid to school first," said a field-team investigator, a father in his thirties.

Every time someone blamed the debacle on the father, their subtext was clear: exonerate the force; he did this to himself.

Every time someone blamed the officers, it was the other way around: substantiate the force; those officers hurt a child.

After the normal relay of bureaucratic delays, Greg was back in an interview room with another tenured investigator. Across from them sat the first officer and his union attorney. The interview began as normal, with the officer reading his memo book into the record verbatim: "We asked him to put child down. He refused, causing child to almost fall and get injured."

Later in the interview, Greg asked, "Did the child at any point fall?"

"No," replied the officer.

"At any point, did the child hit the ground?"

"No," the officer shot back firmly.

The son had been seriously injured, and if not for the second officer's lucky catch, those injuries could have been much worse. It was one thing to twist the facts, but it was another thing to deny them with such impunity. In Greg's eyes, the answer to the Rorschach test was clear: a child almost died, and none of this had had to happen.

Later in the interview, Greg presented the surveillance footage. Until then, the officer didn't know it existed. But even as the footage clearly showed the son crashing to the ground, and even though there was ample documentation of the son's injuries, the officer held firm: "He never touched the ground. The child was never at any time injured."

At the end of the interview, after Greg had turned off the recorder, the officer's union attorney grumbled, "Clearly, this officer didn't use excessive force, as the perpetrator was resisting arrest. If you were good at your job, you'd see that."

A month later, the second officer gave a near-identical statement to the first. In the face of surveillance footage and corroborating documentation, he denied that the son had been injured at all.

Over the course of the next few months, Greg wrote a closing report that substantiated two force allegations against each officer. In addition, he determined that both officers provided false official statements. In 2019, the CCRB didn't investigate false official statements, so Greg forwarded an allegation of Other Misconduct Noted–False Official Statement to IAB.

Until 2020, after voters passed an amendment to the New York City Charter, all false official statement allegations were handled by IAB.[1] Before that year, we could always send IAB supporting evidence that an officer made a false statement. But from 2010 to 2017, as the CCRB sent IAB evidence of eighty-one false official statements by NYPD officers, IAB substantiated only two of them.[2]

Because IAB seldom punished false statements, the CCRB made such allegations only when the evidence seemed irrefutable. In Greg's case, an officer had denied doing something that was clearly captured on surveillance footage, so he sent the false official statement referral to IAB and assumed he'd never hear about it again.

A little more than a year after the incident, the CCRB board agreed with his recommendations, Force—Physical Force: Substantiated, and voted for the highest penalty—Charges and Specifications. The officers would face an administrative trial.

In summer 2020, Greg was working on another case when he stumbled upon a spreadsheet in the agency database. As he parsed through, it offered an odd revelation: IAB had substantiated false official statements against both officers in his kid-on-the-shoulders case. After investigating hundreds of cases over the years, it finally seemed that officers had been held accountable for lying.

But what made the NYPD act against these two officers and not the rest? Neither of them had a long history of misconduct. The first officer, who'd yanked the father's arm, had only two prior CCRB complaints filed against him. For the second officer, this was the first complaint of his career. What was going on?

Without an obvious answer, we dove into each officer's arrest history.

As of July 2022, over the course of his sixteen-year career, the first officer had made 69 misdemeanor arrests, 13 felony arrests, 6 arrests for violations, 2 arrests categorized as "Other," and 1 arrest for an unknown infraction.[3] An average of 5.3 arrests per year, on the low end of the department average of 5 to 8. Over the course of his nine-year career, the second officer had made 34 misdemeanor arrests, 3 felony arrests, and 2 arrests for violations.[4] An average of 4.3 arrests per year.

These officers didn't have high arrest numbers to prop up their performance evaluations. They weren't earners, like Assman or Detective Terrell. Perhaps that made them disposable, or at least vulnerable. Perhaps these two officers would be fired. According to Patrol Guide Procedure 203-08, "Intentionally making a false official statement regarding a material matter will result in dismissal from the Department, absent exceptional circumstances. Exceptional circumstances will be determined by the Police Commissioner on a case-by-case basis."[5] But NYPD commissioners reviewing CCRB cases made "exceptional circumstances" the norm.[6]*

Both officers agreed to plea deals before their public trials. The first officer was docked sixteen vacation days. The second officer

---

* Wrote former Commissioner William Bratton in his memoir *The Profession*, "I, as police commissioner, reviewed all Civilian Complaint Review Board cases regarding the conduct of NYPD officers."

was docked nine days. At some unknown point, someone must have found "exceptional circumstances" allowing both officers to stay on the force because despite their false statements both officers remained on the job, perhaps with black marks on their records.* The first officer stayed in his local precinct. The second officer was promoted to lieutenant and transferred to a training unit.

A 2022 study by LatinoJustice examined 181 false statements in CCRB cases, finding that not a single offending officer was fired in response.[7] Firing an officer for a false official statement was, after all, bad for the brand. It was easier to move on.

SUMMER 2018. Early evening. A man in his late twenties steps out of a yellow school bus at the edge of a housing project in the South Bronx. Laughing teenagers follow behind.

"Get home safe, everyone," booms the man, a program director at the community center nearby.

"Roller coasters are DOPE!" squeals a jubilant teen. "I'm gettin' on that Dragon Coaster next time."

"All right," says the man. "Maybe we'll go again this summer."

The teenagers stream homeward, and the man thanks the bus driver. He turns toward the projects. It's Family Day, where hundreds of new and old residents gather to cook, drink, and reminisce. The party sprawls between the towering brick buildings.

The man strolls toward the crowd. He eyes two male officers—one white, one Black—standing on a footpath nearby. "What's up, Russia?" he asks the white officer.

"Not much," Russia replies.

"You guys having a good one?"

---

* Perhaps the commissioner determined that the false official statement was not about a "material matter," or that the months between the arrest and the interviews made their lies "exceptional."

"Oh yeah," says the Black officer. "You?"

"Oh yeah," says the man. "You guys be well."

The man strolls to the center of the barbecue. "Anyone need to use the bathroom?" he calls out. "I can open the center right now."

A few party patrons jump up, and the man leads them across the street. He unlocks the community center. They could have used a bathroom in the housing projects, but in those buildings, the police were allowed to stop, question, and demand ID from anyone who entered.

"WHAT'S THE DIFFERENCE BETWEEN LIVING here and under communism?" seven-year-old Greg had asked his mother, who'd grown up in Poland.

"Here, the lines are shorter, the supermarkets are full, and the police don't stop you and say, 'Let me see your papers,' wherever you go," she said. "That's what makes America beautiful, Greg. We have freedom."

But in New York City's housing projects, life was not as free as it was for other Americans. In public housing under the New York City Housing Authority (NYCHA), police were permitted to enter and question anyone suspected of trespassing.[8]* When officers stopped someone and took their ID, they could run that person's name through a digital database. This was a warrant check.

If at some point that person hadn't paid a fine or had missed a court date, there would likely be a warrant out for their arrest. This was true for even minor violations, like hopping a subway turnstile, littering, or drinking beer in public. For officers, running a warrant check served as an easy way to stumble upon an arrest.

---

* Until late 2020, some occupants of private apartment buildings were subject to the Trespass Affidavit Program (TAP), which permitted police to enter a building and question anyone inside.

And because it was easy, officers found excuses to stop people left and right.

"Excuse me, you live here?" an officer might say. "Can I see some ID?"

If the person didn't live in the complex and none of their friends were around, they could be arrested for trespassing. But even if they had friends around, that officer could conduct a warrant check.

"Sorry, it says here you've got an open warrant. We've gotta go down to the stationhouse and figure it out." (Hint: that probably means you're under arrest.)

As of 2023, there were nearly 1.3 million outstanding warrants in New York City, 64 percent of which stemmed from "common low-level offenses."[9] This four-step formula of (1) sending more police to Black and brown neighborhoods, (2) issuing a summons to a poor Black or brown person for a minor violation, (3) that person missing their court date for one of a variety of reasons—sometimes they couldn't pay their fine, had a personal emergency, or simply forgot to attend court, and (4) rearresting the same person for a procedural violation was a spectacularly effective way to criminalize both poverty and race in one fell swoop. And we know this formula criminalized race because Black and Latino people were, after all, far more likely to be stopped by the NYPD.[10]

Running a warrant check was easy, arresting someone was time-consuming, and it all ensured that the police were consistently doing *something*. So it's no wonder that this formula was widely embraced by politicians and police leaders alike.

Some readers might ask, if these people hadn't done anything wrong, why worry? Just let the officer check your ID and move on. But New York's most heavily policed communities were keenly aware of two truths in policing:

1. Officers could summons or arrest anyone for actions that were socially normal or seemingly innocuous.[11]* Standing on the sidewalk could be considered blocking pedestrian traffic and result in an arrest for disorderly conduct.[12] Spitting on the ground could get you a summons for violating the Health Code.[13]
2. Officers stood to personally benefit from issuing summonses and making arrests.

It's been widely reported that, at various times, officers across America have been subject to quotas. Police quotas are "formal and informal measures that require police officers to issue a particular number of citations or make a certain number of arrests."[14] For example, NYPD officer Adhyl Polanco reported an unwritten "20 and 1" rule that officers issue twenty summonses and make one arrest every month.[15]

In 2010, the New York State legislature passed what has been described as a "ban on quotas," prohibiting police departments from disciplining officers for failing to meet quotas.[16] In theory, this disincentivized random or unnecessary policing. In practice, the law failed to address a core issue: a ban on quotas was only a ban on negative reinforcement—punishment for doing too little. Police departments like the NYPD could still give officers praise and promotion—positive reinforcement—for higher numbers of arrests and summonses.

At the CCRB, we saw many an officer's performance evaluation. On every one, their number of arrests and summonses was front and center. We saw notorious officers, with sky-high arrest numbers,

---

* Jaywalking, one of the most common pastimes in New York City, was a liability for Black and brown men. In one nine-month period of 2019, Black and Latino people made up 89.5 percent of people issued jaywalking summonses by the NYPD. In the first three months of 2020, 99 percent of jaywalking summonses were issued to Black or Latino people.

dodge discipline on a regular basis. It became clear that an officer's value was largely judged by their "activity"—summonses issued and arrests made. While there was no minimum quota, the more action, it seemed, the better. Because when officers had more arrests and summonses, the NYPD could show the politicians that they were doing *something*.

SO, WITH THE UNDERSTANDING THAT *it's best to avoid interactions with the police, the partygoers opt to walk across the street and use the toilets in the community center. The man stays at Family Day late into the evening. The party dies down, and around 1:00 a.m., about twenty stragglers head to the local deli. While five people go inside to order sandwiches, the remaining fifteen, including the man, wait outside.*

He sees lights and sirens, and approximately twenty officers surround the deli. A plainclothes officer, a short white male in his thirties with bright-red hair, walks toward the man. "We got a call that somebody here has a gun. Guy with a yellow headband."

"Cody?" says the man, gesturing to his friend. Cody wears a yellow headband, but he looks confused. "He doesn't have anything on him," *says the man.* "But you can search him."

The officer searches Cody, and sure enough, he doesn't have a gun. "Okay. He doesn't have anything. He's clean."

"But you still gotta get the fuck out of here," says another officer.

"We're gonna leave," says the man, raising his hands. "We're just waiting for people inside."

But a conflict has already begun.

"What the fuck is your problem?" yells someone in the man's group.

"What the fuck is your problem?" yells one of the officers.

"Y'all need to get the fuck outta here," booms another officer. "You guys are just standing here for no reason."

The officers line up shoulder to shoulder, completely blocking one end of the sidewalk.

"Your group is blocking a pedestrian walkway," yells an officer. Disorderly conduct.

As the line of officers advances, the crowd loudly objects.

"What the fuck you doing?" someone yells from the deli.

"What's the problem?" yells the man.

The officers start to push the crowd back, extending their arms forward and shoving whomever they can reach.

"I'm sorry," pleads the man. "I'm sorry. We're gonna leave."

"You," yells the red-haired plainclothes officer. He points at the man. "You. Come here." The officer reaches out and grabs the man's wrist.

"What's the problem?" yells the man, pulling his wrist back.

"Come here!" demands the officer.

The man throws his hands in the air and yells to the crowd, "Everybody put your hands up!" It's a last-ditch effort, but if everyone puts their hands up in unison, then perhaps the officers will stop, and everyone can leave in peace. It doesn't work.

The red-haired officer lunges forward to grab the man's arm. Knowing that an arrest could cost him his job at the community center, the man turns around and runs as fast as he can.

The officers chase the man into the street.

"You fucking pussy!" huffs an older white male officer. "You fucking pussy!"

Another officer, a white male in his twenties, runs faster. He pulls his Taser from its holster and aims it at the man's back. A red dot flickers on the man's white T-shirt, the Taser's laser sight. Without a word, the officer fires.

Two Taser prongs fly through the air. Two barbs pierce the man's shirt, hook into his skin, and charge him with fifty thousand volts of electricity. Every muscle in his body seems to contract. He flies into the air, landing face-first on the concrete. His front teeth tear into his *lower lip, his head rattles, and in an instant, he's knocked unconscious. He begins to seize.*

Another officer, a Latino man in his thirties, runs toward the man's unconscious, convulsing body. He kneels next to the man's head as two white officers pull his limp wrists behind his back and into handcuffs. Blood streams from the man's head onto the concrete.

"Cuff him up, cuff him up, cuff him up," yells the Latino officer, leaning down and wrapping his palm around the man's head. The officer grinds the man's face into the concrete and lowers his voice. "Yeah. Yeah. Yeah. You talkin' shit, right? You pussy-ass n—a." The officer freezes for a moment, seeming to realize that his body-worn camera is recording. He silently turns it off.

THREE WEEKS LATER, Mac sat across from the man in an interview room.

"And then what happened?"

The man told Mac about waking up in the emergency room, how a doctor pulled out the Taser prongs too quickly. "Oh shoot," the doctor said to his medical students, "I should've done that while you were watching." Was the man just a test dummy to them?

He believed that police could have a positive impact on his community and that there were some officers, like Officer Russia, who truly did. But when he'd tried to de-escalate the situation, he'd been knocked unconscious and charged with inciting a riot. His public defender told him it was best to plead guilty to disorderly conduct, so he did. Still, he was afraid he'd lose his job at the community center.

The day after the interview, Mac received dozens of BWC videos. One showed the officer yelling the racial slur. Another showed an officer yelling, "You fucking pussy." More videos showed unknown officers chasing yet another man, forcing him to the ground, and barraging him with an array of profanity.

"Talkin' all this shit. Fuck," said one officer.

"Give us your fucking arm, motherfucker," said a second.

"Motherfuckers in the Bronx think you can run on a white boy," said a third.

Another video showed an officer at the precinct stationhouse trying to process a man's arrest. A young man complained that officers were searching him too roughly, twisting his arms in protest. "Calm the fuck down," replied an officer. "Don't try that shit right here. We're not the ones, motherfucker. We're not the ones."

Although there were dozens of BWC videos, it was clear that many more officers failed to record. The arrest report said no force was used. All the Family Day partygoers were refusing to provide statements to the CCRB.

One afternoon, Mac passed by one of the agency's few tenured Black investigators. He'd already watched the video. "I want to look him in the eyes while he explains why he said that," the investigator told Mac.

Months later, Mac and that tenured investigator sat across from the Latino officer and his union attorney, a thin white man in his early seventies.

"From beginning to end, can you tell me what happened?"

The officer provided his account but left out the most troubling parts of the incident.

Midway through the interview, Mac cut to the chase. "Did you see the man on the ground?"

"Yes," replied the officer.

"Did you say anything to him?"

"I believe so."

"Do you remember what you said?"

"I, um, I believe I was like, uh, 'We got you' . . . I think I said something like, 'What's up. We got you.' I think I was like, 'Pussy. You pussy. Pussy-ass . . .'"

Would he say it? For five long seconds, they sat in silence.

"I'm gonna pull up the body-cam footage," said Mac. He played the footage. The desktop computer's speaker crackled.

"Yeah. Yeah. Yeah. You talkin' shit, right? You pussy-ass n—a."

Everyone stared at the computer screen, where the officer was grinding the man's head into the pavement.

"Was that you speaking in the video?" asked Mac.

"Um, yes," said the officer.

"And was that your hand on his head?"

"Yeah."

Mac turned to the tenured investigator next to him.

"Any questions?"

The investigator took a deep breath. "Why?" For a moment, the investigator's tone lost its veneer of impartiality. "Why did you say that to him?" The investigator glared at the officer and leaned across the table.

"Honestly," the officer stammered, "I didn't know I said it until after I reviewed my body camera."

The union attorney cut in. "So basically, you said this in the heat of the moment?"

"I mean—" started the officer.

"I mean, this guy threatened you?" the attorney said.

The officer took his cue. "Yeah. This guy had just threatened me. And after that, people started throwing stuff at us. There was a whole bunch of groups all around us. So, in the heat of the moment . . ." The officer explained that he didn't mean anything by what he'd said, that he'd simply blurted it out in the chaos. Perhaps that was his only defense.

A few weeks later, Mac interviewed the officer who'd fired the Taser and asked why he had pulled the trigger.

"When you have a Taser, usually they immediately comply," said the officer. "It's our safer, more, I would say, humane option, than to fight somebody."[17]*

A few months after that, a witness officer told Mac that his BWC had been recording throughout the incident. NYPD Legal had denied that this officer ever recorded at all. Mac pressed the issue with NYPD Legal, and after some back-and-forth, their attorneys admitted withholding forty-two BWC videos from Mac's investigation. They apologized, promising to share the footage shortly. Mac followed up every few weeks, but after four months of cajoling, NYPD Legal changed its tune, refusing to provide the videos because they depicted people whose arrests had since been sealed. Because those arrests were sealed, Mac had no idea who was depicted, so he couldn't have them sign paperwork consenting to the CCRB getting access to the footage. He didn't know who they were. The case was almost a year old, and as far as we knew, those forty-two videos were never watched by a member of the CCRB.

Meanwhile, at one of the CCRB's public board meetings, the man who'd been tased asked why his case was taking so long to investigate. New York Civil Rights Law 50-a prevented the CCRB from disclosing almost anything about its cases, so no one was allowed to explained why.

A few months later, Mac condensed the thousand-page case file into a twenty-page report. Thirty-one allegations. Nine substantiated. Thirteen closed as officer(s) unidentified. The board agreed with Mac's recommendations. And although one board member complained that the report was too long, all three voted for Charges and Specifications, the highest penalty possible.

---

* Traditionally, Tasers have been classified as "less lethal," despite the fact that they can kill you.

Three officers would face an administrative trial. But it'd be years before we knew the results. And as one manager taught Mac, it was best to wash your hands and to move on to the next case.

FALL 2019. Early morning in the North Bronx. A young boy, an inch short of five feet tall, sits in an apartment-complex stairwell. He sits beside three friends. They're just entering their teenage years, and they play Call of Duty *on their cell phones, passing a joint between shrieks of laughter. After half an hour of games, they hear footsteps from the stairwell below. A skinny uniformed officer steps into view.*

One of the boys sees him. "Run!"

The boys scramble upstairs.

"Don't run!" the officer yells wearily. "I don't know why you're running!"

The boys make a break for it, sprinting through the hallway and down a second stairwell. In the building lobby, a burly white officer blocks the door. That's the only exit.

"Stand against the wall," he booms.

The boys give up and line up against the wall.

Yet another officer, a short white male wearing blue jeans and a baseball cap, emerges from the stairwell. A silver badge dangles from his neck. He's the Neighborhood Coordination Officer, or NCO, a linchpin of the NYPD's push for community policing.[18]*

"Well, look who you ran into," he says, looking from the boys to their burly captor. "You know," he adds, "we might have to arrest you."

"Can you just take us to school?" asks the first boy, trying to talk his friends out of trouble.

---

* Neighborhood policing was Mayor de Blasio's favored approach to mending relationships with overpoliced communities. Wrote Greg B. Smith of *The City*, de Blasio "repeatedly praised this effort as an unqualified success—while offering no metrics."

"No," says the officer. "Turn around and put your hands behind your back." He grabs the boy's arms, locking handcuffs around each wrist. "Sit down."

"Nah, man," says the boy. "Floor's dirty."

The officer presses his open palm into the handcuffed boy's chest, pinning him against the lobby wall. "Get. On. The. Ground." He grabs the boy by his sweatshirt and shoves him toward the floor.

The boy struggles, attempting to stand back up. "What the fuck?" he yells. "Get off me!"

As the boy scrambles back to his feet, the two other officers start to walk away, as if foreseeing a confrontation they don't want to witness. One meanders into another room.

"I hate these n—as," yells the boy. "Fuck-n—as!"

"Fuck-n—er doesn't work for me," yells the short white officer. "You look like you're six years old, bro. Grow the fuck up."

"I don't respect you," shouts the boy. "I'm gonna treat you like I treat Assman!"

"I'm not Assman. I'll treat you the way I treat people who disrespect me. Sit down! I said sit down!"

The officer grabs the boy—one hand clenching his shoulder, the other hand grasping the center of his hooded sweatshirt. In one motion, he swings the boy clear off his feet, so fast that his feet fly toward the ceiling. In a second motion, the officer slams the boy headfirst into the ground. The boy's head thuds against the marble floor. The other boys scream.

"You done trying to be tough?" bellows the officer. "Because nobody's impressed."

TWO WEEKS LATER, Greg received a referral from IAB: an officer had allegedly picked up a young teenager and thrown him to the ground. IAB's memo made it seem like a relatively minor incident, but the field team drove to the North Bronx and downloaded surveillance footage from the building lobby. Greg reviewed the footage, which showed an unknown officer slamming a handcuffed boy's head into a marble floor.* The footage was brutal. IAB hadn't bothered to retrieve it.

Even worse, when Greg compared the footage with a photograph of the officer IAB had identified as their subject, he realized they'd identified the wrong officer.

Based on the video, Greg suspected that the officer had committed a crime. Assault, probably. Greg drafted an emergency report to the agency's higher-ups—required whenever a case might be referred to a district attorney's office for criminal prosecution.

A day later, a CCRB higher-up rushed to Greg's desk. "Greg!" he exclaimed. "I just got off the phone with the IAB chief. He's *disgusted* by that video."

The IAB chief had assured the CCRB that he'd take swift action. First, he promised to assign new investigators to IAB's case, ensuring the highest investigative quality. Then, he'd personally deliver the damning surveillance footage to the Bronx District Attorney's Office so that the officer could be criminally investigated.[†]

"You should have heard him on the phone," the higher-up told Greg. "He was so angry."

For a moment, it felt like the system was working. Then two weeks later, Greg received an email from NYPD Legal. His request for BWC footage had been denied. It depicted a group of minors, and unless Greg obtained signed waivers from each juvenile and their parents or guardians, the NYPD would maintain its refusal to

---

* There is some debate as to whether the boy's head hit the floor, the marble siding along the floor, or both. For the purposes of a clear narrative, we're going with the floor.

† The implication was clear: IAB would recommend that the Bronx DA's office open a criminal investigation.

provide the footage. Of course, those arrests had been dismissed and sealed, so he had only the name of the boy who'd been slammed to the ground.

Two months later, Greg sat at the kitchen table in a first-floor apartment in the North Bronx. Across from him sat the boy, whose mother was watching *Maury* in the next room. Greg's CV provided a clear, detailed statement. But he only knew the first names of the kids he'd been playing with, so Greg still had no way to find them or have them sign unsealing waivers for the BWC footage. That footage was still out of reach.

A month later, Greg and a tenured investigator interviewed the main subject officer. As usual, when they first walked in to the interview room, the officer sat waiting beside his union attorney. But this time, a manila envelope had been placed at the center of the table.

"These are for you," the officer grumbled, sliding the envelope across the table. It was labeled "Character References for Truly One of New York's Finest." The officer's arms were crossed, and he glared at the investigators as they sat down. Greg was intrigued. Usually, officers were cagey, quiet, or friendly in these moments. But this officer had an air of hostility.

Leafing through the envelope's contents, Greg found a series of glowing letters penned by senior citizens and business owners from the officer's precinct.

"Do you have any questions before we get started?" Greg said.

"I want to see that video," the officer said.

Greg wasn't going to show his hand, yet. "What video?" Greg asked, wondering if the officer had seen it.

"The video that's affecting my career," said the officer indignantly. It sounded like he hadn't seen it.

"We should discuss any video footage on the record," said Greg, and he turned on the recorder.

The officer began his initial statement. "I grab a hold of the kid, who's telling me, he keeps repeating, 'Fuck-n—a, fuck-n—a,' at me, and I, on my body camera, say, 'Fuck-n—er doesn't work for me. You can call me officer, you can call me anything, but that's not how this interaction is gonna go.'"

Greg had never heard a white officer say the N-word so casually.

"So far, I've treated everybody with respect. And then he says, 'I'm gonna treat you like I treat Assman,' which is a reference to— I don't know, somebody else he's dealt with in the past. I don't know. I grabbed ahold of him. I didn't use any tools, weapons, no Taser, no Mace, no baton. Nothing. I physically grab hold of him, and I force him in a seated position. As I recall, he gets back up, all the while telling me that I can't arrest him because he's on probation. I was like, 'You should be proud of yourself, you look like you're six years old, that's nothing you should be bragging about to your friends.' And I recall sitting him down a second time, where he says he hit his head against a wall. I said, 'Not a problem, I'll get you medical attention.'"

The officer's testimony directly contradicted the surveillance footage.

"For the record," asked Greg, "who's Assman?"

"*He* says Assman is another officer. But I don't know."

The officer worked in the same precinct as Detective Williams, aka Assman, whom "everybody in the Bronx" seemed to know.

"Are you aware of any officer whose name or nickname is Assman?"

"No."

Before having the officer describe the force, Greg asked about the letters.

"I got those in the mail," said the officer. "Letters from the community I serve. Character references. I didn't write or organize them." The letters all referenced the officer's ongoing disciplinary proceedings, so clearly they hadn't come out of nowhere. Later,

Greg would learn that additional copies had been mailed to the chief of Internal Affairs and a sergeant at IAB.

"I also have these for you." The officer slid over a stack of arrest reports. "These are the criminal histories for each kid, in case you didn't have them."

Officers aren't allowed to disclose sealed records, especially for minors.

"Thanks," said Greg, stuffing the arrest reports into his case file.

The letters were an easy subject. But as the interview progressed, the officer seemed to object to even the most basic questions.

"Was he ever picked up off the ground?"

"Not—Not that I know of," replied the officer. "Not intentionally."

"When you say 'not intentionally,' can you be more specific?"

"I don't know what you have for video," said the officer, "but you're trying to *catch* me. I grabbed ahold of him, and I sat him down. I didn't pick him up. I didn't lift him over my head."

After over an hour of painstaking follow-up questions, it was finally time to discuss the video.

"Are you aware of any video depicting this incident?" asked Greg. "Besides the body-worn camera?"

"Yes," the officer replied.

"And what are you aware of?"

"Internal Affairs told me there's a lobby camera of the incident."

"Were you interviewed by Internal Affairs?"

"No."

"Have you reviewed the video?"

"No."

"What did Internal Affairs say about the video?" asked Greg.

"They said the mother CCRBed me, that you guys sent investigators out to the building to retrieve video, and based on that I'm modified."

This meant he'd been assigned to desk duty.

"Who told you this?"

"The two IAB lieutenants who took my guns. I don't know their names. In December I didn't get promoted because of this."

"When were you placed on modified?"

"The eve of Thanksgiving. About a month after this incident."

That was right after Greg sent the video to IAB.

"Okay," said Greg, turning to the computer monitor. It was finally time to watch the footage. As the video played and the officer watched himself slam the boy to the ground, he slumped in his chair. It seemed he finally realized what all the commotion was about. The modified duty. The guns taken away. The lengthy CCRB interview.

"Would you like to amend your statement about how you took the boy to the ground?" asked Greg.

The officer coughed.

"From the video, his feet came off the ground. And me trying to sit him down because he was trying to keep his feet under him. So, it was— It looked like I pulled him toward me, and I pushed him back and down, and his feet came out from under him."

"What parts of his body made contact with the ground at that point?" asked the tenured investigator.

"I believe his butt."

"Anything else?"

"I'd have to watch it again. I recall his butt hitting the ground and his back and head hitting the wall."

"Which part of his head hit the wall?" asked Greg.

"The back of his head."

The officer had admitted to what the video already showed. And from there, it was all downhill.

After the interview, Greg called the Bronx DA's office for a status update. By this point, he figured IAB had given them a copy of the surveillance footage. Would they pursue criminal charges? But when Greg was transferred to a high-ranking prosecutor, he learned their office had no information about the officer's slam. Despite the

IAB chief's prior indignation and his promise to make a criminal referral, the incident had stayed in-house.

But suddenly, the prosecutor wanted the slam footage and requested it from the CCRB's records department. Perhaps there would be an investigation after all.

But about a month later, Greg caught Reilly, the agency's mystery man, drifting from desk to desk.

"You know if we sent that footage to the Bronx DA's office?" Greg asked.

"Why would you ask me that?"

"They asked for it a month ago. They emailed a request."

"None of these cases matter. Don't you see?"

Reilly held his hands up and focused on the ceiling.

"All your cases," he continued. "All those videos. They're part of a black market, records shared between the criminal-justice offices across the entire city—the entire state—the entire country."

He looked back at Greg.

"Your video?" Reilly flipped his wrist dismissively. "It's just one cog in a machine of favor trading and leverage. You see, we might not give them the videos until he gives us the videos we want. He's been holding out on us, so that's how it works. And the whole system is backlogged by a few years. Our records are part of an economy—an economy of political leverage. There's literally thousands of these videos going around. And yours will get to the DA's office, eventually. And whenever it does, they'll probably just do a brief review and decline to pursue criminal charges. You'll never hear about it again."

"When are we sending them the video?" asked Greg, exasperated.

"I don't know," said Reilly. "Someone will probably get around to it." A week later, Reilly resigned.

A month later, the office shut down because of COVID. It would be nearly two years before the case was closed. Greg's manager decided that the officer's use of the N-word was not offensive language because he was mirroring the young boy's words. But the officer's slam was substantiated, and the CCRB board voted for the highest discipline, Charges and Specifications. A public trial was scheduled.

While Greg had been conducting his investigation, IAB had quietly docked the officer fifteen vacation days for using excessive force and for providing an inaccurate statement to IAB itself (the officer had falsely told IAB that he slammed the boy to the ground because he saw a gun on the ground).* IAB then docked the officer another thirty days of vacation for "wrongfully disseminat[ing] confidential Department information." Had the officer been disciplined for giving Greg those sealed arrest records? It certainly appeared that way.

Years later, the CCRB quietly dropped the charges against the officer because he'd already been disciplined by IAB. He was never disciplined for using the N-word, and no public trial was ever held. As of November 2024, with over 500 career arrests under his belt, he was working as a Narcotics officer.[19] Another win for the Black Hole.

In 1987, the United States Supreme Court ruled that police officers are expected to "exercise a higher degree of restraint" than the average citizen, especially in the face of verbal taunts.[20] With that in mind, our experience at the CCRB made us wonder: Why did police unions insist that *every officer* keep their job?

Wouldn't it be sensible to live in a world where we could zoom out and say, "Maybe this guy isn't cut out for policing"? In that world, that officer could apply the skills and intentions that led him to befriend senior citizens and business owners without having to

---

* The inaccurate statement was not added to the NYPD's "comprehensive" public database as of November 2024.

wear a badge and carry a gun. But in the real world, the officer had thin skin, and he threw a boy to the ground so hard that it seemed his skull might crack open. He screamed the N-word, lied about the incident afterward, and tried to blame it on everyone else. Maybe, in a better world, we could all agree that he wasn't a good fit for the job.

The 2017 book *Law Enforcement, Police Unions, and the Future* by Ron DeLord and Ron York, labeled by some as the police-union playbook, notes that "Rule Number One" of dealing with a high-profile incident is "Do not defend the indefensible."[21] But police unions and police departments are very good at keeping their incidents from becoming headlines, and if we learned anything at the CCRB, "indefensible" is a very high bar. There's a defense for almost anything.

It took the CCRB three years to investigate this incident, try to prosecute the officer, and then ultimately drop the charges. The boy's mother filed a lawsuit against the NYPD. But in 2021, a little more than a year after the officer first slammed her son to the floor, she called 9-1-1 in the middle of a family argument. When officers responded, they opened a Children's Services investigation, which risked her son being taken into state custody. She believed this was in retaliation for her lawsuit.

A year after that, the boy was shot in front of his own home. He survived, but according to his mother, the precinct arrested the wrong suspect, refusing to investigate the real shooter, whom she'd captured on camera. She believed this was additional retaliation for her lawsuit. She told a CCRB investigator, "Even when I went to the hospital, they said, 'Oh, those police officers know that you're suing the police department.' No one's guarding my son. He's scared."

Because the CCRB didn't investigate retaliation, the mother's accusations were forwarded to IAB. We never heard from her again.

In 2021, once the case had been closed for good, IAB mailed the CCRB a CD. On it was a copy of an IAB interview from

2019—their interview of that same subject officer who slammed the boy on his head. As we listened, for the first time we heard an IAB interview in which the questions were comprehensive. Their tones were harsh, their questions piercing. It was an NYPD interrogation fit for the box office:

"That was not just your regular force," boomed a deputy inspector. "You picked this kid up handcuffed, and you slammed him down. Okay?"

The deputy inspector and a sergeant grilled the officer like he was a murder suspect. "You're an NCO. You're a hard worker, I'll give you that. You're out there. You're making collars.* You're doing what you have to do. I understand he's mouthing off. But we have to have thick skin as police officers. This kid is handcuffed, okay? You gotta have proper tactics. That's definitely excessive. That's not called for. I mean, do you agree that that force is more than the minimum necessary?"

The officer sighed. "Yes."

The interview was a stunning revelation. We'd never heard IAB take one of our incidents so seriously, but that wasn't necessarily good news. To learn that IAB could grill an officer for using excessive force was to know that in most of our incidents, their half-assed investigations probably weren't a by-product of incompetence. More likely, they were a by-product of neglect.

And despite this grueling interrogation, in the end the officer was only docked a handful of vacation days. For Greg, the whole process reminded him of his Catholic upbringing and the never-ending ritual of confession. Enter guilty. Confess. Repent. Exit forgiven. Case closed.

---

* "Collar" is NYPD slang for "arrest."

13

The Chokeholds

Well into the 20th century, researchers continued to exper-
iment on black people based in part on the assumption that
the black body was more resistant to pain and injury.

—KELLY M. HOFFMAN, SOPHIE TRAWALTER,
JORDAN R. AXT, M. NORMAN OLIVER, PROCEEDINGS
OF THE NATIONAL ACADEMY OF SCIENCES[1]

*S*ummer 2019. A mother in her forties has just returned to her
South Bronx apartment from a twelve-hour shift as a nursing
assistant. She can hardly stand, so she lies sprawled on the living
room couch.

"Mom. Mom. Mom. Mom. Mom."

Her son, a tall teenage boy, is imitating a joke he saw on Family Guy.
He and his younger brother giggle.

"Mom. Mom. Mom. Mom. Mom."

"Shut. Up."

"Mom. Mom. Mom. Mom. Mom."

"If you don't stop, I'm gonna call the police."

"Can I have laundry money?"

"What? Leave me alone."

"Can I have laundry money? Can I have laundry money? Can I have
laundry money?"

"I'm calling the police."

"What you gonna tell them?"

"You're harassing me."

Although her local precinct is among the most notorious in the NYPD, she picks up the phone.

FOR MANY, calling the police on anyone, let alone your own child, is a cardinal sin. But this wasn't the only time we saw a parent make such a call in a CCRB case. It seemed to reflect something deeply cynical about a person's relationship to policing.

A 1998 study published in the *Law & Society Review* defined "legal cynicism" as "'anomie' about law."[2] "Anomie," according to sociology PhD Arthur Niederhoffer, a former NYPD lieutenant, is "a morbid condition of society characterized by the absence of standards, by apathy, confusion, frustration, alienation, and despair."[3]

According to Yale Law School professor Monica C. Bell, simply characterizing people in poor Black communities as distrustful of the police fails to capture the complexity of their relationships to the law. Because "African Americans, women, and residents of high-poverty neighborhoods are equally or more likely to call the police" than their peers in other neighborhoods.[4] In these communities, Bell explains, "Mothers in particular sometimes exact social control over partners and children through police notification."[5] Bell theorizes four frameworks for why mothers request police intervention despite their "anomie":

1. "Officer exceptionalism": " . . . Mothers hold cynical views of the police, but sometimes view officers they personally know as more trustworthy."

2. "Domain specificity": Mothers make *strategic choices* about when to trust the police. While they do not

believe that "the police," overall, protect them from street crime, officers can be strategically used to remove violent partners, find runaway children, or quiet disruptive neighbors.

3. "Therapeutic consequences": Mothers are more likely to call the police when they believe the police will either resolve a conflict or administer punishment that the mother cannot administer alone.

4. "Institutional navigation": " . . . Mothers believe that calling the police sometimes protects them from, or gives them leverage with, other institutions" (e.g., Children's Services, housing project management, etc.).

In places devoid of adequate education, childcare, and other social services, mothers turn to the police when all else fails. Bell defines these decision-making processes as "situational trust." Sometimes, these mothers are in a state of anomie, weary of law enforcement's shortcomings and pitfalls. Other times, police can be used as tools to exert power in otherwise powerless situations.[6]

"NEW YORK CITY 9-1-1. Do you need police?"

"Emergency," the mother says. "My son acts like a drug addict. He's begging for drugs. He's bugging the fuck out. Harassing me. I need help. I don't know what else to do."

Fifteen minutes later, two officers stand outside the apartment door. One knocks. The son cracks the door open. "Hello?"

"Hi," says the first officer, a white male in his mid-thirties. "We got a call?"

The second officer, a Latino male in his mid-twenties, pushes the door open ever so slightly, trying to see inside.

"Excuse me, why y'all open my door?" asks the son. "Y'all got a warrant?"

"Bro," grumbles the Latino officer, "we don't need a warrant."

Both officers push past the son, forcing their way into the front hall-way. The mother stands behind her son, arms crossed.

"We got a call? Emergency?" asks the white officer.

With the two wide-shouldered officers standing inside, there's an air of claustrophobia. The Latino officer stands chest to chest with the son.

"He was being rude to me," explains the mother. "I just want him to leave me alone."

The Latino officer points at the son. His finger grazes the son's shoulder.

"Why y'all touching me?" asks the son. "Why y'all touching me? Why y'all touching me?"

"I'm not touching you, bro," says the Latino officer, standing only an inch away. "Relax. Relax. Relax."

"Why y'all touching me, pussy?" yells the son.

"Easy," the mother yells at the officers. "He's gonna act like that."

The white officer grabs the son's arm. The son flails.

"Stop!" yells the mother. "Stop! Let him go! Don't do that!"

The officers try to pin the son against the wall. As he struggles to break free, his back compresses the light switch, causing the front hallway lights to flicker off and on.

"I didn't do anything!" yells the son. "Stop!"

"He's just being rude!" yells the mother. "I just wanted—"

The officers wrench the son out of the apartment and into the stairwell landing. The son screams from the landing, and the mother screams from the doorway to their apartment.

"No! No!" yells the son, flailing to get back into his apartment. "Why you touching me?"

"Somebody record!" the mother screams. "They're gonna hurt my son!"

The white officer grabs the son's head, clutching the strands of his short black afro and bending him forward.

"Relax," says the Latino officer.

"You just pulled me out my house!" yells the son, twisting from the white officer's grasp and holding up his hands.

Both officers push the son chest first against the apartment-complex wall. Two neighbors open their doors. One starts to record with a cell phone. Everyone yells over one another; voices echo through the building.

Help. Stop. Stop resisting.

The son continues to struggle, and the mother continues to scream. The white officer pulls out a pair of handcuffs. He gets one cuff on, but the son spins around to face him. The officer presses his forearm into the son's chest.

"Relax!" screams the officer. "Relax! Relax! Relax!"

"I! Am! Calm!" screams the boy.

Suddenly, he freezes, closing his eyes and taking a deep breath. Then, he makes a break for the apartment door, twisting out of the officers' grasps again. The white officer wraps his forearm around the son's neck, stops him in his tracks, and tightens his grasp. Chokehold. He lowers the son to the ground. The mother braces herself in the doorway, preventing her younger son from entering the fray.

"I can't breathe!" yells the son. "I can't breathe!"

"He's only a child!" screams the mother. Inside the apartment, the younger son tries to push past her. He believes the officers are killing his older brother.

The white officer loosens his grasp, releasing the chokehold. It seems the son is safe, but he immediately twists away from the officer, sitting upright, chest heaving.

The Latino officer points a Taser at the son's face. "Get on the fucking ground or you're going to get fucking tased!"

"I am on the ground!" yells the son.

"He's only a child!" yells the mother.

The first officer swivels back and points his Taser at the mother's chest. "Stay back!"

The white officer yells into his radio for backup.

The Latino officer slaps the son in the head.

The son puts his hands over his face. The Latino officer slaps his hands away and, from a foot away, points his Taser at the son's head again. A red dot flickers on his right cheek.

A STANDARD AXON TASER X26P has three main settings. In the first setting, the default, two prongs fire forward like harpoons for fifteen to twenty feet.[7][*] In the second or "drive-stun" setting, the Taser is pressed directly into the subject's body. In the third or "warning arc" setting, officers can pull the Taser's trigger to emit two arcs of electricity, ostensibly as a de-escalation method. According to the Axon website, "With a Warning Arc display, the user may deter a subject without having to use actual force."[8] Much like a rattlesnake's tail, this setting signals that danger is near.

THE LATINO OFFICER SWITCHES HIS Taser to the "warning-arc" setting and pulls the trigger. Two arcs of electricity bend at the Taser's tip, emitting a sharp crackling sound.

"Oh," gasps a neighbor.

The son freezes in place.

"Turn the fuck around!" yells the Latino officer, kicking the son in the ribs. He grabs the son by the hair, flips him onto his stomach, and finally locks the second handcuff in place. The son begins to sob.

As the mother protests, the officers lift the son to his feet and carry him down the stairwell. At each floor, heads poke out of apartment doors, and residents yell at the officers.

"What the hell is wrong with y'all?"

On the ground floor, they bump into another dozen officers responding as backup. One grabs the son by the hair.

---

[*] This distance was what we were told in training. However, Axon advertises newer models that travel as far as twenty-five feet.

"*You wanna act like a fucking animal?*" booms the Latino officer. "*That's how fucking animals get treated.*" He turns to the lobby full of officers. "*Let's fucking go!*"

Two new officers take the son and carry him outside and down the front steps. As they walk, they lift his handcuffs up and push his head down. With each step, it seems that one officer is kneeing the son in the head.

Thud. Thud. Thud.

"*Ow! Ow! Ow!*" yells the son. "*Help! He's kneeing me!*"

"*Nobody's kneeing you. Nobody's kneeing you,*" an officer drones through gritted teeth.

"*Ow! Ow!*"

The officers drag the son into the street. His younger brother races outside and stands at the base of the front steps. Going any farther would be too dangerous. "*You're gonna have to kill me before you hurt my brother,*" he yells from a distance.

The Latino officer, now standing closest to the base of the front steps, turns his attention to the younger brother. "*Do me a favor,*" says the Latino officer. "*Go back upstairs.*" He points his Taser at the younger brother's chest. "*Go the fuck back upstairs or I'll fucking tase you.*" He shoves the younger brother, who stumbles backward up the front steps. The officer follows, then shoves him to the ground.

"*Get the fuck upstairs, bro. Get the fuck upstairs before you're next.*"

The younger brother runs back into his home.

As this is happening, an unknown man happens to walk by the apartment complex.

"*Back up,*" the Latino officer tells him. "*Back up from the workspace, bro.*"

"*Get the fuck back,*" snaps another officer.

The bystander quickly walks away.

The mother races out of the building and approaches the Latino officer. "*Why did y'all do that to my son? You didn't give me a chance to tell you—*"

"You didn't help the situation at all," says the Latino officer. "Your son was about to get fucking tased in front of you." The officer waves away the mother and walks over to the son, who's handcuffed at the back of an ambulance, beginning to tell other officers what just happened.

"He just kneed me in my head, like, forty times!" says the son, looking at the officer who hauled him from the apartment complex.

The Latino officer leans down so that he's face to face with the son. "Dude, do me a favor. Shut the fuck up! Shut the fuck up!" He walks away.

Eventually, the officers leave the son in an ambulance. At the hospital, the staff doesn't know what to do with him, so they release him right away. His mother pays for a cab home.

A MONTH AFTER THIS INCIDENT, Mac sat in a booth in a near-empty diner in the South Bronx. Next to him sat a new investigator. Across from them were the mother, her older son, and their civil attorney, a Black man in his forties.

"Would it be all right if we did this somewhere more private?" asked Mac.

"No," replied the attorney. "We can do it right here."

"I just don't want anyone else to overhear. This is a confidential investigation, and we're discussing a very sensitive incident."

"It's fine, man. What do you care? You guys at the CCRB—I've dealt with you before. You take the most egregious incident and exonerate, or unsubstantiate . . . Let's just get on with this. I don't trust you to help this family. And we're only here because she wants to be here." He glanced at the mother.

The man had a point. Even outside observers had heard of the CCRB's wavering investigative quality. A *New York World* headline in 2015 said, "Under intense pressure, young and largely inexperienced staff at CCRB tasked with investigating police misconduct."[9]

From a civil attorney's perspective, filing a CCRB complaint might not be worth the hassle. At the time, the CCRB only substantiated 10 to 12 percent of allegations, so filing a complaint added an unpredictable variable to a civil lawsuit that might bring in tens or even hundreds of thousands of dollars in damages.[10] If we exonerated an allegation, perhaps the city would lower its offer to settle. It was no surprise then when a renowned civil rights attorney asked Mac over drinks, "Why should I advise anyone to file a CCRB complaint at all?"

Mac interviewed the mother, who'd thought the officers were going to kill her son. Then Mac interviewed her son, who'd been choked, kicked, and kneed in the head.

Six weeks later, Mac received BWC footage from NYPD Legal, and it corroborated everything. He also interviewed the younger brother, who'd listened to his brother yell, "I can't breathe."

Over the following months, Mac kept calling and emailing their building management, hoping he could get surveillance footage that would more clearly capture officers seeming to knee the older brother in the head, but no one got back to him.

Five months after the incident, Mac interviewed the Latino officer. "Did you ever tell him you were going to treat him like an animal?" asked Mac.

"If I did, it was in regard to the way he was acting, but I don't recall saying that."

"What does it mean to treat somebody like an animal?"

The room was silent for a solid five seconds, until his attorney interjected. "Do you mean it . . . literally?"

"I don't know what I meant."

"Did you kick him in the side?" Mac asked, looking at a still image of the officer's foot in the older brother's ribs.

"I wouldn't call that a kick. I was trying to gain compliance."

His attorney interjected again. "So, you were moving toward his body to grab his arm?"

"Right," the officer said.

"What was your right foot doing?" asked Mac.

"My right foot was trying to gain compliance."

"Did your right foot make contact with the civilian?"

"It made contact, yes."

"And what was the purpose of that action?"

"To gain compliance."

"Did you intentionally kick him?" asked the officer's attorney. "That's what they're asking."

"No," replied the officer. "I didn't."

"So, was that action unintentional?" asked Mac.

"It was an unintentional action to gain compliance."

The other officer interviews were more of the same.

Over the next few months, Mac gathered more evidence. Eventually, in late 2020, Mac wrote up the closing report and substantiated nine allegations. The case was sent to the CCRB board. The board voted to terminate the white officer, and to dock the Latino officer weeks of vacation.* In late 2024, both officers agreed to plea deals for ten days of vacation. Case closed.

IN 1993, the NYPD banned officers from using chokeholds. But not every rule is strictly enforced. Jaywalking, perhaps a New Yorker's favorite pastime, was, after all, illegal until fall 2024. And

---

* In early 2021, the CCRB and NYPD agreed upon a new framework to standardize CCRB discipline recommendations (known as the disciplinary matrix), and the Board began recommending specific discipline instead of "Charges and Specifications," for example. Unfortunately, in the years that followed, NYPD commissioners continued to ignore CCRB recommendations on a regular basis.

so, on the eve of the trial of Daniel Pantaleo, there was great uncer-
tainty as to whether the chokehold ban would be enforced.

Summer 2019. Inside a courtroom at One Police Plaza, the two of
us were sitting with the prosecution on the last day of the weeks-long
trial. Media coverage had been at a fever pitch, with the city on pins
and needles. Immediately behind us sat Eric Garner's family. To
our left was Daniel Pantaleo, the officer on trial, and his attorney,
Stuart London, the top-tier defender of cops in New York City.
Before us sat Suzanne O'Hare and Jonathan Fogel, the CCRB's top
two prosecutors. On the bench sat Rosemarie Maldonado, NYPD
deputy commissioner of trials, presiding as the administrative judge.
The courtroom was packed with a who's who of academics, activists,
journalists, and cops.

"This is like our Super Bowl," a deputy inspector told Greg on
the way in. "Between our guys and your guys."

The judge slammed down her gavel, and the proceedings began.
At stake? Whether Pantaleo would be fired for using a chokehold
to kill Eric Garner.

The former sergeant who trained Pantaleo at the academy testified that he'd taught Pantaleo that chokeholds were prohibited.[11]
A medical examiner from St. Louis dubiously testified that Garner
had died of a heart attack, not the chokehold in question.[12] Both
faced grueling cross-examination.

CCRB prosecutor O'Hare asserted that "the video is not biased,"
and that "the manner of death in this case is classified as a homicide." Defense attorney London said that his client had actually
saved Garner's life by bringing him to the ground and that, although
Garner had died afterward, "It doesn't matter." He told the judge
that "you can't second-guess cops," adding that Garner had caused
himself to have an asthma attack by yelling, "I can't breathe."

Midway through London's incendiary arguments, Gwen Carr,
Eric Garner's mother, stormed out of the courtroom.

It was a courtroom drama that evoked *To Kill a Mockingbird*, but in the press, the events of this day would only be mentioned in passing, if at all. The media was most focused on the judge's final ruling.

Determined and exceptionally prepared, the CCRB's O'Hare closed by arguing that Pantaleo should be fired, emphasizing to the court that when Eric Garner first yelled, "I can't breathe," Pantaleo's forearm bulged, and he tightened his grasp around Garner's neck.

"That's proof of intent," she noted.

Her closing statement lasted nearly eighty minutes. And as it came to a grand conclusion, she stood before the court with her arms outstretched and cried out as if calling to someone higher than the police commissioner.

"He couldn't breathe," she exclaimed. "God help us! He could. Not. Breathe."

14

The Shootings

From the very beginning of their occupational careers, both police officer and physician must come to terms with the shock of their daily experience. In their preliminary training they learn to keep their equilibrium in an environment where blood, excrement, and death are normal conditions. Constantly, they are exposed to the backside of humanity with all its sordid and guilty secrets. To keep their sanity, and even to survive, most of them build a protective shield of cynicism around them as insulation against this human misery. Without it, many would crack under the battering. Many do go under. Others feel guilt as a result of the frequently necessary lapses from professional ethics and idealism. Drug addiction, alcoholism, and suicide become occupational hazards.

—ARTHUR NIEDERHOFFER,
The Police Family[1]

Fall 2018. Frank Dwyer, one of three NYPD appointees to the CCRB board, addressed a group of tenured investigators. "I read these closing reports," he said, "and I keep thinking—some of these are impressive, complex investigations. I wish we could get some of you working homicides."

Greg turned to Mac.

"I'm pretty sure we already do."

WINTER 2018. A man in his fifties walks through the front door of his apartment building in the Bronx. He's behind on rent. A few months earlier, he was fired from his job as a bank teller. He's been living in poverty for a long time, and with rising rents, working as a bike messenger isn't paying the bills. His landlord is waiting in the stairwell.

"You have to pay the rent, right now."

"I can get it to you next week," says the man.

"Right now," says the landlord. "Or this is it. You gotta go."

Before that moment, the man had been well respected in his neighborhood. He was known as a mentor to young children, and his friendly affect as he biked from delivery to delivery had earned him a reputation as something of a street legend. But at this moment, the man does not know what he is going to do or where he is going to go.

The man pulls out a box cutter and charges at his landlord. Another tenant runs in, managing to pull him off the landlord before the knife finds skin.

The man screams. "I want to die!" He runs upstairs and into his apartment. He rummages for the largest knife he can find and charges back downstairs.

Another tenant calls 9-1-1. "Help! He's got a knife!" they scream to the operator.

The man chases the landlord out of the building and onto the dimly lit street. He slashes the air as the landlord runs for his life. Two male officers, one white, one Latino—perhaps the youngest duo in their precinct—pull up in a marked NYPD vehicle.

"I wanna die!" screams the man, still chasing his landlord.

The officers jump out of their vehicle and stand at the front bumper with their guns pointed.

"Drop the knife!" screams one officer.

"Drop the knife!" screams the other.

"Shoot me!" screams the man, walking toward the officers.

The man suddenly turns away. Wandering into the street, it's as if he's turned into a zombie, ignoring the officers, lumbering forward aimlessly, and yelling the words, "Shoot me! Shoot me!" like they're the only ones he knows.

"Drop the knife! Drop the knife!"

The man lumbers around the police vehicle. The officers follow behind.

"Drop the knife! Drop the knife!"

"Shoot me! Shoot me!"

The officers double back to the front of the police vehicle and root their feet in place. The man lumbers around a parked car and then pivots back toward the officers.

"Yo, this guy's got a gun. He's coming at me," yells someone behind the officers.

There isn't a gun. Is that the landlord?

"Drop the knife! Drop the knife!"

"Shoot me! Shoot me!"

The man staggers toward the officers. One step. Two steps. When he is about ten feet away, they open fire. Four bullets into his chest. One into the open field behind him. His body collapses to the ground. He is dead.

THREE WEEKS LATER, the man's best friend filed a complaint with the CCRB, and the case was assigned to Mac. The shooting had been all over the news: "NYPD: Police Shoot Knife-Wielding Tenant Dead After Dispute with Landlord in the Bronx," CBS News reported. "Officers Fatally Shoot Bronx Man Chasing His Landlord with Knife, Police Say," said the *New York Times*. "NYPD bodycam footage shows fatal shooting of knife-wielding man," read a *New York Post* headline.

When the NYPD released a partial clip of the BWC footage to the press, Mac watched it on the *Post* website. When he requested the footage from NYPD Legal, they denied it even existed. As usual, there was little to stop them from lying.[2]

After several rounds of wrangling with NYPD Legal, they admitted that the footage existed but refused to release it because it was being investigated by the Force Investigation Division. FID refused to release the footage until their investigation was complete and blocked the CCRB from receiving any other documentation of the incident. "There's nothing we can do," said a CCRB higher-up. Mac had to proceed without the full video or a ballistics report.

Mac and Greg went to the incident location together, knocking on doors and scouting for surveillance footage. None of the nearby cameras were working, and none of the witnesses wanted to talk about what happened. Standing where the man had been shot down only a few weeks before, Mac looked up at the street signs marking the nearest intersection. A grim irony was clear: the incident had begun on Kalief Browder Way.[3]*

A month later, Mac scheduled the two officers for interviews at the CCRB, but the NYPD canceled them both. Then came a call from the Bronx DA's office, advising Mac that they were investigating the shooting, as well. Because they might decide to criminally charge the officers, they needed the CCRB to pause its investigation. As per CCRB policy, the case was put on hold indefinitely.[4]†

---

* Kalief Browder was a young Black man from the Bronx. In 2010, when he was sixteen years old, Browder was arrested for allegedly stealing a backpack. He was held without bail for nearly three years, placed in solitary confinement for over two of those years. The charges against him were ultimately dismissed. Two years later, Browder hung himself in childhood home, which is located on the now-named Kalief Browder Way.

† As of 2025, Chicago's Civilian Office of Police Accountability (COPA) is required by ordinance "to pursue an administration investigation within its jurisdiction concurrently with an active federal or state criminal investigation." Across police oversight, this subject is challenging—civilian oversight entities do not want to impede or taint criminal investigations, but it is relatively rare for officers to be criminally prosecuted, and criminal investigations tend to drag on for a long time. For effective

Months later, when the DA's office decided not to prosecute and lifted their hold on the CCRB investigation, the NYPD still refused to provide the BWC or the ballistics report, and for a while, they refused to let the officers appear for a CCRB interview. Nine months after the shooting, Mac and a tenured investigator finally sat in an interview room facing the officer who first pulled the trigger.

"Why are we even doing this?" asked Stewie, placing his arm around the officer's shoulder. "Why are you gonna make him relive this?"

The officer, ash white, looked like he was running a fever.

"You know we gotta do this," Mac told Stewie.

"Just go easy on him. He's the one who's gotta live with killing a guy."

Moments later, the interview began. "From beginning to end, can you tell me what happened?"

This interview was different. The pace was very slow, and there were long pauses between each question and answer. The officer narrated the incident, starting when he received the radio notification for a man with a knife, to when he saw the man chasing his landlord, to when the officer screamed, "Drop the knife! Drop the knife!" over and over. But the man didn't drop the knife, and he said, "Shoot me."

"What did that lead you to believe?" Mac said.

The officer's voice dropped to a hush. "It was going to be a suicide by cop." The officer's head drooped forward, and his eyes welled.

"What was unique about this situation," asked the tenured investigator, "as opposed to the others you've responded to in the past?"

"He didn't drop the knife," the officer said, drooping farther down in his seat.

---

and timely accountability, an oversight entity must have enough resources to walk that fine line.

Stewie threw up his hands, exasperated. "He came at you with the knife. And is this the first time you ever shot anybody?"

"Yes," replied the officer.

Stewie glared at the tenured investigator. "I'd say that's a little unique."

"So when the man said, 'Shoot me,' what did you believe was his intention?" asked Mac.

"I thought he was gonna kill me."

"And was it you or your partner who said, 'Drop the fucking knife'?"

"I said it."

"Can you explain why you used profanity in that statement?"

"I was scared for my life. I've never been put in a situation like that."

"Who fired first?"

"I did."

"How many times did you fire?"

"Four?"

"Were you aware of how many times you fired, or was that something you later learned?"

"That was something I later learned."

Stewie turned toward the officer and spoke softly, like a therapist. "Do you remember firing first, or were you told that later?"

The officer shook his head. "No, I remember firing first."

Forty minutes later, Mac sat back at his desk, ready to transcribe the interview when a higher-up appeared.

"Can you close this case without interviewing the second officer? Stewie's furious. Says the officer's a wreck."

"NYPD Legal won't give me the full body cam or the ballistics report. It'd be nice to interview the second officer, even if this ends up being exonerated."

"I don't want to put the second officer through that for no reason. Could you just exonerate it with the evidence you have?"

This was phrased as a question, but a direct order was implied.

"Yeah," said Mac. "I can close the case."

A few months after the interview, a former FBI instructor came to the CCRB to teach investigators how to use a cutting-edge video-analysis software. Over two days, the instructor taught us how different types of cameras recorded motion differently and that depending on the camera model, software, and the time of day the video was recorded, the same incident could look completely different. Some police incidents went viral, he said, because bad software made motion seem much faster and, thus, the incident more violent. The opposite was true, as well, with some videos making it seem as though officers had been moving more slowly, so the video was less upsetting. But perhaps most interestingly, he showed us how to tell whether a video had been edited. And if so, by whom.

"Would you mind taking a look at a video in one of my cases?" Mac said to the video instructor, who'd consulted for police departments across the country.

The instructor parked himself at Mac's desk and ran the footage through his fancy software. "Where'd you get this?"

"The NYPD website," Mac said.

"This video's been edited at least four times. Look at the metadata. You definitely couldn't use this in court. I wouldn't use it for an investigation at all. There's no way to know what changed. You're gonna want the original footage."

Mac sighed. "This is all we got."

IN THE FALL OF 2018, Mac was at a hotel in St. Petersburg, Florida. He'd been sent to represent the agency at the annual conference for the National Association for Civilian Oversight of Law Enforcement (NACOLE). Over the course of a week, he met the leaders of police oversight agencies across the country and found that the world of police oversight was much larger than he'd imagined.

In Seattle, at the Office of Police Accountability, civilian investigators and sworn police officers conducted their investigations as
teams. In Denver, at the Office of the Independent Monitor, civilian
investigators immediately responded to the most serious incidents,
interviewing officers on scene. But instead of directly asking questions to subject officers, they passed questions to Internal Affairs
officers, who then repeated those questions into the record. In San
Francisco, at the Department of Police Accountability, civilian
investigators were guided by attorneys throughout the investigative
process. At the Los Angeles Police Department Audit Division, a
team of professional auditors reviewed random batches of LAPD
documents, which sometimes led them to discover issues that other
oversight agencies never could.

In one presentation, the court-appointed monitor for the Puerto
Rico Police Bureau explained that police oversight only worked
when every employee had a holistic understanding of their role in
data collection and never just "checked the box." In another, a former homicide detective proposed that data collection should always
revolve around the premise that "officers are concerned about how
they will be viewed by their peers." In yet another, a Department
of Justice official revealed that their office mostly learned about
officer-involved incidents through Google Alerts.[5*]

It was Comic Con for police oversight, and as Mac buzzed from
panel discussions to happy hours, every conversation seemed like an
invitation to a much larger landscape than New York City's.

"Oh, you think you have it bad in New York?" asked a woman
from Baltimore's Civilian Review Board. "We've got it ten times
worse than you'd think."

In every city, there was a different story of policing and a different
story of police oversight. Some agencies had been thrown together
in the aftermath of some awful incident, and some agencies had been

---

* This practice has since changed, and DOJ now has an online complaint portal.

carefully designed without a crisis to spur them on. Some agencies seemed to have access to every police document they wanted, while other agencies had none at all. More than anything, NACOLE was a treasure trove of ideas and experience, where everyone seemed to have a fresh new insight into how to change policing for the better.

Sometime after midnight, Mac sat at a picnic table in front of a pizza place downtown. Across from him sat Dennis, whose speech during Mac's training still rang true.

"So, you're investigating shootings now?" said Dennis, taking a sip from his beer. "Welcome to the big leagues."

"I wouldn't have stuck around for it if it weren't for people like you," said Mac.

At the CCRB, Dennis had mentored almost everyone that Mac and Greg most admired. He exemplified how one person's force of personality, optimism, and commitment to the facts had shaped generations of public servants.

"Can I get your thoughts on a shooting?" asked Mac.

"Always."

Mac walked Dennis through the incident. The confrontation with the landlord. The chase into the street. The "drop the knife." The shooting.

"I just can't shake the feeling," said Mac, "that none of this needed to happen."

At a presentation earlier that day, an officer had talked about how police can justify actions when they fear for their safety, but they're not always held responsible when they intentionally place themselves into scary situations where using force out of fear seems, at least in retrospect, like an inevitability.

"I don't think these officers should get fired," said Mac. "Legally, they're in the clear. But really, couldn't they have stepped back? Wasn't there another way?"

"That's not what they're trained to do," said Dennis. "Can't blame one officer for the system that handed him a gun."

Mac sighed.

"But there's something you can do," said Dennis. "Set a precedent. So, you think there were problems? Write them in your report. You can exonerate the officers. But you can still criticize the policies that led them to kill this man. Someday, the public will see what you wrote. Something awful happened, and nothing illegal happened. Maybe that sends a message that something needs to change."

Back in New York, Mac wrote the closing report. He exonerated the shooting. He wrote that the split-second nature of the incident "precluded [the officers] from more broadly assessing [the man's] wellbeing." The report weighed whether the officers might have first viewed the man as someone who was unwell before accepting his request for suicide by cop. And because of this consideration, perhaps this would set a precedent, and in future instances, when the officers had a little more time to react, the green light to "shoot first, ask questions later" would be scrutinized a little more closely. It wasn't clear who would be doing the scrutinizing, but at the CCRB, where there was rarely a moment that felt like victory, sometimes you had to make your own.

In 1969, former NYPD lieutenant Arthur Niederhoffer, also an attorney with a PhD in sociology, conducted an unprecedented survey. Asking urban police officers what they thought of their own jobs, he found a single sentiment that prevailed over all others: cynicism. The basis for this sentiment, Niederhoffer argues, is the French word "anomie." Just as Black and brown communities experience anomie—"a morbid condition of society characterized by the absence of standards, by apathy, confusion, frustration, alienation, and despair"—so too did the police. As one retired Washington, DC, officer reported, there was an inevitable "emotional or psychological crisis which seems to come to every active and sincere policeman . . . I have seen good men completely ruined by this hopeless feeling."[6]

Based on his survey and his own experiences as a police lieutenant, Niederhoffer wrote that officers in the lower ranks felt uncertain of their own positions in society. In their work, officers learned to manipulate the law "as nothing but a means to an end."

> The policeman realizes that for much of his time on duty he is above the law. Paradoxically, society has granted him the license to disregard the law in order to enforce it. He may kill where necessary, he may destroy property and invade privacy; he may make arrests merely on grounds of suspicion; he may disregard traffic regulations. The sense of power often corrupts him into a belief that he is superior to the law.[7]

But over time, an officer's exposure to the worst of humanity, "the ill-willed, exploitative, mean, and dirty," and anomie, the sense of confusion and despair, is replaced by resentment.[8] The officer feels hostility toward the people who commit crimes, professional pressures that render him increasingly aggressive, and a powerlessness to change anything.[9]

And in turn, anomie becomes the prevailing sentiment of a police organization as a whole. Asked in 1962, "Are you inclined to be pessimistic about the future of our society?" LAPD Chief William Parker replied:

> I look back over almost thirty-five years in the police service, thirty-five years of dealing with the worst that humanity has to offer. I meet the failures of humanity daily, and I meet them in the worst possible context. It is hard to keep an objective viewpoint. But it is also hard for me to believe that our society can continue to violate all the fundamental

rules of human conduct and expect to survive. I think I
have to conclude that this civilization will destroy itself,
as others have done before it. That leaves, then, only one
question—when?[10]

His apocalyptic pessimism becomes far more startling when you
learn that Chief Parker founded and produced *The Thin Blue Line*, a
seminal 1950s talk show on policing, and played a significant role in
the production of *Dragnet*, America's first major police procedural.[11*]

Niederhoffer identified four stages of cynicism in a police officer's career.

1. "Pseudo-cynicism": When officers first attend the
    academy, they begin conforming to the already cynical
    culture of policing. But they still hold on to their
    idealism and commitment to public service.
2. "Romantic cynicism": In the first five years of officers'
    careers, idealism meets anomie, and they form a
    love-hate relationship to their jobs. Cynicism builds,
    bonding officers who understand one another's
    experience, and increasingly isolates them from the
    outside world.

---

* The concept of the "thin blue line" derives from the idea that the police are the
line that separates society from disorder and chaos. The term was first used in reference to soldiers holding the line in battle. However, in the American imagination,
Parker tethered the term "thin blue line" to American policing. Parker's mission was
to reform public perception of the department. He personally propelled the production of radio and television shows that focused on the most compelling aspects of
police work, while omitting negative or mundane content. *Dragnet*, America's first
police procedural, began as a radio show in 1949 and was developed into a television
show in 1951. From 1952 to 1955, it ranked fourth, second, third, and eighth among
the most-watched television shows in America. Parker was a hands-on consultant,
opening select case files to Hollywood producers and ensuring that he had a major
influence on the way Americans were visually introduced to policing.

3. "Aggressive cynicism": Cynicism boils into resentment, which manifests as open hostility.
4. "Resigned cynicism": Nearing retirement, resentment recedes into resignation, and apathy prevails.[12]

The average CCRB investigator's career was much shorter than a police officer's—two years, perhaps—but as we observed it, our stages of cynicism closely paralleled theirs. The cases kept on coming, but to many, the job could feel like it mattered less and less.

AFTER TRAINING, every new CCRB investigator was required to go on a ride along. In 2016, Greg had chosen the South Bronx's 44th Precinct for his. He spent four hours with a pair of officers from Sector C as they drove from job to job. A cyberbullying complaint at an apartment. An assault complaint in the ER. A gas leak in a housing project. Another gas leak. After a while, the officer in the passenger seat, a white male in his early thirties, turned back toward Greg.

"On our first day at the academy, they told us we all just got a front-row ticket to the greatest show on Earth."

"Oh?" said Greg, looking down at his borrowed bulletproof vest.

"Yeah. And I want a refund."

LATER THAT SUMMER, Mac was in the lobby of the 73rd Precinct stationhouse waiting for his own ride along. Officers milled in and out, and a man stood just outside, banging on the front window as he demanded to speak to the commanding officer.

"Hey," said a sergeant, poking his head out of a briefing room. "You guys wanna sit in on roll call?"

Mac, Castor, and the officers set up folding chairs in a large circle.

"Okay, what have you guys been seein'?" asked the sergeant.

Mac started to realize something was off. The first officer who spoke looked at least seventy years old (in the NYPD, you had to retire at sixty-three). He looked more closely at another officer's uniform and noticed a patch that said, *Auxiliary Officer*. He and Castor sat through the meeting as the sergeant debriefed the auxiliary officers, who turned out to be volunteers, on the comings and goings of crime in the neighborhood.

There were more than four thousand auxiliary police officers who patrolled neighborhoods across New York.[13] They weren't really police officers, but they wore police uniforms, drove police vehicles, and from what Mac could see, were briefed like officers at the beginnings of their tours. Only five police departments in the United States had more officers than the NYPD had *auxiliary* officers. On one hand, this seemed like an efficient, wholesome participation in local government. On the other hand, Mac thought, there had to be a downside.

LATE NIGHT, SPRING 2015, A security guard stands inside the entrance of a Dumbo nightclub. A bartender walks up.

"*Hey, that asshole just touched my ass.*"

The security guard walks up to the bar. He sees a man in his thirties who is very drunk.

"*Sir, don't touch the staff.*"

"*I wanna talk to the owner of this place.*"

The security guard goes into the office upstairs and returns with the owner in tow.

"*Sir, can I help you?*" *asks the owner.* "*You can't touch our bartenders.*"

"*Yeah, yeah . . . I wanna . . . talk to you about something more important . . . I wanna invest in this restaurant . . . What do you say? Twenty K?*"

"Sir, we don't do that here. I'm going back up to my office. Enjoy your evening."

As the owner walks away, the man turns to the security guard. "I'm investing . . . in this restaurant . . . You understand me?" The man takes off his jacket, exposing what appears to be a gun holster on his hip.

"Oh, I understand," says the security guard, laughing and slapping the man on the back. "I totally understand."

The security guard reaches down to the man's waistband and feels the holster. The man is too drunk to notice. Does he have a gun? It feels like it.

Moments later, an off-duty officer from the 77th Precinct receives a phone call. It's one of the precinct's auxiliary officers.

"Hey, man, I'm working security in Dumbo. There's a guy in here, and he's got a gun in his waistband."

"Okay, sit tight. I'll call you back."

Then, a plainclothes sergeant receives a phone call from the off-duty officer.

"Hey, sarge, one of our auxiliary guys, he's working security in Dumbo, and he's got eyes on a guy with a gun."

"Where at?"

The sergeant calls the auxiliary officer. He gets a description of the man and the address of the nightclub.

"Keep eyes on him. We'll head over."

The nightclub is only three blocks from the 84th Precinct stationhouse, and the 77th Precinct is four miles away. There are at least five other precinct stationhouses closer to the nightclub. Even so, the sergeant assembles his team of plainclothes officers in the 77. Some are Anti-Crime officers, others are Conditions officers, a sort of junior varsity Anti-Crime unit. The sergeant and two officers head out in an unmarked black sedan. Three officers pile into another. No lights. No sirens. They cross several precincts and park around the block from the nightclub.

According to the NYPD Patrol Guide, the sergeant was required to notify the 84th Precinct of his team's presence in the area.[14] It's not normal for their Anti-Crime team to leave the confines of the 77. But they do not alert the local precinct of their presence, and they do not alert anyone else about the presence of a gun.

Back at the Dumbo nightclub, the man with the gun holster walks outside. He's spent most of his adult life in prison. In 1996, when he was fifteen, he watched his cousin shoot and kill a young man. Although his cousin had been the shooter, they were both convicted of second-degree murder. After thirteen years in prison, he'd been released on parole.

An unmarked vehicle pulls next to him. Are these the police or is he being robbed? The man turns around and runs.

"Stop! Freeze!"

Does the man hear their commands? Across the street, he sees a park. He makes a run for it, passing between two parked cars. He pulls something from his waistband. He looks up, and he's suddenly face-to-face with a second group of officers. Their guns are drawn, pointed at his chest.

"Freeze!" yells an officer.

The man takes one step away from the officers, eyes on the park. One gunshot. The bullet grazes the man's elbow. Second gunshot. The bullet pierces the man's hip. He twists around in agony. Third gunshot. The bullet pierces the man's back and lodges itself into his spine. Fourth gunshot. The bullet misses, shatters the front windshield of a parked car, and lodges itself between a couple on their third date. The man collapses to the ground.

An officer runs up to him, kicks the gun away, then kicks the man to see if he's alive.

"Why'd you shoot me?" the man groans.

"Relax, buddy," says the officer.

The man blacks out.

HE WAS ARRESTED for criminal possession of a weapon and sat in Rikers Island for the next four months. One day, he wrote a letter to the CCRB, and an investigation was opened. But as quickly as it was opened, the man's attorney called and asked for it to be closed due to the pending criminal charges. For two years, his case file lay untouched in the CCRB's archive. Then, in fall 2017, he wrote another letter from Rikers Island requesting that his CCRB case be reopened. The original investigator was long gone, so the case was assigned to Greg.

That fall, Greg and Mac met the man and interviewed him through the bulletproof glass of a Rikers Island visitor's booth. He slid Greg a redacted copy of the IAB case file and revealed that he'd been using a wheelchair since the incident. He insisted that the officers who arrested him shot him in the back and planted the gun and promised that a family member would deliver surveillance footage that proved it.

Two days later, Greg got an unexpected call from the downstairs lobby. "There's a little girl here to see you," said a security guard.

Greg took the elevator down to the ground floor and saw a girl, no older than thirteen, with short, braided hair and a flash drive in her right hand.

"Are you Investigator Finch?" she asked.

"Can I help you?"

She stretched her right hand up. "My uncle told me to give this to you."

Greg took the flash drive.

"My mom's waiting in the car," said the girl. "Bye!" She waved and ran toward the lobby's revolving doors.

Upstairs, Greg opened the flash drive's files, and a group of investigators gathered around his desk. Was this the video that would exonerate the man? Would it show officers planting a gun? Would it show the shooting?

The footage was from a surveillance camera that had been temporarily attached to scaffolding around the corner from the nightclub. It was grainy, but it captured a man—Greg's CV—walking down a dimly lit sidewalk. An unmarked vehicle pulls up next to him, and plainclothes officers jump out with their guns drawn. The man runs. For a moment, it seems that he's pulling something from his waistband. Is that the glimmer of steel? It's hard to tell, but it looks like a gun. The man runs out of frame, and the officers run out of frame, too.

The video didn't show the shooting. And it didn't show the officers planting a gun, either. It did appear to show the man pulling a gun from his waistband before he ran off-screen. But it was hard to tell, so Greg asked around.

"I don't know," said one investigator.

"That's definitely a gun," said another investigator.

"I think you're gonna have to exon this one," said a third.

Greg polled dozens of investigators, and despite some ambiguity, the general consensus was that the man did indeed have a gun. But there was still the question of whether he'd been shot in the back.

Over the next month, Greg requested NYPD documents and asked for IAB's unredacted case file. IAB declined Greg's request.

At that point, all Greg could do was interview the officers. One month later, he and Mac walked into an interview room to find one of the officers wearing a hooded sweatshirt and a mischievous grin. His attorney was grinning, too.

"You know he's faking it, right?" the officer said. "He's not paralyzed."

"What do you mean?"

"My buddy arrested him last summer. After a foot pursuit."

According to our records, he'd been at Rikers for nearly three years straight.

The interview began, and the officer gave his side of the story.

"The male with a gun ran on the sidewalk toward me and my partner. We exited our vehicle. I was on the sidewalk. My partner was in the street. And as he was running toward me, he started pulling his gun out. I drew my weapon. I told him, 'Drop the gun. Police. Don't move.' And at that time, he was crossing between cars toward the street. As he went to turn, that's when I saw him dig under his jacket, and I'm watching the gun come out at that point. And that's when— The shots were fired."

Officers tended to use the passive voice in moments like this— "the shots were fired" rather than "I fired my gun."

"And at that point, what led you to believe he had a gun?"

"I've made numerous gun arrests. I know what a gun looks like."

"And what did you see?"

"I saw a gun coming from his waist. I don't know how else to tell you." The officer laughed nervously.

"What color was it?" asked Greg.

"It was shiny. That's all I remember."

"Did he ever look at you?"

"I think once he saw me, he started cutting into the street."

"How far away was he, when he saw you?"

"The distance between me and you right now."

Mac and the officer were about six feet apart.

"Where was the gun pointed?"

"The gun was pointed out."

"Was it pointed at a person?" asked Greg.

"I couldn't— There's cars in between—"

The officer's attorney interrupted. "It's a dynamic action!"

The officer continued. "That gun was up in a threatening manner. I felt threatened for my life. Being in a shooting is one of those things where . . . you get tunnel vision, and everything happens so fast."

To the officer, it was simple: he feared for his safety, so he shot the man. But for Greg, there were still lingering questions. Had the officers seen the gun? Had it really seemed like the man was going to shoot them? Had the man even seen the officers in the first place? Did this really need to happen?

The officer thought so. And he also said that the man had pretended to be paralyzed.

"At one point he was let out of jail and officers stopped his car. The guy jumped out and ran like a banshee. I guess he was showing up to court in a wheelchair, claiming he was paralyzed, and then walking around fine with no problem."

Greg had no way to independently verify this strange allegation, and it didn't really impact the case. But it spoke to a sentiment deeply rooted in the NYPD's culture: everyone was out to game the system.

Three months later, the two of us interviewed the second shooter. Stewie was his attorney.

"I get out the car. I'm out in the street. The guy turns and runs toward us. Pulls out a gun. I didn't see it initially, but I hear the other cops yell, 'Drop the gun, drop the gun.' So, I focus more. That's when I see the gun in his hand. He turns in between two cars. I'm in the street. Coming into the street, he raised the gun, and I fired three rounds at his direction."

At his direction.

"Well, did you hit him?" Stewie asked with an eyebrow raised.

The officer ignored Stewie. "Then he fell. The gun fell in front of him. I went over to the gun. Stood over the gun. Called over EMS. Put over . . . 'Male shot.' Then someone cuffed him. I don't remember who."

"At the point where you heard your partners say, 'Drop the gun,' where was your attention focused?" asked Mac.

"On him. Running."

"Were you able to see a gun at that point?"

"Once they said, 'Please drop the gun,' I noticed the gun."

"And what exactly did you see at that point?"

"A *gun.*"

"Can you specifically describe this? Color? Size? Was he waving it in the air?"

The officer shook his head. "This is three years ago now. It's all a blur."

"Which hand was it in?" asked Greg.

"I don't remember."

"How far away was he when you first noticed the gun?"

"I don't remember."

"Halfway from where he started?" Mac asked. "Quarter of the way? Can you give an approximate range?"

Stewie erupted. "He said he doesn't remember. The bottom line is a guy pointed a gun at this officer and he defended his life!"

"Understood," said Mac, trying to move along.

"It's not understood," barked Stewie. "Because you wouldn't be here if it was understood."

There was a long pause.

"Do you remember the approximate range between where he was first stopped and where he was shot?" asked Greg.

"No."

"Did the man point his gun at any officers?"

"I don't know."

"And when he turned into the street, how far away was he from you?"

"Fifteen feet. Maybe ten feet."

"At that point, when he turns, does he appear to be aware of you?"

Stewie sighed. "How could he possibly answer that question?"

"Somebody could make eye contact," Mac said.

"Maybe he could point a gun at you!" yelled Stewie. "Has anyone ever pointed a gun at you?"

"How long did the man raise the gun?" continued Greg.

Stewie's eyes widened. "Well, not *too* long," he boomed, turning toward the officer with arms outstretched. "Because you *shot* him. Right?"

"I don't know the time," replied the officer. "It was quick."

"Before this incident, had you ever discharged your firearm while on the job?" asked Greg.

"Don't answer that question," interjected Stewie. "Why is that relevant?"

"It goes to his experience," replied Mac.

"Don't answer the question," Stewie told the officer. He turned back to Greg. "You want to know if he discharged his firearm? Pull his records. But that's totally irrelevant to this interview. Totally irrelevant. I'm not letting him answer it."

"He's got to answer," Mac replied.

"*Fine*," said Stewie. "Get the sergeant in here to order him to answer.* Listen—he shouldn't even be down here. He's not answering the question. His training—*whatever*. You have no jurisdiction over whether he ever fired his gun before this day. So, if you want him to answer it, call the sergeant."

Greg paused the recorder and Mac left the room to find the sergeant. Greg, Stewie, and the officer sat in silence. After about thirty seconds, Stewie calmly turned to the officer and asked, "By the way, *had* you ever discharged your firearm?"

"No."

"That's what I figured." He looked at Greg and shrugged.

A few minutes later, Mac returned with the friendly sergeant. Stewie raised his arms. "Never mind, sarge. It's all good." Between the officer, the sergeant, and the two of us, at least fifty taxpayer dollars had been wasted on this outburst.

Greg resumed the interview. "So, the previous question was— had you ever fired your weapon before?"

"No."

Near the end of the interview, Stewie turned to the officer and asked, "By the way, when he pointed the gun at you, what did you think would happen?"

----

* From time to time, reps would advise their officers not to answer a question. If the officer held fast, we'd have to pause the interview and find the sergeant who worked as the NYPD's liaison to the CCRB. He'd walk over from his windowless office and into the interview room. "Officer, I'm ordering you to answer the question," he might say. Then, the interview would continue. Officers might refuse to answer our questions, but they wouldn't risk facing charges of insubordination.

The officer chuckled, as if he'd forgotten to say it. "I feared for my life."

Stewie looked at us and smiled.

TWO MONTHS LATER, the two of us interviewed the sergeant who'd orchestrated the incident from beginning to end, failing to notify the local precinct.

"Was any notification made to the local precinct before you arrived?

"No. I didn't get to actually call them. We were busy setting up." It was a twenty-minute drive, across several precincts, from his stationhouse to the nightclub where it all began. "I mean, things happen quick," the sergeant said. "I can't let a guy with a gun just be in a club. Imagine if it's a mass shooting."

If the sergeant's top concern had in fact been public safety, it might've made it a good idea to notify the local precinct, which was just three blocks away.

"I just don't feel comfortable letting that happen," continued the sergeant. "I wanted to get there as soon as possible so I could stop the man with a gun from hurting somebody. So, notifying the local precinct wasn't, like, top of my list. I just don't want anyone to get hurt, you know?"

This sergeant had crossed precinct lines on a covert mission that ended with two bullets lodged in a man's body, a bloody bullet on the ground, one bullet in a shattered windshield next to two bystanders' heads, and a gun arrest that would prove his unit was doing *something*—all without raising the crime rate in his own precinct. This gun arrest was also a prize in the game of policing, leading to lots of paperwork and lots of overtime and furthering perhaps the sergeant's main concern, a promotion to lieutenant that came a year after the shooting and a promotion to captain only three years later.

Greg dreaded writing the closing report. When he first received the case, he saw an opportunity to make a real impact. A man had claimed that officers shot him in the back and planted a gun to conceal the real facts. But now it seemed the facts were not in the man's favor. Although he had in fact been shot in the back, it was likeliest that he'd been shot in the hip first, twisted around, and then been shot in the back in quick succession. Although the video wasn't perfectly clear, he probably had a gun. There was no evidence that the officers had planted one on him. It was both New York State law and NYPD policy that an officer could use deadly force *only* with the reasonable belief that doing so was necessary to prevent "death or serious physical injury."

In this instance, the officers, trained to see threats of death or serious physical injury around every corner, appeared to believe that they faced a genuine threat. A man with a gun ran toward a group of officers. It didn't matter that he was running away from other officers. It didn't matter that the officers had forced themselves into this situation. It didn't matter that the officers hadn't notified the local precinct, that they'd come up with a shoddy plan that put everyone in danger. In this specific context, it only mattered that they "feared for their safety," if only for an instant, and that their fear made sense. And after much deliberation, it did make sense—a man running at you with a gun might reasonably make you believe that shooting that man was necessary to prevent your own "death or serious physical injury."

Greg still believed that the allegations should've been unsubstantiated. To some, the key word in "preponderance of the evidence" isn't the first word, but the last. In this case, the evidence was incomplete—the NYPD denied Greg access to crime scene evidence, key witnesses, and other unknown contents of their own investigation. The officer interviews boiled down to "I feared for my safety." How was Greg to exonerate a shooting when he didn't have all the facts?

But he didn't make the final call. That came from the higher-ups, who faced a kaleidoscope of pressures to exonerate rather than unsubstantiate. To unsubstantiate would be to leave a lingering question mark. A black mark on each of the officer's records. Was there a chance that the shooting was unjustified? Sure. But Greg's manager delivered him the news: the sergeant would receive a referral to IAB for failure to supervise—a relatively minor infraction—and the shooting would be Exonerated. It was easier that way.

In the end, a scramble for a gun went wrong, and while the officers may have been justified in their actions, the NYPD obstructed an impartial investigation. This was no surprise to anyone at the CCRB. In fact, it was so normal that we didn't even weigh the department's obstruction when deciding the case's outcome. That was the unspoken agency policy: obstruction was just part of the process, missing evidence was inevitable, and it was best not to talk about the Black Hole.

In his memoir *Blue Blood*, Edward Conlon wrote that "when a cop shoots his gun, either punishment or praise is allotted, as a matter of course: either you get a medal or you lose time, from a loss of vacation days to a potential prison sentence."[15] In reality, praise was the far likelier outcome. In a department where there had been at least 3,779 firearm discharge incidents from 1994 to 2023, the CCRB had substantiated fourteen "Force - Gun Fired" allegations.[16] That's another drawback of insisting the police do *something* without defining what *something* is. When it's all spelled out, an incident like this can seem unsafe, unnecessary, and arguably a waste of taxpayer dollars. But when the headline reads, "Ex-con on 'lifetime parole' shot by police after pulling handgun in Brooklyn," as it did in this case, maybe it even feels reassuring. Maybe it feels like the police are keeping you safe from the bad guys. At least they're doing *something*.

Although most police shootings are often avoidable, they're usually technically legal—arising when officers are thrust into dangerous situations by their higher-ups, their own professional ambitions, or simply a sense of public service.* Then something scares them, they fear for their lives, and they shoot.

---

* In 1989, the United States Supreme Court established a national standard to assess whether a use of force is lawful, ruling that force must be "objectively reasonable." Some communities have created more stringent standards—requiring that a use of force (shootings included) be not only reasonable, but necessary.

15

Slave Patrols

The Barbadians endeavor to rule all.[1]

—JOHN LOCKE, 1671

Although shootings are relatively rare, they're just the tip of the iceberg when compared to everyday policing in Black and brown communities. The most heavily policed communities exist in a world beyond the media's gaze. They're relentlessly governed by laws that simply aren't enforced in other neighborhoods. Consequently, summonses and arrests extract wealth from them like pump jacks on a Texas oil field.[2]* And although police shootings are rare, the police themselves become reminders of the collective psychological toll of a million smaller moments, moments not sensational enough for the headlines but big enough to keep you up at night. Moments that might make one wonder: Am I next?

---

* For example, in fiscal year 2015, Ferguson, Missouri budgeted 23 percent of its revenue based on fines and fees. In addition, "City officials evaluated the performance of criminal justice actors based on the amount of revenue they produced."

IN 2001, SALLY E. HADDEN wrote the definitive book *Slave Patrols: Law and Violence in Virginia and the Carolinas.* This text has been widely cited as evidence that modern American policing descended from one institution: Southern slave patrols. In 2020, citing Hadden, the NAACP Legal Defense Fund submitted an amicus brief to the United States Supreme Court noting that "policing in America has its roots in the control of African-American communities in the Southern colonies" and that "the transformation of antebellum slave patrols into late-nineteenth-century police forces was thus a change in name only."[3] More recently, as reformers have strained to explain the brutality of modern-day policing, media outlets from *The New Yorker* to *Time* have repeated the adage that all American policing is an institution descended from antebellum slave patrols.[4]

Yet somewhere between Hadden's book and the millennial zeitgeist, something important was lost in translation. In her book, Hadden explicitly downplays the relationship between modern policing and slave catching, noting that many have "jumped to the conclusion" that slave patrols of an earlier century in a distinct region of America explain the violent confrontations of modern policing nationwide. She cautions:

> After all, the complex police and racial problems that our country continues to experience in the present day are, in many cases, the results of failings and misunderstandings in our own time. To blame the 1991 beating of Rodney King by police in Los Angeles on slave patrollers dead nearly two hundred years is to miss the point.[5]

The founders of Charleston, South Carolina, immigrated from a different land from the rest of the United States' colonizers. They arrived from Barbados, a tiny Caribbean island, and they did so under unique circumstances.

In 1670 as "the oldest, richest, and most densely populated colony in British America," Barbados began expanding its territory to the Eastern Seaboard of North America.[6] Barbados was a colonial oligarchy, that had developed with relative independence from the English Crown. Its exceptional wealth relied on an exceptional system: a uniquely brutal version of chattel slavery, so jarring that it shocked even its colonial contemporaries. Founding Father John Dickinson described Barbados as "a few lords vested with despotic power over myriad vassals and supported in pomp by their slavery."[7] In the British colonies, indentured servants had initially performed most labor. But over the course of the 1600s, Barbadian overlords "gained the reputation of being a hell for the working class," and it became difficult to retain a functional workforce.[8]

Around 1640, Barbadians traveled to Dutch-occupied Brazil, where they learned the practice of enslaving kidnapped Africans to manufacture sugar.[9] As the labor force in Barbados transformed into outright chattel slavery, the rate of slave mortality was twice that of Virginia, and at a far greater scale.[10] Barbados became "the richest and most horrifying society in the English speaking world."[11]

While the Barbadian version of slavery was staggeringly profitable, the oligarchs wanted to bestow land to their children. On a twenty-one-mile long island, they felt they had run out. So, they chose what is now South Carolina as the new territory for their expanding slave state. Their unique system of chattel slavery traveled with them. South Carolina's founding charter gave each planter 150 acres for every servant or slave he imported. And as the Barbadian oligarchs imported more and more African slaves, they came to own most of the land in South Carolina's coastal low country. They founded the city of Charleston as their capital, modeled after Bridgetown, the capital of Barbados.[12]

But to run a profitable slave state, there needed to be someone to keep the slaves from escaping. In 1704, the governor and council of Carolina enacted America's first Patrol Act, which required militia captains to "take up all slaves which they shall meet without their master's plantation which have not a permit or ticket from their masters, and the same punish."[13] This was the institutional beginning of slave catching in what would become the United States. Between 1712 and 1729, North Carolina and South Carolina split.[14] By the middle of the eighteenth century, Barbadian-style slave laws, and the system of slave catching used to enforce them, existed everywhere south of the Mason-Dixon.[15]

In 1739, a group of about fifty slaves in South Carolina tried to fight their way to Spanish-occupied Florida, killing plantation masters on their way.[16] Although the insurrection was unsuccessful and most of the "Stono Rebellion" participants were executed, the uprising fueled a growing sense of dread in the white people of South Carolina. "On this occasion, every breast was filled with concern. Evil brought home to us within our very doors," wrote South Carolina legislators. "We could not enjoy the benefits of peace like the rest of mankind and that our own industry should be the means of taking from us all the sweets of life and of rendering us liable to the loss of our lives and fortunes."[17]

As slave insurrections became more common throughout the Americas and the population of enslaved people grew, white fear grew, as well. In 1804, enslaved people of Haiti, along with a coalition of poor white immigrants, successfully overthrew their French captors. Haiti declared independence from France, fueling fears that a similar revolution might take place on American soil.[18]

In 1822, Denmark Vesey, a free Black pastor in Charleston, planned a major slave rebellion. His plans were foiled, but in response, the South Carolina legislature voted to create an arsenal and guardhouse to fortify Charleston against future slave rebellions.[19] In 1829, the construction of "the Citadel" was completed in downtown Charleston. In 1842, the legislature created a military academy at the Citadel to train cadets for future wars and to defend the city from the threat of a slave insurrection. Meanwhile, the original Charleston town watch evolved into the City Guard and continued to enforce slave law in cooperation with members of the Citadel. In 1856, the City Guard was formally established as the Charleston Police Department, and the enforcers of slave law had finally become the local police.[20]

As has been illuminated by cultural geographer Wilbur Zelinsky in *The Cultural Geography of the United States*, historian David Hackett Fischer in *Albion's Seed: Four British Folkways in America*, and journalist Colin Woodard in *American Nations: A History of the Eleven Rival Regional Cultures of North America*, the various regions of the United States are profoundly distinct. These regions have different cultural, spiritual, and political origins that inform not only the manner in which oppression impacts Black and brown people, but the very roots of the government institutions within that region's bounds. It's easy to forget that prior to the invention of cars, airplanes, and the Internet, America was far more provincial. So too with its institutions, and indeed its police.

According to Hadden, the institutional influence of slave patrols is limited to those Southern cities where there were direct evolutions from slave patrols to police departments, like Charleston.[21] And in many Southern cities, slave patrols more clearly evolved into local branches of the Ku Klux Klan than police departments.[22] The Chicago Police Department, Los Angeles Police Department, and Minneapolis Police Department did not experience the same evolutions as departments founded in the American South. The police in those regions have their own cultures, laws, and conceptions about race. Inevitably, the presence of the Klan or the role of the slave catcher impacted some American regions more than others.[23]

There's no doubt that mass incarceration is an institutional descendant of slavery and Jim Crow. And there's a rich historical record of police departments across America enforcing slave catching laws in various forms and fashions. Some corners of today's political discourse would prefer to whitewash that history. Further, it makes sense that some aspects of modern policing look and feel like slave catching, especially to the people being policed. But as Hadden warns, to overemphasize the influence of slave patrols on modern policing is to miss the point. It broadly labels all modern police and their predecessors as a lineage of pure racists, and to simply claim that cops are racist is to ignore the complex and often well-meaning reasons that might lead one to join law enforcement today. This framework also ignores the extent to which individual opinions, biases, and even outright bigotry can recede into the background when the much more deeply entrenched structures of systemic racism drive policy choices and, indeed, mass incarceration. Not only that, it fails to distinguish between the institution of policing and its various and distinct cultures.

If Americans want to change policing, it will take separating these two concepts: institutional history and cultural history. Institutionally, we can look back at the legal roots of the criminal-justice system: the English common law, the Southern laws that enforced slavery, Jim Crow, mass incarceration, and more. But to change the culture of policing, we'll need to first identify what that culture is and how it pulled us so far from the principles of de-escalation, impartiality, and deference to the public that Sir Robert Peel first enshrined in London.

Today's policing culture—which in some places permits police to use discourteous and offensive language about women, people of color, and the LGBTQ+ community—is a modern problem unto its own, with unique variations in every department. These cultures fester in a profession of over 85 percent men.[24] In many cities, the culture roots itself in an Irish tradition of anti-colonial resistance. The culture grows when the public demands the police do *something*, and by *something* they mean *anything at all*.

The problem with modern policing isn't just that officers are sometimes personally racist, it's that the institution of policing thrives on *ease.* When the public demands that you put people into cages, it's easiest to take the people with the least power. And an institution where the easiest thing to do is cage poor Black and brown people is the textbook definition of "structural racism.'" Indeed, Ta-Nehisi Coates underscores the point in his groundbreaking book *Between the World and Me*:

> The truth is that the police reflect America in all of its will and fear, and whatever we might make of the country's criminal justice policy, it cannot be said that it was imposed by a repressive minority. The abuses that have followed from these policies—the sprawling carceral state, the random detention of black people, the torture of suspects—are the product of democratic will.

There are many symptoms. But when the problem is that the institution of policing makes an entire population of Americans disposable because of their race and lack of access to power, the symptoms will remain. To successfully address the problem, we must, as Coates implores us, challenge more than the police. We must challenge ourselves.

---

* Further, to blame modern policing on slave catching absolves those making that claim of failing to learn the history of policing in their own communities. It allows white reformers to broadly blame the police, rather than reflect on policing, slavery, and perhaps mass incarceration as social institutions that their own friends and families might have benefited from, advocated for, or refused to change. Just as mass incarceration provides benefits to stockholders and employees alike, the benefits of slavery were not limited to the confines of the Charleston low country, or to the slave catchers who patrolled the South. For over two hundred years, slavery was an American pastime, from which white Americans benefited, North and South alike.

16

The Protests

The more controversial the incident, the more time is your friend.

—RON YORK AND RON DELORD,
Law Enforcement, Police Unions, and the Future[1]

June 2020, one week after Derek Chauvin has murdered George Floyd in Minneapolis. A group of officers sit in an NYPD van at the base of the Brooklyn Bridge. They're all on overtime. One officer accidentally activates his BWC.

"Oh, my goodness. I have squirters. Bro, like no exaggeration I got like thirty different sheets because every bitch I fuck, if they're not bleeding all over the place, they're fucking squirting all over the place. Regardless, it's always wet. I always have to change my sheets…. I'm like, 'What the fuck?' Jesus. God damn, man. I can't have fucking girls in my house. If they don't invite me to theirs, I'm like, 'Fuck it.' It's not even worth it anymore. I'm tired of being in the laundromat. All the little Mexican girls are looking at me like, 'What the fuck is with this guy? He must have a huge dick.' And then I got one bitch. It's like every time I touch her, she's squirting in the fucking car. I'm like, 'This is a brand-new car. Fuck you. Don't fuck up my car.'"[2]

The officers look over Cadman Plaza, where a protest was dispersed a few hours before.

"I have the sudden urge," says the officer, looking out the front windshield, "Johnny, I have the sudden urge to throw rocks all of a sudden."

"Oh my God," says a second officer, "It's the best feeling man, it's better than sex."

"Throwing rocks?"

"When you stone somebody."

A third officer chimes in. "Usually, it's the ex-wives."

They all laugh.

NYPD Legal accidentally sends this footage to the CCRB. An investigator listens to the audio, and reports it to his supervisor. The audio is sent to IAB, and we never hear about it again. As of November 2024, the first officer was still employed by the NYPD.

THROUGH THE EARLY STAGES OF 2020, investigators worked remotely. On one March day, around 1 percent of new COVID cases nationwide were among members of the NYPD.[3] Our investigations continued, but officer interviews were put on hold indefinitely. In BWC videos, we saw a blanket of apathy fall over the department, as officers stopped wearing masks early on and appeared to resign themselves to the virus.

Thousands of New Yorkers were dying, particularly in the most policed neighborhoods. As more and more people stayed indoors, the crime rate plummeted. At one point, nearly 20 percent of the NYPD officers called in sick.[4] Dozens of officers died.[5] From the isolation of our apartments we continued to receive complaint after complaint of stop-and-frisks, vehicle searches, and chokeholds.

One day in late May, Mac took a virtual training on advanced forensic video analysis. There was a handful of other CCRB

investigators present, but most of the several hundred other participants were members of law enforcement from all across America.

"I've got a brand-new video to show you today," said the instructor. "An incident in Minneapolis."

Over the course of the training, Mac watched Derek Chauvin
murder George Floyd from what seemed like every angle: cell phone,
BWC, and multiple surveillance cameras. Much of it was footage
that wasn't in the public eye until Chauvin's trial a year later.

"This is a bad one," said an officer. "Everyone should prepare for
protests."

There was something strange about watching these videos
for the first time, especially in a teleconference with hundreds of
cops. Those who spoke seemed openly disgusted with Chauvin—
disgusted with the murder and disgusted because they could see this
would lead to other officers' suffering.

And for this group, who had likely all seen horrific videos of
police violence that never captured the public's attention, we knew
one thing: the better the camera angle, the bigger the protests. But
none of us would have guessed what happened next.

As the protests spread from Minneapolis to New York and across
the world, the CCRB received hundreds of complaints.[6] In New
York City, protesters marched by the tens of thousands, chaper-
oned by a department of officers who had spent the previous three
months accepting the possibility of death by COVID. Morale in the
NYPD was low.

In early June late at night, the two of us sat on the roof of Mac's
Crown Heights apartment building. A mass of protesters marched
by on their way toward Downtown Brooklyn. Hip-hop blared as
residents cheered from their fire escapes. An alert buzzed on Greg's
phone: protesters had overtaken the 88th Precinct stationhouse.
Another precinct was under siege.

"A year from today, I'd bet policing looks exactly the same," Mac
said. "Everyone's been trapped in their apartments. Sports are all on

pause. There's gonna be another George Floyd when things go back to normal. And when that happens, I don't think everyone will care this much. They didn't before."

During the protests, notorious officers, normally assigned to police poor Black and brown communities, were suddenly face-to-face with throngs of millennials of all races cheering, "Black lives matter," and "Defund the police." The story of George Floyd's murder also became a story about police violence at protests. The CCRB, an agency that had always seemed virtually invisible, was thrust into the national spotlight.

In one case, an officer called a twenty-one-year-old protester a "stupid fucking bitch" and shoved her to the ground.[*] In another, officers drove through a crowd. There were the mass arrests, in which thousands of batons struck thousands of protesters' arms, legs, and ribs. Often there was no way to identify those involved beyond the relative few who filed online complaints. Our investigations seemed as chaotic as the incidents themselves.

Mac had a case that was broadcast live on CNN and narrated by Don Lemon, but because the cameras cut away at the wrong moment, every subject officer went unidentified. As the media searched for answers, a reporter unearthed the same Assman transcript that Greg had found in the federal courthouse and used it for a profile in *The Intercept*.[8] The rapper Ice Cube retweeted the article, writing, "Very sick people."[9]

Greg had a case where a sergeant posted an online rant claiming that "black people are stupid" for "burning down their own cities." Offensive language, as per agency policy. But shortly thereafter, the sergeant retired. In one case, Mac's CV was one of New York City's highest-ranking elected officials, who'd been recording a protest on his cell phone. Though the footage documented an officer beating

---

[*] After her head struck the concrete, she suffered a seizure and a concussion, among other injuries.

a woman with a baton, his shield number was blurred in the fray. Witness officers denied knowing who the officer in the video was, so the case was closed—Officer Unidentified.

Mac was assigned a case in the South Bronx where legal observers (volunteers trained to ensure that protests were policed lawfully) were illegally arrested as officers beat a mass of protesters they'd intentionally encircled. In September 2020, Human Rights Watch would condemn the violent police response as "serious violations of international human rights law."[10] NYPD commissioner Dermot Shea praised the operation, claiming it was "executed almost flawlessly."[11] Greg sat in on interviews with top NYPD chiefs who denied wrongdoing at every turn. In 2021, Chief Terence Monahan, who orchestrated the Bronx debacle, retired with a $235,635 vacation-day payout, the largest in the history of the NYPD.[12]

Amid the protests and police violence, there was alarming violence toward officers, too. A brick thrown into a lieutenant's face, a Molotov cocktail thrown into an empty police vehicle. Hundreds of officers were injured.[13] We checked in on those officers we knew personally, and on our friends who went to protest day after day. We knew how ugly it could get for everyone. We were at home watching the footage.

Ironically, the NYPD responded to more than one protest by funneling marchers along preplanned routes, then beating or arresting those who didn't go home on command. As a sergeant told a young officer in conversation captured on BWC, "Protests? You may not have done these before. But we do. They're so orchestrated. They're like a *symphony*." But if the protests were to lead to lasting change, we knew those changes wouldn't happen on the streets. They'd happen in the fine print of the policies that governed policing and the voices of the leaders who shaped it.

As Mayor de Blasio publicly congratulated the NYPD for using "tremendous restraint," CCRB investigators were inundated with their new complaints.[14] In some cases, the NYPD withheld footage.

In others, they provided so much irrelevant footage that it took months for one investigator to sort through. IAB officers were reassigned to patrol the streets, so even basic document requests went months without a response.

The CCRB was not prepared to investigate such large-scale demonstrations.* Why would it be? With rare exceptions, our cases revolved around a single incident with a set number of potential subject officers and civilians. When the protests exploded across the city, individual investigators worked alone handling protests involving thousands of people. But the boundaries of every protest blurred, and sometimes, coworkers investigated the same incidents for months without knowing it. Meanwhile, the police unions refused to allow for investigators to conduct virtual interviews, adding turmoil to our already massive backlog of cases.

Months would pass before the NYPD or police unions could be persuaded to cooperate. Journalists asked why the CCRB was taking so long to conduct its investigations. Internally, investigators were pressured to close their protest cases even faster. But we all knew it would be a long time before those cases were closed, let alone the cases from before the protests. There was simply too much to investigate and too much stonewalling from the Department.

As the protests waned, policing drifted back to normal. At a July CompStat meeting, NYPD commissioner Dermot Shea stood up and pledged to retake the city, describing the protesters as "the one percent fringe lunatics."[15] And although 65 percent of US adults supported the protests and 11 percent of Americans had attended at least one, the largest protest movement in American history wound down almost as

---

* Prior to 2020, the CCRB had a few meager procedures for investigating mass protests. But they were sorely outdated. The documents they relied on either weren't in use or would take months to find. And because any of the thirty-five thousand members of the NYPD could have been randomly assigned across the city, perhaps marching beside protesters for hours on end, it was nearly impossible to track where they might've been at a given moment.

fast as it had arrived.[16] Politicians largely ignored their demands, the media lost interest, and the police kept on doing *something*.

From the BWC footage, we could understand why many officers had missed the point of the protests. From their perspective, the protests were Armageddon, a nightmare of burning vehicles and walls of protesters that looked like they'd come seeking battle. "Hold the line," the officers would yell, as if reenacting a scene from *Band of Brothers* or *Game of Thrones*. There were two different movies playing out in America. In one, it was a peaceful revolution, a chance to relive the Civil Rights Movement of the '60s marred only by the occasional bad-faith actor. In the other, it was all-out war. Both sides saw themselves as the protagonists and struggled to realize that's how the other side saw themselves, too. Politically, the result was a stalemate.

While the protesters were out chanting "Defund the police," the chiefs had placed officers on mandatory overtime. In June 2020 alone, the pay for those extra hours cost the city $179 million.[17] Many chiefs retired. Others were promoted to take their places. None, to our knowledge, faced meaningful consequences.

Months after the protests later, a lieutenant was interviewed about a protest gone awry. Midway through the interview, angered by the investigator's line of questioning, he demanded to have the CV's name. He said he was going to arrest him. We never learned if he did.

IT WOULD'VE BEEN ONE THING if inner-city police officers were a happy-go-lucky bunch, needing only a loud wake-up call from their fellow American citizens to make them aware that their system needed to change. But for those of us behind the blue wall, we knew that most officers weren't thrilled in the first place. Many already lived behind a protective shield of cynicism, counting down their days to retirement. Protesters thought they were protesting policing itself, but they were largely confronting the rank-and-file officers ordered by the brass to show up as security. Across America, the brass remained largely untouched and unchallenged, so policing didn't change.

In the years that followed, pundits and politicians spoke of a brighter future, proposing a series of solutions that had already failed years before. They seemed not to know, for instance, that male officers of color don't seem to commit less misconduct than their white male colleagues or that training is only as effective as a trainer and only useful for as long as it's remembered, enforced, and retaught. Yet for some reason, old and discredited proposals for change were presented as new and responsive, with the implication that police departments were ready and willing to embrace them.

On the inside, we had seen how the NYPD dodged reform, distracted the public, and denied access whenever possible. The public hadn't seemed to realize that reforming a police department is an extraordinarily daunting task, that there is typically massive institutional resistance to even minor changes, or that all along, police chiefs can usually say whatever is necessary to convince the public to move on.

Echoing the "defund the police" mantra, some reformers proposed massive cuts to the NYPD budget. But as legislative proceedings wound through New York's city council, most of the resulting cuts proved to be mainly performative, as when more than five thousand School Safety Agents—unarmed peace officers—were transferred from the NYPD to the Department of Education under the guise of reinvesting in education. This would have had little impact on the number of officers out on the street, let alone education. But that didn't matter because, in 2022, well after the glow of the protests had faded, the transfer was canceled.[18]

At times, the public discussion turned to civilian oversight of the police. Some reformers proposed abolishing the CCRB, arguing that it failed to hold officers accountable. Others proposed changing the CCRB to an elected board.[19] Writers for the *New York Times* suggested that the CCRB was "all but toothless."[20] Few, if any, focused on the series of bureaucratic hurdles that made oversight so difficult. At times, the agency was required to defer to the New York City Law Department whenever there were disputes with NYPD policy, as when access to documents was repeatedly restricted.[21] The New York City Law Department also served as legal counsel to the NYPD, creating a potential conflict of interest that seemed clearer every day.

Yet even with attention focused on the CCRB's power, or lack thereof, there was rarely attention paid to the NYPD appointees to our board. Some, if not all, were in frequent contact with the NYPD and police unions, and so worked to water down CCRB policy at every turn. There was no meaningful reason for NYPD appointees to be on the CCRB board, as CCRB recommendations were just that: recommendations. Once a CCRB case reached One Police Plaza, the NYPD could do whatever it wanted. But the department's appointees to the CCRB board remained.

Others proposed expanding the CCRB budget but without also ensuring that we had the access necessary to conduct thorough and timely investigations. Our budget did expand slightly, but the issues that plagued our investigations remained.

In the months and years that followed, America went through its newest phase of "crime is up." Police departments nationwide would claim that shootings had risen at extraordinary rates, while, somehow, murder rates were declining.[22]

Meanwhile, we started to see a strange new pattern in CCRB cases. Officers would respond to an incident because ShotSpotter, a recording device installed throughout most Black and brown neighborhoods, would "recognize" what sounded to its software like a gunshot. When officers responded, they'd report that a gun had indeed been fired, even if there was no evidence to support the claim. Perhaps someone would be frisked, everyone would leave, and the incident would be recorded as a shooting.

We came to suspect that the NYPD was juicing their shooting numbers. And sure enough, a *Vice* headline in 2021 said, "Police Are

Telling ShotSpotter to Alter Evidence from Gunshot-Detecting AI."[23] Chicago's Office of Inspector General issued a scathing report asserting that ShotSpotter routinely mistook fireworks and car backfires for gunshots—leading law enforcement to a gun-related crime *only 9 percent of the time*.[24] How were the other 91 percent of cases documented? That was up to the police.[25]*

Across America, many officials failed to examine the frailty of this data, let alone report on its unreliability, and crime rates were rarely if ever audited by an independent body. Still, headlines kept reporting versions of "Crime Is Up." And because America needed someone to do *something*, police budgets continued to grow.

By 2025, the NYPD budget would be 5.83 billion dollars, about 4 percent higher than when George Floyd was murdered in Minneapolis in 2020. IAB's budget would go up by about 10 percent, as well.[26] Without addressing the root cause—America's inability to define *something*—policing would continue to grow.

IN THE PHRASE "BLACK LIVES MATTER," the word "matter" sets a low bar. Black lives have always mattered to America, though initially as a source of free labor and profit. The wealth generated by the enslavement of Black people built large swaths of this country. So what does it mean to "matter" today? The answer is ultimately confusing, because Black Lives Matter is both a decentralized organization fighting to highlight racism, discrimination, and inequality and a slogan adopted by people across the world. Over time, as leaders have been unable to agree on precisely what it means, or what should change, or how that change should be achieved, "Black lives

---

* In 2024, Brooklyn Defenders, a public defense office, published a report that found the NYPD could corroborate the accuracy of ShotSpotter only 16.57 percent of the time, and that over 99 percent of ShotSpotter alerts "did not lead to the recovery of guns or identification of those involved in gun violence, costing taxpayers millions to fail at its stated purpose."

matter" has become less of a call to action and more of an invitation to discuss racial inequality in the aftermath of yet another tragic, unnecessary, unjust death. Minds are changing, but political decisions are lagging far behind.

At the CCRB, where we saw Black people suffer wanton beatings all too often, we had to ask ourselves: Would Americans have come to say that George Floyd's life mattered if he hadn't been killed by the police? Would protesters think his addiction mattered? That he lost his job? Did America believe his life mattered when he was still alive? We all knew the answer.

We also pondered whether police were prepared to change. Studies and experience showed us that a significant reason people become police officers is for job security.[27] Did officers see reform as a threat to the most stabilizing force in their lives? And could the protests have possibly shocked the police as much as they'd shocked the public?

The chief of the NYPD's Internal Affairs Bureau from 1996 to 2014, Charles Campisi, published a memoir in 2017 titled *Blue on Blue: An Insider's Story of Good Cops Catching Bad Cops*. In it, he draws a straight line between the 1894 Lexow Committee, the first civilian investigation into NYPD misconduct, and today's calls for reform:

> In New York City, [it] happened every twenty years or so, almost as regular as clockwork. The Lexow Committee in 1894, the Curran Committee in 1912, the Hofstadter Committee in 1931, the Helfand Commission in 1951— they all reveal widespread corruption in the NYPD, ranging from bribery to extortion and even to murder. The 1970–72 Knapp Commission . . . And after every one of those scandals, the Department brass announced that it was establishing new protocols to eliminate corruption from the NYPD ranks forever.[28]

He described demands for police reform as part of a predictably scheduled cycle—a part of any NYPD officer's career:

> Suddenly newspaper headlines would be screaming about it, clergymen would be denouncing it from the pulpits, reformers would be demanding change, and the politicians—who were always shocked, shocked, to learn that there was corruption in the ranks of New York's Finest—would appoint a committee or commission to investigate the problem. In the end, a few high-level Department heads would roll, and some dirty cops might be sent off to prison—and everybody would forget about it until the next major scandal came along.[29]

To cops, calls for police reform are temporary. The reformers cry wolf for a few years, and once they're finished, the gears keep turning. Campisi summed it up this way: "If you're an NYPD cop, you have to get used to the fact that in today's headlines you may be a hero, but in tomorrow's headlines you're going to be a bum."[30]

The 2020 protests might have stunned the world, but for most in the world of policing they were part of a familiar ritual: After a triggering incident comes outrage followed by calls for reform leading to performative changes, if any. And then it's back to business. However unpleasant, it is a ritual to which officers simply have to adapt. And adapt they do.

A system refined to sophistication over the nineteenth, twentieth, and twenty-first centuries, this ritual is as fixed in its ways as policing itself. Unless there is structural change so significant that the cycle is broken forever, we won't have to wait until 2040 for the next George Floyd.

SHORTLY AFTER THE PROTESTS, the New York State legislature passed a law making it a felony for police officers to use chokeholds.[31]

A few days later, Mac received a new case. An officer had choked a man in broad daylight, and the incident made international news. Mac's case was put on hold because of the pending prosecution. At CompStat, an NYPD chief publicly bragged that every district attorney in New York had promised never to bring such charges. In fall 2021, the charges were dismissed.

The NYPD never did fire that officer, even though he'd previously been caught on camera beating someone else. It was only when the officer was found, standing on a beach, firing a gun into the Atlantic Ocean, that he quietly resigned from the department. In June 2022, he was sentenced to a prison sentence of up to four years—for the firearm charge, not the chokehold.[32] As of early 2025, the chokehold ban has never been successfully prosecuted in New York State.[33]

In 2020, Mayor de Blasio announced that the NYPD was disbanding Anti-Crime, but soon enough, they reappeared, rebranded as Public Safety Auto. "It's all the same," a union attorney joked to Mac. By the time former police officer Mayor Eric Adams had settled into office in early 2022, it was called the Anti-Gun unit, then the Neighborhood Safety Team, then Anti-Crime again, with more rebrands sure to come.[34]

After all that, the CCRB was still getting scammed by IAB. In late 2022, IAB even gave us a roll call with fake names: PO Dickhurtz, PO Schmegma. The jokes continued, and the beatings did, too. In 2024, complaints to the CCRB were up 51 percent, and the Police Commissioner was ignoring 45 percent of CCRB recommendations, up 29 percent from 2021.[35]

FOLLOWING THE PROTESTS, Greg's cases were piling up. There was no clear way to investigate all of them well, so he would focus on the most pressing. But did any of it really matter? What was waiting for him on the other side? A never-ending deluge of cases that could be sunk at any moment by an unsympathetic IAB detective,

an ornery union rep, a skeptical store manager, a stonewalling officer? America had just gone through mass protests to change policing, and nothing had really changed.

Then, in January 2021, Greg got a call from his union: "They're
offering you a new job."

In this new role, Greg would work directly with the higher-ups.
Though technically still an investigator, he wouldn't have any cases.
Instead, he'd manage recruitment campaigns and agency social
media, coordinate public events, write grant applications, and help
HR draft disciplinary memos for other employees' infractions. He'd
be present for public CCRB board meetings and at votes by the
board, which were held behind closed doors.

Greg took the job.

In the years that followed, working with the board, legal counsel, and HR, Greg gained access to some of the CCRB's most
sensitive inner workings. He drafted confidential memos to the
police commissioner and watched the board deliberate on almost
every case. What seemed strange to Greg was that he did all of
this while receiving more praise than he ever had as an investigator, all while doing maybe 5 percent of the work. He listened as
the higher-ups openly disparaged investigators, as if completely
unaware of who worked longer hours, under far more pressure, for
less than half the pay.

Greg had moved to another part of the agency, where the profound pressure that governed an investigator's life seemed far, far
away. And he'd finally found a stable job, surrounded by people who
treated him with dignity. But he couldn't shake the feeling that he
was simply doing *something*. *Something* was what had led to the pain
and trauma that defined his old cases. *Something* would ensure that
the next new investigator saw the same. *Something* was what made
the cycle continue.

17

Termination

Well, let me make it simple for you. There's a ritual. You're part of the ritual now. And there's only one rule to the ritual. *Don't fuck with the ritual.* If you go through the ritual, your career keeps on going. If you don't, you get forced out.

—ADVICE FROM ONE CCRB
INVESTIGATOR TO ANOTHER

In a saner world, police would be held to a higher standard than people in other professions. After all, policing is one of the few professions that empowers one not only with the authority of the law, but the ability to take a life. But at times, the NYPD made you wonder what an officer had to do to get fired.

In one extreme case, officers pulled a man over for street racing and jumped into his car. One put a gun to his head and told him to drive. It was all captured on a secret audio recording, in which the officer said, "Drive or I'll blow your fucking head off." Four years later, the CCRB recommended termination, but at trial the officer claimed he jumped into the complainant's car because of inclement weather. The NYPD kept him on the job. We wondered what else that officer had done in his career. And now, exonerated, what else might he do?

When the NYPD did fire an officer, they could still file an appeal with the state courts. If that appeal failed, there were often opportunities in other departments.[1] Fired in New York? Try Long Island—there's better pay there, anyway. This is a national issue, too. In 2020, 3 percent of police officers in Florida had previously been fired by other departments.[2] The Cleveland police officer who fatally shot Tamir Rice in 2014 had, in his previous job in another Cleveland suburb, been deemed an emotionally unable recruit—unfit for duty.[3] In 2024, the San Francisco Chronicle reported on the widespread use of "clean-record agreements," described as "a secret system of legal settlements that has whitewashed the corruption, criminality and other misconduct of law enforcement officers throughout California for decades," and allowed officers to quietly land new jobs with other departments.[4]

Beyond individual actions of corruption or brutality is the police practice of building networks of criminal informants. CIs, typically in need of money, are usually paid in cash for the information they provide. Many informants use that cash to sustain their addictions, even while sometimes informing on their own drug dealers. CIs have been known to intentionally give false information to the police, leading to raids and break-ins into the homes of innocent people, terrorizing their families in the process.

Harvard Law School professor Alexandra Natapoff estimates that as many as 4 percent of young Black men in urban centers are CIs.[5] The NYPD creates sprawling athletic leagues to keep kids "off the street," but little prevents them from recruiting these same kids to become CIs.[6] Some risk being entrapped, forced to become informants or face the wrath of their local precinct. Sometimes, CIs are killed for snitching.

What we observed at the CCRB was consistent with previous criticisms of the shadowy world of criminal informants, that the NYPD's CI system tore communities apart—keeping drug addicts addicted and putting young Black and brown men in danger.[7] The

NYPD might argue that CIs are integral to fighting crime, but that claim would be much more credible if the CI system had meaningful transparency and accountability. You'd think that's the type of system that would be carefully scrutinized in a free and fair society.

Overall, it was rare to find a case where the CCRB recommended termination, let alone where the NYPD implemented it. Most officers' conduct was, after all, legal. When it wasn't, the infraction was usually relatively minor—a frisk based on poor information, a refusal to take a civilian complaint.

But the exciting thing about working at the CCRB was that any day, a new case might appear on your docket, and that case might grow into something truly extraordinary, something so big that it might escape the Black Hole.

FROM THE CCRB's ADMINISTRATIVE PROSECUTION Quarterly Report (published March 2023):

In August 2019, at approximately 11:30 p.m. in the Bronx, Victim 1, an eighteen-year-old Hispanic male; Victim 2, a sixteen-year-old Hispanic male; and Victim 3, an eighteen-year-old female were sitting on the stoop of their apartment smoking marijuana cigarettes. Victim 4, a Black female in her early fifties, was walking up to the building when she saw Lieutenant Eric Dym (the Respondent) and another officer approach Victim 1 and speak with him. Lt. Dym then left, and Victim 2 and Victim 3 followed Victim 1 into the building. Victim 5, a sixteen-year-old Hispanic male, and Victim 6, a seventeen-year-old Hispanic male, were sitting on the building's fire escape next to a vacant first-floor apartment smoking marijuana. Lt. Dym returned to the building thirty minutes later with a large group of officers. Lt. Dym entered the vacant first-floor apartment, went to its window, and pulled Victim 5 by his foot through the window, off the fire escape and into the apartment. Officers came up the fire escape and pulled Victim 6 into the vacant apartment.

Lt. Dym told Victim 5 and Victim 6 that "you better fucking figure it out" as they were handcuffed. Neither victim had resisted the
officers' attempt to handcuff them. Lt. Dym then went to Victim 4's
apartment door and demanded that Victim 1 open the door. Victim
7, a fifteen-year-old Black female, and Victim 8, a Hispanic male in
his early forties, had both been asleep inside Victim 4's apartment.
Victim 7 was awoken by Lt. Dym's shouts and went to awaken
Victim 8. Victim 1 ran and hid in a closet in Victim 8's bedroom.
Victim 2 was by the front door when Lt. Dym told him, "Open the
fucking door." Lt. Dym knocked the peephole out of the door and
entered the apartment and pointed his gun at Victim 7, Victim 8,
Victim 2, and Victim 3. Lt. Dym pointed his gun directly in Victim
7's face and told her to "get the fuck on the ground." Victim 8 asked
why the officers wanted to arrest Victim 3, and Lt. Dym pointed his
gun directly at him and told him to mind his business. Lt. Dym and
another officer entered Victim 8's bedroom, and Victim 1 was pulled
out of the bedroom closet. He was struck in the face and body by
the other officer. Lt. Dym used his foot to pin down Victim 1's face
to the floor, and the other officer handcuffed Victim 1. Lt. Dym told
him, "You're not a fucking tough guy now." Lt. Dym then instructed
officers to arrest Victim 7 and Victim 8 and to issue a summons
to Victim 3. Victim 4 went down to the precinct stationhouse and
asked Lt. Dym for a business card. He walked away from her without providing her the information. When Lt. Dym was interviewed
about the entire incident, he falsely stated that a junior officer told
him that Victim 1 had been in the third-floor apartment and falsely
stated that the apartment's door had been open and that he heard a
firearm had been racked. The falsehoods were used to fabricate his
account of his entry into Victim 4's apartment. Lt. Dym also falsely
stated that the BWC cameras were dead when he in fact instructed
officers to turn them on to record part of the entry into the vacant
first-floor apartment and to not record the incident in Victim 4's
apartment.

On March 23, 2022, the Board substantiated twenty-one (21) total allegations: seven (7) Abuse of Authority allegations against Lt. Dym for entering the first-floor apartment, for entering Victim 4's apartment, for damaging Victim 4's property, for arresting Victim 7, for arresting Victim 8, for arresting Victim 3, and for failing to provide Victim 4 with a business card; seven (7) use of force allegations for using physical force against Victim 5, Victim 6, and Victim 1, for pointing his gun at Victim 2, Victim 8, Victim 7, and Victim 3; five (5) discourtesy allegations for speaking discourteously to individuals, speaking discourteously to Victim 2, speaking discourteously to Victim 7, speaking discourteously to Victim 8, speaking discourteously to Victim 1; and two (2) untruthful statement allegations for providing a misleading official statement and a false official statement to the CCRB.

Facing termination, in 2022 Lt. Dym settled several pending cases, including this one, in exchange for forty-six vacation days. He then retired as the most complained about cop in modern NYPD history.[8] As of early 2025, aspects of this case relating to junior officers remain pending administrative trial.

. . . .

To some, police misconduct can be reduced to an argument about bad apples, a smattering of awful aberrations in an otherwise honorable profession. To others, policing is an irredeemable profession, hence the refrain "all cops are bastards." But recent scholarship indicates that the reality is more complex.

From 2016 to 2022, four groundbreaking studies presented a new model to identify a problem at the heart of American policing: networks of misconduct. In 2016, a study published in the *University of Chicago Legal Forum* proposed that misconduct was learned through "networks" of officers, and spread like a "contagion" from the most violent officers to the officers who watched them get off scot-free.[9] Three years later, a study from the American Sociological Association built on this idea, mapping misconduct in the Chicago Police Department to determine that "police misconduct, like deviance more generally, is a networked phenomenon" and that "beyond individual bad apples and bad institutions, officer networks appear to play an important role in the emergence and possibly even persistence of misconduct."[10] That same year, the Georgia State University Department of Criminal Justice and Criminology published a study that built on these insights, finding that officers who worked in the same networks as bad apple officers were more likely to commit misconduct themselves.[11]

In short, small networks clustered around the most violent officers account for a significant proportion of police misconduct. It isn't just the bad apples; it's also everyone the bad apples taught to be bad, and the people they then teach to be bad, and on and on. These networks tend to thrive in Black and brown communities, where public demand to do *something* is high.

A 2022 study published by PLOS took these studies to a new level. Analyzing networks of officers in the Chicago Police Department from 1971 to 2018, researchers identified 160 potential "formal and informal networks," or "crews," that were able to coordinate "abusive and even criminal behaviors." These crews accounted for less than 4 percent of the Chicago Police Department but were responsible for approximately 25 percent of force complaints, lawsuit payouts, and police shootings. The study concluded that the issue isn't bad apples, it's the "groups of officers [who] coalesce into cliques or small groups with the explicit intention of engaging in misconduct, including outright criminal behavior, and the concealment of such activity."[12]

These studies reveal a profound opportunity. By using data mapping, we can predict the groups of officers who are most likely to commit misconduct, even criminal activity. All it takes is access to the data.

The problem with these studies is that they don't effectively answer the question: Why do these crews persist?[13]

From a distance, it would appear these networks exist in the dark, but the brass in major metropolitan police departments are most certainly aware of the problem officers who generate the most lawsuits and complaints. When we wonder why the most violent officers aren't fired for their transgressions, the de facto answer is the unions, who protect even bad-faith actors. But for a union to protect a bad-faith actor, the brass must act first, identifying a bad apple and then trying to fire them. The brass, however, have a good reason to tolerate bad apples, crews, and even networks of misconduct from coming under fire: the officers most willing to operate outside the boundaries of the law are often the officers who generate the most arrests. They're the ones who create something out of nothing.

These networks of officers, particularly in Black and brown communities, are among those who pile contraband on the table for a social media snapshot. They're often the ones who are "proactive," who find guns and drugs, who make the most arrests, issue the most summonses, and keep the gears turning. When arrests are up, even if those arrests were made outside the boundaries of the law, the crime rate goes up. And if the brass have even partial control of when and how the crime rate goes up, they can use this power to go to city leadership and ask for a bigger budget whenever the demand for more *something* is loudest. When their budget increases, the brass and the crews can make millions with higher pay and more overtime. Meanwhile, the public rests assured that something is being done.

It's not a coincidence that crews, usually working in plainclothes, are the usual suspects in your latest local police scandal. Although we aren't aware of the networks-of-misconduct theory being studied yet from the perspective of arrest statistics, we've seen that the officers in these networks typically make so many arrests that they become indispensable to the police brass. As for the lawsuits and civilian complaints, the houses broken into and the evidence manipulated? That's just part of the ritual. If you keep your head down and don't fuck with the ritual, the public moves on to the next scandal. Maybe you even get promoted.

But to push out one bad supervisor is to isolate a single patient when the virus has already spread. Often, bad supervisors don't merely tell their officers how to operate outside the boundaries of the law. They teach them how to do it when they're gone.

At the CCRB, we learned that a single leader with a force of personality could shape generations of public service. We shared the lessons we inherited with scores of investigators, mentoring them to view their profession through a lens of passion, kindness, and rigorous impartiality. Most of those investigators never knew the people who influenced us most. But training is only as good as the trainer. And for every lawless supervisor in policing, there are scores of officers who learned from them and can only help but carry the torch.

IN SPRING 2021, Mac got a call from a CCRB higher-up. Mac's case, the one in which a Latino officer yelled a racial epithet while grinding a Black man's head into the ground, had gone to trial. The NYPD judge ruled that the officer should be terminated. It was only the second time in CCRB history that this had happened. The first was Pantaleo.

"Congratulations, Mac. You should be proud."

But there was a catch. The NYPD commissioner still had to sign off on the judge's ruling. There was a chance that she'd reverse the decision.

"We'll wait and see."

A few months later, the NYPD published the judge's decision. It was damning:

The word "n—r" is unique and unparalleled in American English. In the United States, where a history of slavery and its malignant residuum continue to plague American life, there are few words that when spoken in a derogatory manner are as painful, incendiary, and inextricably tied to racism.

The decision noted that the officer's union attorney, in his opening statement, had suggested that the word "n—r" was a "greet[ing]" for "someone who is from the African-American community." The judge disagreed:

> [The officer's] use of the charged language in this disciplinary matter is a paradigmatic example of the most vile variety of discourteous and offensive language: hate speech . . . The actions accompanying Respondent's words reveal an unmistakable intent to "intimidate [or] attack" in a manner that shocks the conscience, sullies the credibility of the Department, and impedes its ability to serve and protect its diverse constituency.[14]
>
> Decision: Termination.

But below the judge's signature was a bright-red stamp: *Disapproved.* The police commissioner had written her own response:

> I make no attempt to defend [the officer's] remark, but recognize that the statement was made during an otherwise chaotic encounter with a large group of individuals. I find that [the officer]'s statement was made in a moment of time likely without forethought and that he allowed his judgement to fail him as there is no evidence of past racial or gender animus

on the part of [the officer] . . .' [The officer]'s otherwise stel-
lar history and the brief duration of the underlying incident
provide mitigating factors when considering the penalty to
be imposed.

The commissioner ordered the officer to forfeit thirty days without pay (already served), forfeit forty-five vacation days, and be
placed on one year of dismissal probation. With this single decision,
the commissioner seemed to set a precedent: if a situation is chaotic
(and it often is), and if the statement is without forethought (which
you can always claim), and there's no history of racial or gender
animus (which is rarely provable), officers are allowed to use hate
speech and keep their jobs.

In that officer's CCRB interview, the Black investigator had
asked, "Why did you say that to him?" But the union attorney had
interjected, "So basically, you said this in the heat of the moment?"
At the time, it'd seemed like a bullshit excuse. But now, "the heat
of the moment" was the crux of the police commissioner's decision
not to fire him.

As of July 2022, over the course of his eight-year career, the Latino
officer had made 86 misdemeanor arrests, 66 felony arrests, and 1
arrest categorized as "Other."[15] That's 19.1 arrests per year versus the
NYPD average of 5 to 8. It seemed he was a moneymaker, too valu-
able to sacrifice.

The media read the commissioner's decision, as well. On June 27,
2022, a *New York Daily News* headline read, "NYPD Commissioner
Sewell intervenes to save job of decorated Latino cop who called
suspect the N-word."

---

* It came as no surprise that there was no evidence of past racial animus. The NYPD
had a rich history of disregarding allegations of racial profiling.

The commissioner blocked the firing of an officer who ground an unconscious man's head into the concrete, establishing a precedent that effectively allowed high-performing officers to use hate speech and keep their jobs. But the *Daily News* headline led with the commissioner "saving" a decorated officer. Heroism at its finest.

Summer 2019. Greg walked over to Mac's desk. We knew the NYPD commissioner planned to announce his decision any day. Would he fire Daniel Pantaleo? Early one morning, an NYPD memo had been leaked to the press. It told every officer to prepare for mass protests.

"The department just scheduled a surprise press conference," said Greg. "I think they're announcing the decision. We gotta go."

We walked a block from our office on Church Street to City Hall Park, passed the mayor's office, ducked under the arches of the towering David N. Dinkins Manhattan Municipal Building, and went through security at the entrance to One Police Plaza. The press conference was open to the public, but by the time we walked inside, we were too late.

"Sorry," said a young white officer. "Room's full."

We walked outside.

"Wait," said Greg. "I found a livestream."

In the shadow of NYPD headquarters, we huddled around Greg's phone. The commissioner began his speech.

"Good afternoon, everyone," said Commissioner O'Neill, a Brooklyn native and grandson of Irish immigrants. "I'm here to announce my decision."[16]

At that moment, a man about our age, wearing a suit and tie, walked out of police headquarters. "I couldn't get in. You watching the decision?" He joined us.

For ten minutes, the commissioner kept everyone on pins and needles, and then, he said it. "I agree with the deputy commissioner of trials' legal findings and recommendation. It is clear that Daniel Pantaleo can no longer effectively serve as a New York City police officer."

"I can't believe they did it," said Greg.

"I guess we're gonna keep our jobs," said Mac.

"Wow," said the man, shaking his head.

Mac extended his hand. "I'm Mac. What brings you here, anyway?"

They shook hands.

"I'm Eric Garner's cousin," he said. "I just rushed off work to watch."

"Damn," said Mac. "Sorry for your loss."

He nodded solemnly. "Thanks. Have a good one." He walked away, back toward the subway.

A few hours later, we were back at the office. The CCRB staff, all two hundred or so, stood gathered around the executive director's office for an emergency all-staff meeting.

"I know the commissioner told the press there were no victors today."

He looked around the office floor, resting his gaze on Suzanne O'Hare and Jon Fogel, who'd spent months preparing for the trial. He pointed at them. "But I respectfully disagree. These two prosecutors just led the greatest prosecution in our agency's history. I couldn't be prouder. And today, we're gonna celebrate a win."

The staff erupted into applause. For a moment, all the petty bureaucratic vengeance took a back seat. In its place was a resounding sense of relief. "Today, New York City is a safer place thanks to you all. I know everyone here is underappreciated. And until somebody goes Hollywood"—he chuckled to himself—"things are gonna stay that way. But tonight, you should all go home proud. You're part of something important. For one day, the whole world was watching."

FALL 2015. Late at night, before Mac joined the CCRB, he sat at a bar in a New England fishing town. On the television, Donald Trump declared that he would build a wall and that Mexico would pay for it.

"You see this guy?" asked a white man in his forties from down the bar.

"Oh yeah," said Mac neutrally.

The man nodded.

"It's gonna be interesting," he said.

"Definitely," said Mac.

The channel changed to ESPN.

"Sox suck this year," said the man.

"Shouldn't've signed Sandoval."

"Man, I'm rooting against the Sox at every turn. I'm from New York."

Over the course of the evening, Mac and the man spent hours discussing the finer points of baseball-roster construction, Long Island politics, and how best to reel in a false albacore.

"What do you do, anyway?" asked the man.

"I worked in politics," Mac replied. "But right now, I'm looking for a job. You?"

"I run a few businesses back home, but I'm former NYPD."

"What was that like?"

"I'm here now. Quit and didn't look back."

They started buying each other drinks, and by closing time, they were suitably buzzed. "I've got a six-pack in my car," the man said, "Want to go catch some squid, drink by the dock?"

"Aren't you a cop?"

"Not anymore."

Not long after, Mac and the man stood at a dock lit by cool fluorescent lights. The man took a drag from his cigarette. "You see, the key to squidding is just finding them. You get a good warm night, have your rod ready, and you'll have fifty in no time."

Mac looked down at the glassy water. Squid seemed to fill the harbor wherever the dock lights beamed. The man dropped in a small barbed lure and jigged it up and down. A few seconds later, a squid wrapped its tentacles around the barbs. The man yanked the lure out of the water, and out came the squid. Black ink shot into the night air.

The man dropped the squid into a white five-gallon bucket. "More where that came from. Grab a rod."

Over the next few hours, the bucket filled.

"It must have been pretty crazy being a cop in New York," Mac said. "What was that really like?"

The man took a long drag from his cigarette.

"I'll tell you a story from when I was a rookie."

WINTER 2005. Two officers drive through a housing project in northern Manhattan. One officer's been on the job for five years; the other's only a week in. The radio blares: "Neighbor reports finding man shot in head. Sector B?"

"Oh, shit," says the older officer. "You ever seen a dead body?"

"No," says the rookie.

"Fuck yeah," says the older officer, face lighting up. "You're about to."

The older officer speaks into the radio: "Sector B to dispatch. We'll pick up the job."

They drive to one of the tallest towers in the housing project, taking the elevators to the sixteenth floor. They talk to the neighbor, then open the apartment door. Inside, an older man sits slumped at a kitchen table. Before him is a bowl of cereal, soggy. A bullet hole marks the center of his forehead.

"Oh shit, rookie," says the older officer. "Lock the door."

The rookie locks the door and asks, "So, how do we set up the crime scene?"

The older officer starts to laugh.

"After this," he says, smiling.

The older officer walks up to the dead body and, in one swift motion, punches it in the head as hard as he can. The body falls sideways and hits the ground with a thud.

"What the fuck?" gasps the rookie.

The older officer straddles the dead body and begins to pummel its face. One punch. Two punches. He keeps going. The rookie freezes in terror.

"What the fuck, man? What the fuck are you doing?"

The older officer keeps punching the dead body over and over. He stops for a moment, chest heaving, and looks up at the rookie. He's grinning from ear to ear. "Can't you see?" says the older officer.

"What? What? What the fuck?" says the rookie.

"Don't you get it?"

"Get what?"

"Nothing matters."

"What?"

"Nothing. Matters."

He goes back to beating the dead body. Later, he falsifies a report to say the man was assaulted, then shot.

BACK ON THE DOCK, Mac stared at the man in horror.

"What the fuck?"

"Yeah, man. That was the most fucked up thing I'd ever seen."

He took another long drag from his cigarette, then shook his head. "But you know," he said, "five years later, I had my own rookie. I did the exact same fucking thing."

He paused, looking over the water.

"And when *I* said, 'Nothing matters,' I fucking meant it." He looked Mac dead in the eyes.

"*That's* what being a cop did to me."

MAC WAS PROMOTED TO SUPERVISING Investigator in 2019. He left the CCRB in late 2022. From 2023 to 2025, he served as the Executive Director of the Community Police Review Agency in his hometown of Oakland, California.

Part III

BREAKING THE
FIXED SYSTEM

18

A Better World

Who's the face of American democracy? The president? The governor? The mayor? Who are the real representatives of this democracy? Who among them do we meet in person? Who shows up at a moment's notice? Who do we call in times of need? Who takes the laws we democratically pass and makes them real, enforcing them against real people? It's the police.

And when you think of the police, whether you think of the brass, the unions, or the officers who patrol your neighborhood, do you know what they do? Or do you just know that they're the police and that they do *something*? When you read a headline that says, "Crime Is Up," do you know what it means? Or do you just assume it means things are getting worse?

Americans' faith in the criminal-justice system is low. In 2024, only 21 percent of Americans reported having "a great deal" or "quite a lot" of faith in the criminal-justice system.[1] It may have appeared contradictory when a Gallup poll taken after George Floyd's murder found that 81 percent of Black Americans wanted "more" or the "same amount" of police in their neighborhoods. But everyone wants more public safety. Yet over the past fifty years, we've been conditioned to believe that only the police can provide it. At least they can do *something*.

And even though *something* has left Americans disillusioned, Black and brown people are still being placed into cages at extraordinary rates. The system is deeply flawed, effectively rigged against our most vulnerable communities, and in dire need of top-to-bottom reform. Yet still we mainly demand *more* of what we've had, clinging to the discredited notion that more officers on the street will automatically keep us safer.[2] When the choice is between more gruel and no gruel, well, the choice is easy.

But when we ask for more of a fixed system, the cost is anomie.[3]* What does it mean when we have a sense of anomie toward the same system that's supposed to protect us? Our anomie spreads, from our feelings about the criminal-justice system to our feelings about politics, government, and democracy itself. Soon enough, nothing really matters.

As citizens of the world's most powerful democracy, we might ask ourselves: Is this the country we want to live in? A country that prides itself on the rule of law, but where poor Black and brown people and police officers alike live in a state of anomie?[4] A country where the most violent police officers are allowed to thrive with relative impunity, terrorizing communities and coworkers alike? A country in which the most patient and professional officers are often sidelined while the crews and networks of misconduct are promoted and protected because they make so many arrests, because they do *something*? Are we in a country where progress should be measured by arrests and easily manipulated crime statistics? No.

This system can seem fixed in its ways. In 2020, we lived through the largest protest movement in American history under the banner of "defund the police" and Black Lives Matter. And in response,

---

* According to one study, being subjected to a single police stop makes someone 1.8 percent less likely to vote.

statistically suspect crime rates skyrocketed. Police budgets did, too. Where the system changed, it grew. How could American policing possibly be reformed?

In the 1980s, when New York City was at the peak of a very real crime spike, one man began to create a system that would revolutionize policing across the globe. And perhaps surprisingly, he was an investigator, too. Jack Maple was a detective for the city's subway police well before it was merged into the NYPD. At a time when the NYPD was rife with "brutality, theft, abuse of authority and active police criminality," Maple made it his mission to focus on fighting violent crime.[5] His mantra was to treat every crime victim as though they were his own mother. This approach led him to create a revolutionary system of data mapping designed to detect patterns of crime, identify the small minority of repeat offenders who were preying on the public, and arrest those people who were doing the most harm.[6] The system, initially called Charts of the Future, would come to be known as CompStat.[7]

As Maple built this system, he faced extraordinary resistance. Despite being threatened with demotion and even termination, he kept on building. And his system appeared to work, reducing crime by roughly 70 percent over a decade.[8] By the early 1990s, the system's success got Maple promoted to deputy commissioner of the NYPD. But lower-level supervisors still tried to get him fired. Their objections boiled down to one basic issue: they simply did not want to change.

Prior to Maple's innovation, conventional wisdom in law enforcement held that the police had almost no control over violent crime (and, by extension, little or no responsibility for its ups and downs).[9] Maple demonstrated otherwise: among the relative few who committed violent crimes over and over—usually armed robbers and burglars—there were in fact patterns to their behaviors. Maple believed that if police identified those patterns and brought serial offenders to justice, they could reduce the pain, suffering, and loss they inflicted on society. Maple proved his system worked by forcing officers to tell their bosses exactly what they did, why they did it, then—when that wasn't working—showing them an alternative that would truly improve public safety.

But over time, CompStat lost its way. When crime went down, Maple told Mayor Rudy Giuliani that the number of arrests should go down, too. It was a logical conclusion, but Mayor Giuliani told him that when crime went down, arrests had to go up. The mayor needed the police to do *something*. Ultimately, Maple resigned, and the NYPD had less and less incentive to treat every crime victim like their own mother.

And as the broken-windows theory of policing spread across America, more police resources were dedicated to minor violations, while many violent crimes—assaults and robberies, rapes and murders—were left unsolved. "That's like giving a facelift to a cancer patient, all right?" said Maple of broken windows, which some described as "quality of life" enforcement. "If you only have quality of life enforcement . . . you will be living in a fool's paradise."[10]

Maple abruptly died in 2001, and his policing revolution was hijacked before he could see it through. In his absence, CompStat morphed into a productivity scoreboard for broken windows, a tool used by police brass to micromanage and embarrass subordinates who weren't doing enough *something*. The system that sprang from the mind of a truly humanist investigator—*treat every crime victim like they're your own mother*—devolved into a managerial weapon, which, in 2022, former DOJ inspector general Michael Bromwich simply called "crude scorekeeping."[11]

Following Maple's death, as other cities tried to emulate New York's seemingly miraculous crime decline, CompStat was adopted by police departments across the nation and the world, institutionalizing a form of policing that focused more on numbers than people. Proponents defended it as data driven, which implied sophistication and accuracy. But its innate flaw was that it incentivized police departments to protect and promote the most statistically productive officers, whether or not the statistics provided meaningful data, and whether or not those officers were treating their communities well.

Jack Maple and CompStat offer both a lesson and a warning. Municipal policing can be revolutionized. But unless its values are revolutionized in concert, eventually, it'll all revert back to what the Irish built back in the 1800s: a money game.

IF OUR DEMOCRACY had an opportunity to create a new criminal-justice system from the ground up, it would bear little resemblance to what we have today. That's something we can all agree on, from the cops to the academics, to the journalists, to the public, to us. While nobody can prescribe exactly what that reinvented and more perfect system might be, here is our modest proposal, as any change must begin with a new vision of what is possible.

Within the complexities of our current law enforcement's fundamental problems are signposts pointing to their solutions. We believe the process of lasting reform must begin by taking a moment to abandon the chaos of the present and envisioning an American criminal-justice system truly deserving of the word "justice." On the ground, this system would have three central roles: protectors, investigators, and conflict-resolution specialists. When a citizen called 9-1-1, the options would expand beyond, "Police, fire, or medical?" Perhaps as simply as, "Protection, fire, medical, or conflict resolution?"

Protectors

A person in need could call upon protectors—depending on the situation, either mental health experts, police officers, or social workers—to provide safety at a moment's notice. Protectors would aim to stop violence as first responders. They'd separate abusers from the abused, calm people in states of crisis, and would not personally benefit from placing people into cages. A wide body of research shows that incarcerating people has catastrophic social consequences, breeding violence, poverty, and anomie, so for the protector, incarceration would always be a last resort.[12]

Each type of protector (mental health expert, police officer, and social worker) would be trained to diagnose complex social situations and encourage nonviolent resolutions whenever possible. Protectors would have many more tools at their disposal than arrests and summonses, prisons and jails. They could divert citizens to rehabilitation centers, mental health clinics, housing programs, jobs programs, and more. Protectors would be mediators and problem solvers, with the primary goal of reducing violence in the moment and connecting the public to services that foster growth and public health. When protectors improved public health, they'd be financially rewarded for doing that, not for merely making an arrest at the end of their tour to earn overtime pay.

Some of the protectors would be armed. When absolutely necessary, protectors would use violence to defend their communities and themselves. But violence would truly be the protector's last resort; and when a protector used violence, that action would be included in measurements of community violence—and recorded as an increase.

Investigators

Whenever protectors observed systems of violence—saw patterns of robberies, assaults, rip-offs, and so on—they would notify investigators. These investigators—agents, detectives, analysts, whatever title you prefer—would use the tools of detective work to identify criminal networks, typically small groups of people disproportionately responsible for community harm. Investigators would focus on the big picture, identifying networks that indulge in sex trafficking, weapons trafficking, and wage theft, rather than arbitrarily chasing after people who "look like criminals."

In this future, the war on drugs would be retired as a relic of a darker past. Protectors and investigators, with a clear division of power and responsibilities, would prioritize their work using Jack Maple's mantra: *Treat every crime victim like they're your own mother.* They would focus on the acts that lead to the most social harm, leaving minor violations such as noise complaints, shoplifting, and petty disputes to conflict-resolution specialists.

Protectors and investigators would work for separate institutions and would not flow back and forth, as is so often the case with officers and detectives today.

Conflict-Resolution Specialists

Conflict-resolution specialists—unarmed but highly trained mediators—would be available at a moment's notice, too. Reporting a distressing family argument but don't want anyone arrested? Concerned about someone having a combative mental health crisis? You could ask for conflict resolution, letting the 9-1-1 operator decide if a protector needed to join in tandem.

IN THIS SYSTEM, we'd all have more options than simply calling 9-1-1 or doing nothing. We'd be able to do *something* ourselves.

Protectors would respond to public safety issues. Investigators would identify the people who committed egregious and systemic offenses. Conflict-resolution specialists would work to diffuse the conflicts most prone to lead to violence. They would all rely on independently verified data to improve their violence-reduction strategies. They'd have district guardrails, unique to each profession, preventing them from disproportionately criminalizing any one group. In their own ways, each role would work in a system simultaneously endeavoring to reduce poverty and violence and to address those problems as far upstream as possible—going after the root causes, not the downstream effects.

The protectors, investigators, and conflict-resolution specialists who attained these goals most effectively would be offered promotions, and those who abused their powers would be promptly relieved of their duties. If they engaged in criminality or other misconduct, they'd be held to a higher standard than the public. Discipline and punishment would be swift, fair, transparent, and effective.

In this system, jails and prisons would be financially incentivized to reduce recidivism rates, not public perceptions of crime, and they'd be required to provide quality education and job training to every incarcerated person. If we were to still call it "correction," it would need to be truly rehabilitative.

This new system would not be judged by whether "crime is up" or "crime is down," but by whether the American people were actually safer and better positioned to flourish in their own lives and perceived the American criminal-justice system as fair and just.

We know—there is ample and incontrovertible evidence of it— that what permanently reduces crime is employment, education, housing, health care, and the equitable enforcement of law. That would also involve addressing the underenforcement of laws on institutions that inflict harm on vulnerable communities, through criminally antisocial behaviors such as wage theft and environmental pollution. The system would not be an arms race between competing industries, whose primary incentives are directed by profit. The system would be officially chartered as a public service and its employees dedicated to public service in the truest sense.

Overcoming Resistance

Sounds like a better world to live in, right? Building it won't be easy. Police brass and police unions will resist these proposals, for both would struggle to imagine a safer world with fewer police officers. But because overburdened officers are asked to do everything, a task which is simply impossible, we'll need to narrow the scope of police services and use the savings to fund the new structure. The public, however, will need to press lawmakers to pass new local laws and budgets and will have to hold public officials accountable when they cling to the failed practices and policies that got us into this mess.

For the brass, policing isn't always about representing the interests of the public, or even the interests of the officers in their command; it's about representing the interests of the police departments they run, which usually means making them bigger. That's how bureaucracies tend to work.

Police unions will resist these changes, too, but in a different way. Unlike the brass, they represent the interests of their officers. And these unions know that their officers are suffering. They know that crime statistics are a game of smoke and mirrors. They see their officers blamed for the brass's mistakes. Police unions understand the anomie, and they want it to stop. They won't voluntarily agree to having fewer members. But if, in exchange for a smaller police force, communities offered to pay those fewer officers better wages and commit to meaningfully improving their working conditions, a negotiation could begin. And perhaps, piece by piece, step by step, we could make it easier for those who fear change to say yes instead of no.

If, however, police unions refuse to negotiate, then communities must consider a complete reset. For what is at stake in this overdue reckoning is the well-being of all our people. Every one of us has a stake in this discussion, and the vast majority of us, many officers included, stand to gain from a wholesale reform of our entrenched, demonstrably inefficient, and socially harmful systems.

Challenging Conventional Wisdom

The need for change demands that we ask ourselves tough questions and challenge conventional wisdom. Law enforcement often relies on the premise that incarceration is a deterrent from committing crime, though many authoritative studies show it is not.[13] Why not create *incentives* that discourage crime? If your car-insurance company can reward you for not getting into an accident, why can't the government pay you for not committing a crime?[14*] What if that kept us all safer? Why couldn't we at least figure out if that worked at scale? And why, after decades of human suffering, are police still fighting a losing war on drugs? From heroin to crack to fentanyl, the cycle has continued. It has to stop. And if someone is going to do *something* about it, we need someone new.

Despite the efforts of many well-meaning officers, modern policing is failing. It isn't "broken," as pundits often say because it works exactly as designed. It criminalizes Black and brown peoples' actions where their white peers often proceed unharmed. It spreads anomie through Black and brown communities and police officers alike. Where policing does reduce crime, the process is brutal and inefficient with life-withering consequences that span generations. National living standards have remained stagnant for most Americans. In many communities, levels of misery and despair have increased. Simultaneously, thousands of government bureaucracies and expansive corporate industries have seen their power, influence, and wealth grow disproportionately.

---

* Richmond, California's Office of Neighborhood Safety, used this method to great effect, cutting the city's homicide rate in half.

19

Six Proposals

Here we offer six concrete steps to get us all a little closer to a criminal-justice system that's truly just. Our cases, interviews, and research all point to these conclusions. They cut to the heart of the problems, including the exclusion of women from the profession, the ongoing war on drugs, the lack of alternatives to modern policing, the failures of Internal Affairs, the lack of public access to police records, and the need for truth and reconciliation. Every solution, of course, will create new problems, but we believe these problems will inevitably pale in comparison to what we face now.

Proposal #1: Policewomen

In *Behind the Shield*, Arthur Niederhoffer discusses what he calls the "authoritarian police personality." He theorizes as to whether police enter the job because they have authoritarian tendencies or whether they develop those tendencies after entering policing. What factors made someone more authoritarian over time? Was it their race? Their religion?

Niederhoffer couldn't find any factor that held up to scrutiny, except for one: gender. He concluded that "police authoritarianism

does not come into the force along with recruits, but rather is incul-
cated in the men through strenuous socialization. The . . . system is
geared to manufacture the 'take charge guy,' and it succeeds in doing
so with outstanding efficiency."[1] Policing clusters groups of men to
control other people's bodies. What could go wrong?

As of 2024, about 19 percent of NYPD officers identify as
women.[2] Nationwide, the number drops to about 14 percent, and
only 3 percent are in leadership positions.[3] In real life and in the
movies, policing is largely a man's world. But that doesn't make our
communities any safer. An array of studies show that female officers
are much more effective in interrupting violence and less likely to
perpetrate it. They generally use less force, they're more likely to
de-escalate conflict, and they're more likely to report other officers'
misconduct. Male officers, no matter their race, tend to use violence
at the same rate.[4]

Female officers respond much more vigorously to violence against
women, and they're far better equipped to investigate such crimes.
As one study found, "Policemen see police work as involving control
through authority, while policewomen see it as a public service."[5] In
1991, the commission convened in the aftermath of Rodney King's
beating found that "female officers are not reluctant to use force,
but they are not nearly as likely [as male officers] to be involved in
use of excessive force."[6] Studies have also found that female officers
were less likely to be the subject of civilian complaints and lawsuits,
saving cities millions.[7] Even among CCRB investigations, female
officers were 50 percent less likely than their male colleagues to
commit misconduct.[8] A more recent study found that male officers are significantly less likely to use excessive force in the presence of their female colleagues.[9] And the 2019 study on networks
of misconduct found that female officers may actually be disrupters
of those networks.[10] Despite these positive indicators, discriminatory hiring practices and discriminatory work environments have

prevented women from entering policing at the rates that might transform the nature of policing itself.

American policing is a fraternity, to the extent that its culture has a throughline: it is one of hazing, violence, and military-style brotherhood, creating more problems than solutions. This won't change until women have an equal place in the ranks of every police department. The 30x30 Initiative, a coalition of police leaders, researchers, and organizations, seeks to close policing's gender gap by having departments pledge to hire 30 percent female recruits by 2030.

But we must also look beyond 2030. Simply put, police departments need to hire 50 percent women. It's a matter of public safety.

Proposal #2: End Prohibition

Essayist Dave Hickey writes that "the trick of civilization lies in recognizing the moment when a rule ceases to liberate and begins to govern."[11] It's clear that America's laws around drugs ceased to liberate a long time ago. Whether it was in the late '60s, when President Nixon first popularized "tough on crime" and the war on drugs, or in the '50s, when narcotics squads policed heroin as a pretense to raid jazz clubs, or in 1875, when San Francisco first criminalized the use of opium to police Chinese railroad workers, these failed policy solutions presented us with an enduring truth: prohibitions often create problems worse than the acts they attempt to eliminate.[12] America's constitutional ban on the production, importation, transportation, and sale of alcohol in 1920 is case in point. Until its repeal in 1933, Prohibition created a black market, prices for smuggled foreign spirits and bootleg booze skyrocketed, and gang violence exploded. As a consequence, America became a much more dangerous country.

In *Blue Blood*, NYPD detective Edward Conlon wrote, "If you got rid of narcotics today, you could send half the cops in this city home."[13] We can't get rid of narcotics, but we could certainly decriminalize their use and pair addiction treatment with harm-reduction practices like safe-use sites, clean-needle exchanges, and Narcan trainings.[14] As with the repeal of Prohibition, this would eliminate the black market, lower prices, reduce gang violence, and make America a much safer country. Recent attempts to decriminalize, as in the case of Oregon in 2020, show that harm-reduction practices must be in place before the decriminalization goes into effect.[15]

Every year, tens of billions of dollars are spent on the policing of low-level drug offenses and a wide array of actions that are arguably unnecessary to police.[16] This misdirected law enforcement comes at the expense of investigating unquestionably harmful crimes, such as human trafficking, murder, rape, domestic violence, and wage theft. Nationwide, the rate at which homicides are solved has continued on a downward trend since the mid-1980s.[17] In some cities, the detectives who investigate the most harmful crimes tend to be overworked and underfunded relative to their peers who are out busy doing *something*.

So often, tragic police incidents start with Black men navigating the indignity of poverty. Eric Garner was choked to death when he sold loose cigarettes. George Floyd was murdered when he used a counterfeit twenty-dollar bill. Michael Brown was killed after shoving a convenience store clerk over a pack of cigarillos. The NYPD bureaucracy makes it easier to rack up overtime on an unnecessary arrest than to run a complex police investigation, to take time resolving conflicts, or truly treat each crime victim like they're an officer's own mother. Today, it's easier to say "Crime is up," and angle for a bigger budget. A continuing war on drugs has made this cycle easier with each passing day because it stands as a glaring reminder that America's criminal justice system prioritizes doing something above addressing the crimes that do the most harm.

Here's what we propose: vote for politicians who vow to end the war on drugs and select local leaders who insist on holding departments accountable for unnecessary officer overtime and the misappropriation of police resources. And in one way or another, America needs the federal government to end the prohibition on drugs once and for all. In contrast to criminalization, regulation of the drug industry will make our communities and our police officers safer, saving billions of taxpayer dollars in the process.

Proposal #3:
Violence Reduction Agencies

"Law enforcement can't fix everything," said Patrick Yoes, president of the Fraternal Order of Police, the largest police union in the United States. "We're not responsible for poverty. We're not responsible for failed school systems. We're not responsible for broken family units. Yet, we find ourselves having to deal with all of those things, and we carry the burden of it."[18]

The police are asked to do everything. The same officer might be asked to respond to a couple arguing, a broken car window, a man going into diabetic shock, a suicide, and a robbery, perhaps all in the same day. That officer is required to document each of those incidents with a level of precision liable to be scrutinized in the media, on a witness stand, or both. It's an impossible task, almost entirely divorced from what Hollywood depicts as the life and work of a cop.

Yet there's a crucial point missing from Yoes's statement: while law enforcement is not responsible for poverty, failing schools, or broken families, officers do issue unnecessary summonses, burdening poor families living paycheck to paycheck. Officers do stop-and-frisk Black students, lowering test scores in the process. Officers do arrest parents, separating them from their children.

Law enforcement certainly can't fix everything, but it can break things, too.

In 2000, the NYPD commissioner reported that well over 95 percent of his officers had never fired their guns while on duty.[19] Today, only 5 percent of officers nationwide have discharged their firearms more than once.[20] In New York, it was common knowledge in criminal-justice circles that more than 90 percent of 9-1-1 calls lead to the disposition of non-crime corrected, a catchall term meaning, in essence, that police intervention wasn't necessary.[21]

Two centuries of modern policing have taught us that the American people want government officials specifically tasked with reducing violence. And because we've learned that so many factors contribute to violence—poverty, addiction, and lack of access to housing, health care, education, and more—violence can't be reduced through policing alone.

We need a new kind of institution in local government, guided solely by the principles of peacekeeping, violence interruption, mediation, and restorative justice and staffed by trained professionals whose abilities to diffuse conflict go far beyond the training afforded to most police officers. We all intuitively recognize such people in our personal lives: A savvy bartender. A beloved teacher. A veteran librarian. A smiling bouncer. An unflappable nurse. These are the kinds of people whose skill sets and incentives make them part of the solution, not the problem. We all know people who seem naturally disposed to diffuse conflict and resolve disputes. Imagine them working for your local Department of Violence Reduction—a precursor to a system of protectors, investigators, and conflict-resolution specialists.

Cities across the country have begun to test different approaches to this concept.

In Eugene, Oregon, a program known as CAHOOTS (Crisis Assistance Helping Out On The Streets) has been operating since

1989. It deploys two-person teams consisting of a medic and a crisis worker who respond to mental health crises, welfare checks, suicide threats, and more. They rely on trauma-informed de-escalation and harm-reduction techniques.[22] They don't carry guns. In 2019, they called for police backup in only 0.625 percent of their responses—160 times out of 24,000 incidents.[23] By 2024 there were more than one hundred American municipalities with new, nonpolice, unarmed crisis response teams.[24]

In Oakland, California, the Department of Violence Prevention (DVP) uses the Ceasefire model of crime prevention, partnering with the Oakland Police Department, to identify people who police believe are driving violence but who are not yet subject to arrest (for lack of evidence). Then, DVP coaches, who are not law enforcement, make daily contact, working to build trust and map out life plans that break the cycle of violence.[25] A Northeastern University study tied the Ceasefire model to a 31.5 percent reduction in Oakland gun homicides.[26]

There are international models to borrow from, too. The UK, Belgium, France, and South Africa use community-safety professionals as unarmed mediators to address low-level crime and disorder. Although these nonpolice responders tend to suffer from low pay and unclear performance metrics, in the United States, we could pay such professionals well.[27] Separated from police departments, they would provide genuine community policing by enlisting actual community members to keep one another safe.

There must be arms of government that aim to prevent moments where a police presence would even be necessary. By pushing to create or expand a violence reduction agency in your city, you can help build an institution that succeeds when it prevents violence, nothing more and nothing less.

Proposal #4: Civilianize Internal Affairs

If you wonder why police aren't held to a higher standard than the public, it's because they're allowed to set their own bar. Many police departments, NYPD included, have their own judges, juries, and executioners. Jack Maple once wrote that "the [police] leader must back the cops when they're right, train them when they make mistakes despite good intentions, and hang them when they betray the public's trust," but the public's trust has been betrayed over and over, and change has been incremental, to say the least.[28]

Charles Campisi, the chief who ran the NYPD's IAB from 1996 through 2014, wrote that "civilians can never truly understand police work because they are not trained investigators."[29] This problem begs for a simple solution—train more civilians to investigate police work. Being a police officer certainly offers insight into another police officer's thinking. But wearing a shield is not the only way to learn the rules and laws of policing.

By all accounts, Chief Campisi was an extraordinarily principled man, but to expect Internal Affairs officers in every city to protect the public above their coworkers is an unsustainable expectation. The internal dynamics of any police department boil down to politics, and because Internal Affairs is an arm of policing, their investigations will by design be subject to politics and bias undermining the independence a truly effective investigation demands.

At the CCRB, we learned that IAB could be excellent when an officer's actions offended the brass's self-image. But in other cases, officers with high arrest numbers had their conduct rationalized away. We saw how, when officers would speak out against NYPD corruption or discriminatory practices, IAB could be used as a tool to silence their voices. "I want to create a true safe haven for whistleblowers," said then NYPD Lieutenant Edwin Raymond, who wrote the critically acclaimed book *An Inconvenient Cop: My Fight to Change Policing in America*, "Internal affairs is just not equipped to deal with systemic corruption. You're literally asking the department to investigate itself."[30] Further, it wasn't uncommon for people to complain that officers were retaliating against them for complaining in the first place.[31] From what we could see, IAB did little to prevent this from continuing.

In the NYPD, IAB was a punishment post, where poorly behaved or ineffective officers were stranded, labeled rats. With this in mind, we must ask ourselves, Why are we forcing cops to do this job? Why should we require them to define the difference between a good cop and a bad cop? Whose benefit does that serve?

The "who watches the watchmen" question is complicated. We understand why the police don't trust the public to police them: the public is largely ignorant when it comes to the mechanics of policing, let alone the psychological toll the job takes on its officers. Like the police, CCRB investigators are frequently frustrated by commentators who talk about police reform but don't appear to know the basics. We wouldn't trust them, either.

But the reality is that professionally trained civilian investigators *can* understand these issues. They *can* understand a police officer's thinking. They *do* empathize with the unique and daunting challenges a police officer faces on the job. Civilian investigators *can* effectively combat police corruption, and they can do it while remaining impartial and without playing favorites. It's a matter of training and letting civilian investigators do their jobs without being undermined.

In a world of policing without Internal Affairs, there must be a robust system of civilian oversight, truly independent from police budgets, police power, and police marketing. Our government can only be *for* the people if it's held accountable *by* the people.

Proposal #5: Tear Down the Blue Wall

To the NYPD, "ongoing police investigation" means one thing: you can't have it. If policing is to meaningfully change, the process must begin with the premise that the police cannot be the arbiters of public access. The current system is fundamentally undemocratic.

In his 2017 book *Unwarranted*, Barry E. Friedman wrote, "Police play an indispensable role in our society. But our failure to supervise them has left us all in peril." For our society to effectively manage policing, however, we need to know what's happening behind the blue wall. We propose that cities and states create independent bodies to determine which police records should be made public.

As the pioneering publisher of investigative journalism S. S. McClure wrote, "The vitality of democracy depends on popular knowledge of complex questions." Policing, as we have seen, can be staggeringly complicated. It can only become democratic if we all learn how it works. Not through the lens of a police department's public information officer, or another city official with a potential conflict of interest, but through the lens of someone who is positioned to value the public's interest over the department's brand.

Although the events of 2020 led to some rollbacks of prohibitive police-secrecy laws, we've seen how the NYPD has circled the wagons, and the public has marginally more access than it did before George Floyd's murder. In fact, one of Mayor Adams's first major changes to the NYPD in 2022 was to fold IAB into NYPD Legal.* Now, NYPD attorneys review every single CCRB document request, providing investigators the absolute minimum with a newfound efficiency.

Police discipline needs to be fully transparent. A proudly progressive state like California still limits records access to the point of absurdity. This needs to end, and transparency needs to be the national standard for police disciplinary records access. Anything less fails to address the urgency of the moment: countless shocking stories are shielded from the public every year. If we've learned

---

* We are not aware of public reporting on this development. But it's what we were told internally and experienced in practice.

anything, it's that the stories in this book are grains of sand on a far-reaching beach. Absent public access, the government won't be forced to learn from these mistakes, and thus, Americans will be prevented from improving our democracy.

Police unions and departments alike have used straw man arguments to keep their records hidden from the public. In New York, union leaders went so far as to tell the state legislature that transparency measures would incite members of the public to assassinate officers in their own homes.[32] New York's Civil Rights Law 50-a was repealed, and the union's hysterical premonitions fell flat. On appeal, a panel of three federal judges found not a single example of increased danger to officers resulting from this most basic form of transparency.[33]

Police disciplinary records, data, and training materials must automatically be made public unless a truly independent arbiter rules otherwise.

A lack of transparency begs many more questions. Why aren't all police training materials public and readily accessible?* Why do police departments decide their own metrics for success? Why are some police departments allowed to have their own teams of attorneys approve internal policies without the consent of other branches of city government? Why don't robust whistleblower and antiretaliation protections extend to rank-and-file officers nationwide?[34] The system cannot be considered truly just until these questions are meaningfully answered.

Today, it's open season on saying, "Crime is up," whether or not the evidence is there to support that claim. But going forward, crime data must be independently audited. As of 2025, departments aren't even required to report their crime data to the FBI.[35] Whether

---

* We can't help but note that in January 2025, the NYPD's several thousand page Patrol Guide was still posted online in four PDFs that were painstaking to sift through, as if by design.

managed at the state or federal level, there must be a national standard for crime statistics, a permanent check on crime-data manipulation that is regulated and enforced by stakeholders beyond a local police department.[36]

To build a truly transparent system, the media must evolve, as well. The media is slow to change. But crime reporters could easily create professional associations that set a higher standard. Imagine if the best journalists had a seal of approval that said, *Crime Reporter Association Approved*. It would parallel other industry accreditations, like Fair Trade USA and the Better Business Bureau. Some areas of journalism are moving in the right direction—shifting away from breathlessly publishing mug shots for mere arrests, for example, despite the fact that suspects are constitutionally presumed innocent until proven guilty. Perhaps in this new world, we could have a better sense of who was reporting the facts and who was chasing clickbait.

There are opportunities for change in the courts, too. Congress has the authority to create new court systems under Article III, Section 1, of the United States Constitution.* We propose Congress create a new court system specifically tasked with addressing police violence, corruption, and discipline when local departments fail to act. We'll leave the details to constitutional scholars and a legislature that's amenable to systemic change, but it may be that the current system has too many political roadblocks to succeed on the state and local level alone.

Police accountability is government accountability, and it can no longer happen in the dark. Our only option is to establish transparency measures that tear down the blue wall for good.

---

* Article III of the Constitution invests the judicial power of the United States in the federal court system. Article III, Section 1 specifically creates the US Supreme Court and gives Congress the authority to create the lower federal courts. The Constitution and laws of each state establish the state courts.

Proposal #6: Truth and Reconciliation

In 2019, the average American lifespan was 78.8 years. In 2022, it was 77.5 years.[37] For Black Americans, the average lifespan dropped from about 75 years in 2019 to 72.8 years in 2022.[38] Only a handful of studies assess an American police officer's average lifespan, but they've generally concluded that officers' life expectancies are "significantly lower than that of the US population," perhaps as low as 66 years.[39] Many causes contribute to this phenomenon, but we can be sure that their respective miseries live in tandem, and largely out of the public eye.

American police departments have used the facade of community policing to appear as if they are responding to community needs. Often, departments will send Black officers to community meetings to negotiate and apologize for the worst parts of *something*. This process is a charade, lacking meaningful dialogue and staving off structural change. Black and brown communities shouldn't have to accept forced apologies from lone Black officers while other officers, perhaps in the same precincts, may break into their homes and put them into cages.

Tearing down the blue wall must go hand in hand with a process of truth and reconciliation. The psychological toll of being policed comes in waves; it can take weeks or months before someone can even articulate why they felt violated, why they couldn't forget what happened. At the CCRB, we saw how most officers were shielded from the impact of the trauma they inflicted. While a CV might cry in front of us for hours, the officer would likely never know. Moreover, that same officer sometimes thought that they'd done everything right.

Driving the crisis of policing is the fact that police officers are often taught to see their jobs strictly through the lens of honor and dignity—as warriors who defend us from violence—when policing, by its very nature, has the potential to inflict extraordinary harm.

How are officers to reconcile this contradiction? How can they be honest about their own anomie?

In the early 1990s, South Africa ended its formal policy of apartheid. In 1995, under the leadership of President Nelson Mandela and Archbishop Desmond Tutu, South Africa's parliament passed a law to form a Truth and Reconciliation Commission. The commission's central purpose was to promote reconciliation and forgiveness among perpetrators and victims, to discover the nature and incentives of human rights violations over the prior thirty-five years, to identify the victims, and to grant amnesty to anyone who fully disclosed their involvement in human rights violations.[40]

In Chile, where Augusto Pinochet ran a military dictatorship from 1973 to 1990, the government killed, tortured, or politically imprisoned more than forty thousand people.[41] In 1990, shortly after Pinochet left office, the new president established Chile's National Commission for Truth and Reconciliation. This commission began to document the cases of disappearance, killing, torture, and kidnapping and included accounts of nearly every victim whose stories it heard.

From 1972 to 1991, one Chicago police commander ordered the torture of more than 120 people to induce false confessions that placed some of the victims on death row. In 2015, the Chicago city council provided a formal apology and voted to provide public education on police torture, free college education for survivors and their families, a counseling center for torture survivors, $5.5 million in financial compensation, and a public memorial.[42]

The model of official truth and reconciliation isn't always satisfying. Bad actors aren't always punished individually, closure isn't a foregone conclusion, and even when it works as designed, the process of moving through collective intergenerational trauma is profoundly painful. Still, this model offers Americans a chance to face the realities that Black and brown communities endure every day. It's an opportunity to transparently assess the scope of policing in America and a forum to say, "Help me understand." America has turned a blind eye to the experiences of both Black and brown communities and officers alike. We need to hear their voices. It's the only way to make their stories really matter. It's the only way to address the anomie.

In our cases, victims told us over and over: "I just want this to never happen to anyone else." Inevitably, it would, and the public rarely knew. For the officers, we saw how heavily the psychological toll of policing weighed on them, too.

Arthur Niederhoffer believed that there are "two kinds of police cynicism. One is directed against life, the world, and people in general: the other is aimed at the police system itself."[43] We need to hear officers' cynicism, listening carefully to their voices. It's the only way we can address the problems police officers face on the beat—the favoritism, the contradictory pressures, the disparate expectations that make their jobs feel impossible.

We need to allow officers to reflect on their challenges in private, too. That's why officers should be provided with mandatory counseling, so that none of them can be retaliated against for seeking mental health care, as has so often been the case. We can't expect the police to treat the public well if they aren't treating themselves well first.

In 2022, former DOJ inspector general Michael Bromwich led the investigative team that wrote a comprehensive report detailing criminal conduct within the Baltimore Police Department's vaunted Gun Trace Task Force. In *Anatomy of the Gun Trace Task Force Scandal: Its Origins, Causes, and Consequences*, the report detailed the task force's corruption and analyzed the department's history, culture, and incentives. Among its recommendations was to enlist officers who engaged in corruption to participate in academy training, explaining to recruits firsthand the devastating impact of police corruption, violence, and misconduct on officers and the communities they served. Bromwich and his team reason that the only way to learn from history is to discuss it out in the open. We couldn't agree more.

Moreover, the report insists, officers must hear from the victims about what its authors describe as "the devastating consequences of corrupt acts on victims and their families, including the loss of liberty, loss of employment, and damage to their relationships with their families and communities."

Police officers and poor Black and brown communities share a significant commonality: they're isolated communities that live with different rules from the rest of American society, and they share lives that are at times blighted by anomie. Only when we hear from them all in a transparent, open forum, on a regular basis, can we begin to unravel the incentives that sustain such a brutal and inefficient system.

Police unions, as we have seen, will undoubtedly stand in the way of truth and reconciliation, for when their officers speak freely, they lose power. But if police unions are unwilling to envision a criminal-justice system without anomie—if they choose to be part of the problem rather than part of the solution—then perhaps police unions shouldn't exist, as is the case in Georgia, North Carolina, South Carolina, and Tennessee.[44]

In some cases, officers and victims will need to speak in private— in the vein of mediation or restorative justice. But more often, their stories will have to be told in public, even if it means granting immunity. We propose creating a national forum for officers and victims alike to share their stories. It won't be *Cops* or *Blue Bloods*, but it's what academics, journalists, and civil rights leaders have been calling for. It's also what the police need—for us to hear their voices without the filters of the brass and the unions. It cannot be merely another political charade, another ritual; it must show America what policing really looks like behind the blue wall, what it really means to the people it touches and changes. If we can do these things, we can break the fixed system of American policing for good.

Epilogue

How does this end? Absent some extraordinary changes, the NYPD is not going to like this book. Of course, they'll misunderstand it. They'll likely see it as an attack, when in truth it's an investigation into something much bigger than them. They have their own press office, whose central purpose is to protect the department's public image. And because this book is focused on facts, not their public image, history shows that they'll see it as something they have to tear apart.

CompStat is a pillar of the NYPD's legacy. Former commissioners and mayors like Bill Bratton and Rudy Giuliani have made mountains of cash tethering their names to CompStat and selling it to departments around the globe.[1] They'll say that by criticizing CompStat, we're putting Americans in danger, we're putting police officers in danger, and we're discounting the hard work of everyday police officers. Simply put, that's bullshit.

Books about police violence make the police look bad. We expect they'll say that we hate the police and resort to character assassination, personal threats, and empty lawsuits. When we say we have tremendous respect for certain officers, that we only want a safer country for everyone, they'll say, "*We're* the experts on public safety. These guys don't know anything about policing." And we'll admit there's a lot left to learn. There's a Black Hole at the center of many city governments, where crime statistics are shrouded in secrecy, where conflicts of interest undermine fact-driven investigations, where cheating scandals plague promotion processes from top to bottom. We would, in fact, love to learn more about the Black Hole, for it sits at the center of an extraordinarily important part of our democracy.

And when they say, "*We're* the experts on public safety," remember that these are the same voices who said that civilians could never investigate police misconduct, that we'd never understand. And they'll say the same thing about crime. They'll say at least they did *something* because *something* ends up meaning *anything at all*. And when the police can do *anything at all*, as we've said before, their budgets grow, their power grows, and the gears keep on turning.

They'll try to brand us as leakers, or perhaps as disgruntled employees who resorted to an exposé for a quick buck. But that would be false. By the end, we were each finding meaning in our work. We could have stayed at the CCRB without rocking the boat. And we could have made several million dollars over the next few decades, collecting sterling pensions at the end. Writing this book was not an easy choice. It was painful to leave. And as you might imagine, this puts us at tremendous personal risk of retaliation. But while our CVs taught us that in the impossibly complicated business of policing, it was never a good idea to be on a cop's bad side, our experiences at the CCRB illuminated abuses of authority, waste, inefficiency, corruption, criminal activity, conflict of interest, and more. Something needed to change.

They might simultaneously claim we leaked stories and that those stories are not true. They'll deny public access as much as they can, of course, and use this all to try to discredit and defund the CCRB, an agency that can only succeed with real independence, unrestricted access, and a budget to match.

They'll try to further conceal public records even as they tell the press that they're more transparent than ever. They might even fire a notorious officer or tweak a column in CompStat, pointing to that as proof they've changed for good, then assure us that the public can stop worrying—that they'll never do it again. They promise.

They'll delay, delay, delay, and hope the public loses interest. If that happens, maybe they'll arrest us on some trumped-up charges, just to plant a flag in their victory. It's happened before.

They'll try everything. Because when you're a master of persuasion, trained both to talk someone into handcuffs and to make the bureaucracy say yes, you don't always take a position and stand by your values. Sometimes, you take every position. You claim every value. And you do everything you can to get your opponent to submit.

The NYPD can lie to you because they're allowed to. They can manipulate statistics. And they can do it because there's no independent oversight of their statistics. They can say, "Crime is up," and they might blame it on us. And they're able to do it because those cops, academics, politicians, and journalists who are in their pockets will rush to their defense without question.

Unfortunately, the same might prove true for the CCRB. More than ever, the agency is beholden to the whims of the mayor's office.* It used to be part of the NYPD, and in many ways, it's compelled to operate in the same manner. They might even be forced to discredit us, as well, for in the game of bureaucratic survival, that's likely their best option.

But there's still a path forward to make this all worthwhile, and it starts with you.

First, it takes challenging your assumptions about crime. That means taking a crime-related headline with a grain of salt. Ask yourself, "Who benefits from this headline?" Because "crime is up" headlines are often clickbait, intentionally skewed to play on your greatest fears. Then, read past the headline.

---

* Given that the mayor is a former NYPD captain with what appears to be little regard for police oversight, we can only expect the worst. And if anyone could use a media distraction, it would be him.

Second, keep learning about the criminal-justice system. We love *True Detective*, but we also know that cop shows reveal little about their real-life counterparts. Consequently, when cops insist, "You don't know anything about policing," sometimes they're on to something. You can change that. And if you've already changed it for yourself, you can change it for someone else.

Third, keep in mind that the United States is a democracy. When our leaders fail to govern effectively, we can and should remove them from office. The same is true for the higher-ups in your local police departments. Unlike lower-level officers, most high-ranking officers are not unionized; with enough political will, they, too, can be replaced.

Fourth, and we know this isn't an easy ask, but take a moment to learn about your local police department. Policing is complicated, and it can only become democratic if we all stop pretending to know how it works. Attend a public meeting and ask someone how the gears turn. Read your department's manual or observe a criminal proceeding at your local courthouse. If "the vitality of democracy depends on popular knowledge of complex questions," it's time to invest in knowledge. All in all, in America the answer to the question—"Who watches the watchmen?"—is simpler than it seems. The answer is you. If you want to break the fixed system of American policing, you have to be willing to police the police. You have to be the cop cop.

If you've taken anything from this book, we hope it includes the investigator's tool kit. The tools of an investigator will empower you to navigate the muddle of rhetoric that swirls around policing, language that is often largely divorced from the facts and the truth, designed to have a persuasive effect but often lacking in meaningful context. At times the rhetoric devolves into a shouting match of vague and undefined slogans—"Black lives matter" versus "blue lives matter," "law and order" versus "defund the police," or is confined to online echo chambers that only seem to add to the confusion.

It isn't only rhetoric that's dividing our nation. It's the absence of definitions. Policing has gone largely undefined. Officers have been asked to do *something*, by which society has generally meant *anything at all*. And *something* has a different meaning in every one of the nearly eighteen thousand law enforcement agencies across America.

When the police speak, listen carefully, and ask them what they mean—insist they define their terms. What do they think it means when "crime is up"? What is a crime? Is it a complaint? An arrest? Are these crimes policed in white neighborhoods? Latino ones? Black ones? Who's keeping count? What do they think "community policing" means—not as a theory, but in practice? Is it getting a criminal informant? Is it searching for guns and drugs? Is anything and everything police do in a community "community policing"? Or is it just a state of mind? What *isn't* community policing?

You can apply the tools of an investigator to any conversation, from a town hall meeting to a dinner with friends. When someone says a neighborhood is dangerous, ask them what they mean. When someone says, "Crime is up," ask them what they mean. When someone says the police are the answers to these problems, ask them why.

WE'RE NOT ALONE IN THIS FIGHT for a better democracy. Many officers yearn to end the bullshit arrests, the overtime rackets, the networks of misconduct, the screaming bosses, the empty datafication of *something*. They hate being despised by the public they serve. And they know, as we learned at the CCRB, that Derek Chauvin didn't create all this anomie. It was policing itself, our society's demand that the police do *something*, even when *something* hurts us all.

Some officers will undoubtedly resent our proposals, some to the point of outrage. Others will argue the solution to our woes is more tough-on-crime policing. Some will say the problem is not enough *something*. But that's because, as John Timoney put it, policing has failed to study its own history. It's a profession fixated on short-term solutions to long-term problems, even when those solutions lead to catastrophe in the long term.

As with Black and brown communities, officers are losing years of their lives, dealing with the suicides, the anomie. When you look at the numbers, it isn't criminals who are killing the police, it's policing itself. We truly believe they can be partners in breaking the fixed system, if we can amplify the right officers' voices—the ones you seldom hear.

As for the two of us, our goal is just to leave America better off than we found it. We believe that's an America where everyone—officers included—is safer and happier, liberated from anomie. That's an America with far fewer people in cages, where social services aren't simply replaced with police because police do *something*. We believe that's an America where the police know their work always matters. It would be easier that way.

Acknowledgments

This was our best shot.

This book is for the victims, who spoke out because they didn't want this to happen to anyone else. To the unnamed officers who shared their perspectives, we believe you can fight the anomie. To the countless public servants enduring the Sisyphean task of civilian oversight, we are deeply honored to have worked alongside you. Sorry for the surprise; this was the only way it could work. And to the past and future investigators seeking meaning in this strange world: Remember that when you feel like shit, you aren't, even if you're surrounded by mountains of shit on all sides.

There is no way to capture the depth of gratitude we have for the many people who shaped our lives, kept us well, and supported us through this process. We know you understand why so many of you will have to go unnamed.

However, thank you to Mark and Barbara for your stalwart support and vision, and Elliot, Mike, Leah, and Jeremy for your brilliant perspectives. Special thanks to Marcellino, who, despite his passing in 2023, will never be forgotten.

To the Zando book team, Molly Stern, Sarah Ried, Quynh Do, and those behind the scenes, thank you for your extraordinary guidance, nuanced understanding, and commitment to getting this right. To Liz Stein, thank you for keeping us focused, motivated, and organized. Larry, thank you for keeping your elbows out, and for understanding so clearly that this isn't about us.

Thank you to Jay Mandel for seeing the potential. We also wouldn't be here without Skyler McKinley and the Board of Directors of Yes Men Know, LLC (a Delaware company), who were remarkably agreeable throughout this process.

And finally, thank you—for reading past the headline.

Notes

INTRODUCTION

1. https://www.criminaljustice.ny.gov/crimnet/ojsa/arrests/nyc.pdf https://www
    .criminaljustice.ny.gov/crimnet/ojsa/jjag-report-2011.pdf https://data
    .cccnewyork.org/data/map/1525/minor-arrests-under-18-years-old#1525
    /a/2/1891/127/a/a.
2. https://www.ntd.com/69-of-nyc-crime-cases-dismissed-after-new-justice
    -reform-law-manhattan-institute_896033.html; https://datacollaborativefor
    justice.org/wp-content/uploads/2021/04/2021_04_07_Conviction_Record
    _Report.pdf.
3. https://www.nyclu.org/data/nypd-discipline-numbers.
4. https://www.ktoo.org/2015/07/19/ntsb-investigates-man-machine
    -environment-fridays-plane-crash-near-juneau/; https://safetycompass
    .wordpress.com/2017/08/14/inside-the-ntsbs-general-aviation-investigative
    -process/.
5. https://pmc.ncbi.nlm.nih.gov/articles/PMC7642213/ https://nyulawreview
    .org/wp-content/uploads/2019/04/NYULawReview-94-Richardson_etal
    -FIN.pdf.
6. https://www.nytimes.com/2014/07/18/nyregion/staten-island-man-dies
    -after-police-try-to-arrest-him.html.

A BRIEF HISTORY

7. https://www.acluct.org/en/news/civilian-review-boards-work-they-must-avoid
    -past-mistakes#:~:text=By%20the%20end%20of%20the,and%20they%20
    remain%20common%20today.&text=Despite%20their%20ubiquity%2C%20
    CRBs%20are,powers%2C%20such%20as%20subpoena%20power; https://
    d3n8a8pro7vhmx.cloudfront.net/nacole/pages/161/attachments/original
    /1481727974/NACOLE_AccessingtheEvidence_Final.pdf?1481727974.
8. https://www.nyc.gov/site/ccrb/about/history.page.
9   Press Conference - Civilian Review Board Reform: Statements By Lindsay
    And Robert F. Kennedy (WNYC-TV, 11/03/1966) https://nycrecords.access

.preservica.com/uncategorized/IO_fc7a5a07-371f-448b-b930-3a8d276
c6fa5/.

10.   https://www.nytimes.com/1971/12/15/archives/excerpts-from-the-testimony
-by-serpico.html.

11.   https://www.usccr.gov/files/pubs/nypolice/ch4.htm#:~:text=The%20
CCRB%20as%20Part%20of%20the%20NYPD&text=In%201986%2C%20
then%2Dmayor%20Ed,commissioner%20appointed%20another%20six%20
members.

12.   https://www.cityandstateny.com/politics/2020/06/meet-the-men-who
-scared-de-blasio-away-from-police-reform/175932/.

CHAPTER I: TRAINING DAY

1.   https://www.usatoday.com/story/news/nation/2019/06/15/nypd-suicides-3
-police-officers-kill-themselves-10-days/1464330001/.

2.   https://www.nytimes.com/2019/06/11/nyregion/steven-silks-cop-suicide
.html?module=inline.

3.   https://pmc.ncbi.nlm.nih.gov/articles/PMC6400077/.

4.   https://pmc.ncbi.nlm.nih.gov/articles/PMC4734369/; https://pmc.ncbi.nlm
.nih.gov/articles/PMC8056254/; https://pmc.ncbi.nlm.nih.gov/articles
/PMC4734369/#:~:text=On%20average%2C%20the%20life%20expectancy
%20of%20police%20officers%20in%20our,29.3%3B%20p%3C0.0001);
https://www.politifact.com/article/2021/jun/08/do-police-officers-have
-shorter-life-expectancy-ge/; https://journals.sagepub.com/doi/abs/10.1177
/1098611112465611.

5.   https://heinonline.org/HOL/LandingPage?handle=hein.journals/polic15
&div=12&id=&page=; https://www.thehotline.org/resources/officer-involved
-domestic-violence-a-survivor-story/.

6.   https://data.cityofnewyork.us/Public-Safety/NYPD-Sectors/eizi-ujye.

7.   https://www.nydailynews.com/1997/01/27/nypd-as-in-ny-polite-dept/;
https://apnews.com/article/nypd-courtesy-professionalism-respect-motto
-63f1c6f6ded00ba42e39d72793612ad9.

8.   https://www.cbsnews.com/news/nypd-police-bias-report-civilian-complaint
-review-board-most-unsubstantiated-2019-06-26/.

9.   https://www.ojp.gov/ncjrs/virtual-library/abstracts/history-new-york-city
-police-department.

10.   https://gothamist.com/news/eric-adams-wants-to-bring-back-the-nypds
-most-controversial-unit.

11.   https://nysfocus.com/2022/03/03/
nypd-plainclothes-anti-crime-unit-neighborhood-safety-team-ccrb
-complaints-lawsuits.

12.   https://www.nytimes.com/2023/06/05/nyregion/nypd-anti-crime-units
-training-tactics.html.

13. https://nysfocus.com/2022/03/03/nypd-plainclothes-anti-crime-unit
-neighborhood-safety-team-ccrb-complaints-lawsuits; https://www.nyclu
.org/uploads/2021/12/nyclu-2021-ccrbdata-report.pdf.

14. https://www.nyc.gov/assets/ccrb/downloads/pdf/policy_pdf/issue_based
/CCRB_BlakeFellow_Report.pdf.

15. https://www.nyclu.org/resources/policy/testimonies/civilian-complaint
-review-board-and-civilian-oversight-policing; https://www.nyc.gov/assets
/ccrb/downloads/pdf/policy_pdf/annual_bi-annual/2023_CCRB_Annual
_Report.pdf.

16. https://www.technologyreview.com/2022/02/14/1045333/map-nyc-cameras
-surveillance-bias-facial-recognition/.

17. See Opinion and Order, 08 Civ. 1034 (SAS) and 12 Civ. 2274 (SAS) in
Floyd v. City of New York, 959 F. Supp. 2d 668 (S.D.N.Y. 2013).

18. https://www.nyc.gov/html/oignypd/assets/downloads/pdf/nypd-body
-camera-report.pdf.

19. *Annual Report 2018* (New York: Civilian Complaint Review Board, 2018),
www.nyc.gov/assets/ccrb/downloads/pdf/policy_pdf/annual_bi-annual/2018
CCRB_AnnualReport.pdf.

20. https://projects.propublica.org/nypd-unchecked-power/.

21. https://www.nytimes.com/2023/03/16/nyregion/nypd-discipline
-recommendations.html; Rules governing the NYPD Commissioner's final
approval over MOS Discipline: Section 434 of the New York City Charter;
Section 14-115 of the New York City Administrative Code; Section 75 of
the New York Civil Service Law.

22. https://www.casemine.com/judgement/us/591471efadd7b0493437600a.

23. https://projects.propublica.org/nypd-disciplinary-records/.

24. https://www.osc.state.ny.us/files/reports/osdc/pdf/report-6-2023.pdf.

25. https://www.nytimes.com/2018/02/19/nyregion/new-york-police-overtime
-pay-trial.html; https://abovethelaw.com/2018/03/collars-for-dollars-an
-unconstitutional-police-practice/.

26. https://www.nytimes.com/2018/03/19/nyregion/new-york-police-perjury
-promotions.html; https://www.nytimes.com/2018/02/14/nyregion/ccrb
-sexual-misconduct-police.html; https://www.cityandstateny.com/policy
/2019/10/how-the-nyc-charter-revision-questions-would-change-the-ccrb
/176778/.

CHAPTER 2: EXONERATED

1. https://nymag.com/news/features/establishments/68511/.

2. According to the Department of Justice, police officers kill about ten
thousand dogs every year. https://www.policinginstitute.org/wp-content
/uploads/2019/07/PF_Dogs_final_7.22.19.pdf.

3. https://www.nydailynews.com/2016/03/24/exclusive-nypd-cop-shoots-kills
   -bronx-familys-beloved-dog-in-incident-captured-on-video-warning
   -graphic-content/.

4. https://www.nypdmonitor.org/wp-content/uploads/2024/09/Discipline
   -Report.pdf.

5. Consolidated Laws of New York, chapter 71, title 7, article 33, section 1213,
   www.nysenate.gov/legislation/laws/VAT/1213.

6. https://ccrjustice.org/home/blog/2016/03/23/requiem-suspicious-bulge.

7. https://www.cbsnews.com/newyork/news/an-unconstitutional-overreach
   -cbs2-investigates-nypd-continuing-banned-practice-of-patrolling-private
   -buildings/.

8. Kevin D. Walsh, *The High Price of Unregulated Private Police Training in New
   Jersey* (Trenton: New Jersey Office of the State Comptroller, 2023), www.nj
   .gov/comptroller/news/docs/police_training_report.pdf.

9. "Current NYPD Members of Service," Civilian Complaint Review Board,
   www.nyc.gov/site/ccrb/policy/data-transparency-initiative-mos.page.
   (December, 2024 Access Date).

10. Edward Conlon, *Blue Blood* (New York: Riverhead, 2004), 257.

11. "DAO-DCT Disciplinary Case No. 2017-17005 states that in prior
    disciplinary cases, the NYPD has held that the use of profane remarks
    during stressful situations or while an officer is trying to get a chaotic
    situation under control, does not constitute misconduct." https://www.nyc
    .gov/assets/ccrb/downloads/pdf/closing-reports/202104639_Redacted
    ClosingReport.pdf.

12. https://www.nysenate.gov/legislation/laws/CPL/690.30.

13. "NYPD Commissioner Dermot Shea defends 'no knock' search warrant,"
    Anthony M. DeStefano. *Newsday*, April 15, 2021, www.newsday.com/news
    /new-york/nypd-commissioner-drmot-shea-no-knock-search-warrant-g35961.

CHAPTER 3: DISCOURTESIES AND OFFENSIVE LANGUAGE

1. https://www.investopedia.com/terms/r/regulatory-capture.asp; https://www
   .oxfordreference.com/display/10.1093/oi/authority.20110803100411608.

2. Daniel Carpenter and David A. Moss, eds., *Preventing Regulatory Capture:
   Special Interest Influence and How to Limit It* (New York: Cambridge
   University Press, 2014), www.tobinproject.org/sites/tobinproject.org/files
   /assets/Kwak%20-%20Cultural%20Capture%20and%20the%20Financial
   %20Crisis.pdf.

3. David Freeman Engstrom, "Corralling Capture," *Harvard Journal of Law
   and Public Policy* 36 (2013), web.archive.org/web/20201030171737/https://
   law.stanford.edu/wp-content/uploads/sites/default/files/publication/370256
   /doc/slspublic/corrralling_caputure.pdf.

4. NYPD Patrol Guide, 203-10 (Effective 08/01/13).

5. "Retired NYPD officer arrested in 105th Precinct bribery plot used racial epithets on the job, say CCRB complaints," Noah Goldberg. *New York Daily News*, May 12, 2021, www.nydailynews.com/2021/05/12/retired-nypd-officer-arrested-in-105th-precinct-bribery-plot-used-racial-epithets-on-the-job-say-ccrb-complaints.

6. Mark J. Lesko to the Honorable Cheryl L. Pollak, May 11, 2021, s3.documentcloud.org/documents/20705756/busch-et-al-detention-letter.pdf.

7. https://www.justice.gov/usao-edny/pr/former-nypd-police-officer-sentenced-97-months-imprisonment-bribery-and-drug#:~:text=Earlier%20today%2C%20in%20federal%20court,and%20attempting%20to%20transport%20heroin; Noah Goldberg, "Weepy ex-NYPD officer gets 8 years in federal prison in bribery, drug schemes," *New York Daily News*, last modified April 21, 2022, https://www.nydailynews.com/2022/04/20/weepy-ex-nypd-officer-gets-8-years-in-federal-prison-in-bribery-drug-schemes/.

8. Kirstan Conley, "WATCH: NYPD Sgt.'s filthy tirade captured in shocking cellphone video," *New York Post*, May 21, 2012, nypost.com/2012/05/21/watch-nypd-sgt-s-filthy-tirade-captured-in-shocking-cellphone-video.

9. https://s3.documentcloud.org/documents/4418987/nypd-cases-437.pdf

10. NYPD MOS Database Lookup, 2025.

11. https://www.nacole.org/police_oversight_by_jurisdiction_usa.

12. Tracey L. Meares, Tom R. Tyler, and Jacob Gardner, "Lawful or Fair? How Cops and Laypeople Perceive Good Policing," *Journal of Criminal Law and Criminology* 105, no. 2 (2015): 297–344, scholarlycommons.law.northwestern.edu/cgi/viewcontent.cgi?article=7558&context=jclc.

CHAPTER 4: ABUSE OF AUTHORITY

1. https://mhanational.org/issues/2022/mental-health-america-adult-data; https://www.nami.org/about-mental-illness/mental-health-by-the-numbers/.

2. https://bja.ojp.gov/sites/g/files/xyckuh186/files/media/document/learn-about-the-issues-transcript.pdf; https://www.tac.org/wp-content/uploads/2023/11/smi-in-jails-and-prisons.pdf; https://www.sciencedirect.com/science/article/abs/pii/S0160252717301954#:~:text=The%20Washington%20Post%2C%20which%20committed,et%20al.%2C%202015.

3. https://gothamist.com/news/nypd-used-body-bags-to-make-122-arrests-in-110-days.

4. https://www.nyc.gov/assets/oignypd/downloads/pdf/Reports/CIT_Report_01192017.pdf.

5. https://www.nyc.gov/assets/oignypd/downloads/pdf/Reports/CIT_Report_01192017.pdf.

6. Rich Calder, "Drug cocktail causes a sickening experience for EMT spit victims," *New York Post*, February 28, 2019, nypost.com/2019/02/28/drug-cocktail-causes-a-sickening-experience-for-emt-spit-victims.

7. https://www.nytimes.com/2024/05/21/health/psychiatric-restraint-forced
    -medication.html.

8. "How Rikers Island Became New York's Largest Mental Institution," Jan
    Ransom and Amy Julia Harris, *New York Times*, December 29, 2023, www
    .nytimes.com/2023/12/29/nyregion/nyc-rikers-homeless-mental-illness.html.

9. https://comptroller.nyc.gov/newsroom/longer-court-case-processing-times
    -inflate-nycs-jail-population-cost-taxpayers-nearly-1-billion-annually
    -comptroller-landers-report-reveals/.

10. Catia Sharp, "Jails: America's Biggest Mental Health Facilities," *HKS Student
    Policy Review*, July 30, 2018, ksr.hkspublications.org/2018/07/30/jails-mental
    -health-facilities.

11. https://www.nytimes.com/2018/02/14/nyregion/ccrb-sexual-misconduct
    -police.html.

12. Charles Campisi, *Blue on Blue: An Insider's Story of Good Cops Catching Bad
    Cops* (New York: Scribner, 2017), 73.

13. Campisi, Blue on Blue, p.74

14. *Annual Report 2018*, 17.

15. Brittany Arsiniega and Matthew Guariglia, "Police as Supercitizens," *Social
    Justice* 48, no. 4 (2021): 33–58, www.jstor.org/stable/27221470.

16. Dean Balsamini, "Police union slashes number of 'get out of jail free' cards
    issued," *New York Post*, last modified August 8, 2018, nypost.com/2018/01
    /21/police-union-slashes-number-of-get-out-of-jail-free-cards-issued.

17. Allison, Steele, "Police say don't confuse courtesy cards with a free pass,"
    Philadelphia Inquirer, June 7, 2010, www.inquirer.com/philly/news/local
    /20100607_Police_say_don_t_confuse_courtesy_cards_with_a_free_pass
    .html; An Sanok, "Recreation struggles to survive," *South Coast Today*, July 6,
    2007, www.southcoasttoday.com/story/news/2007/07/06/recreation-struggles
    -to-survive/52857625007.

18. Andrew Kuntz, "Corruption by Card: How Police Association Cards Allow
    Law Enforcement to Cloak Self-Dealing as Discretion" (New York: Center
    for the Advancement of Public Integrity, 2018), scholarship.law.columbia
    .edu/cgi/viewcontent.cgi?article=1018&context=public_integrity.

19. "Councilman Raps Extra Courtesies," *Los Angeles Times*, November 2, 1927, 22.

20. https://timesmachine.nytimes.com/timesmachine/1955/12/16/81883965.pdf
    ?pdf_redirect=true&ip=0; https://timesmachine.nytimes.com/timesmachine
    /1954/11/14/110072016.pdf?pdf_redirect=true&ip=0; https://timesmachine
    .nytimes.com/timesmachine/1954/11/30/84441069.pdf?pdf_redirect=true
    &ip=0; https://timesmachine.nytimes.com/timesmachine/1927/08/12
    /101505646.pdf?pdf_redirect=true&ip=0; https://timesmachine.nytimes.com
    /timesmachine/1959/04/27/80771577.pdf?pdf_redirect=true&ip=0.

21. https://www.nydailynews.com/2024/09/10/staten-island-cop-who-sued-nyc
    -over-courtesy-card-usage-settles-for-175k/.

CHAPTER 5: STOP-AND-FRISK

1. Terry v. Ohio, 392 U.S. 1, 16–17 (1968).
2. For boys, Goff et al., 2014; for girls: Epstein et al., 2017. https://pmc.ncbi
   .nlm.nih.gov/articles/PMC9248049/#:~:text=Multiple%20studies%
   20suggest%20that%20Black,et%20al.%2C%202017).
3. Philip Bump, "The facts about stop-and-frisk in New York City," *Washington
   Post*, September 21, 2016, www.washingtonpost.com/news/the-fix/wp/2016
   /09/21/it-looks-like-rudy-giuliani-convinced-donald-trump-that-stop-and
   -frisk-actually-works.
4. https://ccrjustice.org/files/CCR-Stop-and-Frisk-Fact-Sheet-2011.pdf.
5. Floyd v. City of New York, 861 F. Supp. 2d 274 (SDNY 2012);
   Taahira Thompson, "NYPD's Infamous Stop-and-Frisk Policy Found
   Unconstitutional," Leadership Conference Education Fund, August 21,
   2013, civilrights.org/edfund/resource/nypds-infamous-stop-and-frisk-policy
   -found-unconstitutional.
6. Nicholas K. Peart, "Why Is the N.Y.P.D. After Me?" *New York Times*,
   December 17, 2011, www.nytimes.com/2011/12/18/opinion/sunday/young
   -black-and-frisked-by-the-nypd.html.
7. https://ccrjustice.org/home/what-we-do/our-cases/floyd-et-al-v-city-new
   -york-et-al#:~:text=In%20a%20historic%20ruling%20on,racial%20profiling
   %20and%20unconstitutional%20stops.
8. https://www.nytimes.com/2024/09/05/nyregion/eric-adams-nypd-gun-units
   -illegal-stops.html.
9. Amanda Geller, Jeffrey, Fagan, Tom Tyler, and Bruce Link, "Aggressive
   Policing and the Mental Health of Young Urban Men," *American Journal
   of Public Health* 104, no. 12 (2014): 2321–27; Cynthia Golembeski and
   Robert Fullilove, "Criminal (In)Justice in the City and Its Associated Health
   Consequences," *American Journal of Public Health* 95, no. 10 (2005): 1701–6;
   Naomi F. Sugie and Kristin Turney, "Beyond Incarceration: Criminal Justice
   Contact and Mental Health," *American Sociological Review* 82, no. 4 (2017):
   719–43.
10. Rod K. Brunson and Ronald Weitzer, "Police Relations with Black and
    White Youths in Different Urban Neighborhoods," *Urban Affairs Review* 44,
    no. 6 (2009): 858–85.
11. Joscha Legewie and Jeffrey Fagan, "Aggressive Policing and the Educational
    Performance of Minority Youth," *American Sociological Review* 84, no. 2
    (2019), journals.sagepub.com/doi/full/10.1177/0003122419826020.
12. Terry v. Ohio, 392 US 1 (1968).
13. Danielle Paquette, "Guiliani: 'White police officers wouldn't be there if you
    weren't killing each other,'" *Washington Post*, November 23, 2014, www
    .washingtonpost.com/news/post-politics/wp/2014/11/23/giuliani-white
    -police-officers-wouldnt-be-there-if-you-werent-killing-each-other.

14. Nick Gass, "Giuliani: 'I saved a lot more black lives than Black Lives Matter,'" Politico, July 11, 2016, www.politico.com/story/2016/07/rudy -giuliani-black-lives-matter-225353.

15. Quint Forgey, "Bloomberg in hot water over 'stop-and-frisk' audio clip," Politico, last modified February 11, 2020, www.politico.com/news/2020 /02/11/michael-bloomberg-stop-and-frisk-clip-113902.

16. *Crime and Enforcement Activity in New York City (Jan 1–Dec 31, 2015)* (New York: NYPD), www1.nyc.gov/assets/nypd/downloads/pdf/analysis_and _planning/year_end_2015_enforcement_report.pdf.

17. Police Department, City of New York, *CompStat Report Covering the Week 8/26/2024 Through 9/1/2024* 31, no. 35, www1.nyc.gov/assets/nypd /downloads/pdf/crime_statistics/cs-en-us-city.pdf; https://www.nyc.gov /assets/nypd/downloads/pdf/crime_statistics/cs-en-us-city.pdf.

18. Alex Goldman and Emmanuel Dzotsi, "#128, The Crime Machine, Part II," October 12, 2018, in *Reply All*, produced by Gimlet, podcast, MP3 audio, 35:17, gimletmedia.com/shows/reply-all/n8hwl7.

19. Steven Lee Myers, "The New Police Commissioner: The Overview; Fire Commissioner to Take Over as Police Head," *New York Times*, March 29, 1996, www.nytimes.com/1996/03/29/nyregion/new-police-commissioner -overview-fire-commissioner-take-over-police-head.html.

20. https://crime-data-explorer.app.cloud.gov/pages/explorer/crime/crime-trend (accessed August 2022).

21. https://www.washingtonpost.com/news/the-fix/wp/2016/09/21/it-looks-like -rudy-giuliani-convinced-donald-trump-that-stop-and-frisk-actually-works/

22. Amanda Terkel, "Ray Kelly On Stop And Frisk: 'No Question' Violent Crime Will Rise If Program Is Stopped," HuffPost, last modified August 18, 2013, www.huffpost.com/entry/ray-kelly-stop-and-frisk_n_3776035.

23. Associated Press, "NYC mayor lambastes stop-and-frisk ruling," Politico, August 13, 2013, www.politico.com/story/2013/08/stop-and-frisk-michael -bloomberg-new-york-95474.html.

24. Yoav Gonen, "Bloomberg: 'We disproportionately stop whites too much and minorities too little' in stop-frisk checks," *New York Post*, June 28, 2013, nypost.com/2013/06/28/bloomberg-we-disproportionately-stop-whites-too -much-and-minorities-too-little-in-stop-frisk-checks.

25. *Adult Arrests 18 and Older: 2011–2020* (New York: New York State Division of Criminal Justice Services, 2021), www.criminaljustice.ny.gov/crimnet/ojsa /arrests/nyc.pdf.

26. "Full transcript: Ninth Democratic debate in Las Vegas," NBC News, February 20, 2020, www.nbcnews.com/politics/2020-election/full-transcript -ninth-democratic-debate-las-vegas-n1139546.

27. "Stop-and-Frisk Data," NYCLU, March 14, 2019, www.nyclu.org/en/stop -and-frisk-data.

28.   Todd S. Purdum, "The Perpetual Crime Wave Crests, and a City Shudders," *New York Times*, August 1, 1990, www.nytimes.com/1990/08/01/nyregion /the-perpetual-crime-wave-crests-and-a-city-shudders.html.

29.   Post Editorial Board, "Mayor de Blasio, do something about deaths in our streets," *New York Post*, last modified July 7, 2020, nypost.com/2020/07/06 /mayor-de-blasio-do-something-about-the-deaths-in-our-streets.

30.   New York City Mayor's Office of Operations, *Mayor's Management Report for Fiscal Year 2013* (September 2013), 6; www.nyc.gov/html/ops/downloads /pdf/pmmr2014/nypd.pdf.

31.   "PBA Statement on Bloomberg's Stop & Frisk Apology," Police Benevolent Association, November 17, 2019, www.nycpba.org/press-releases/2019/pba -on-bloombergs-stop-frisk-apology.

32.   https://nycpba.org/press-releases/2003/evidence-of-ticket-quotas-and-dont -blame-the-cop-campaign/; https://nycpba.org/press-releases/2003/ fewer-cops-more-summonses/.

33.   "PBA President Calls Stop and Frisk Quotas an Unnecessary Source of Friction with Communities," Police Benevolent Association, May 17, 2012, www.nycpba.org/press-releases/2012/pba-president-calls-stop-and-frisk -quotas-an-unnecessary-source-of-friction-with-communities.

34.   https://www.huffpost.com/entry/nypd-stop-and-frisk_n_4066335; https:// www.theguardian.com/world/2013/aug/12/stop-and-frisk-landmark-ruling

35.   Conlon, *Blue Blood*, 244.

36.   https://www.merriam-webster.com/dictionary/top%20brass#:~:text=informal ,that%20no%20action%20is%20necessary.

37.   Chapter 6: "NYPD and the Media: Curbing Criticism." Eterno and Silverman, *The Crime Numbers Game*.

CHAPTER 6: POLICING IN HD

1.   Elliot Harkavy, "In View: Body-Worn Camera Triggering Technologies," Body-Worn Camera Training & Technical Assistance, bwctta.com/resources /commentary/view-body-worn-camera-auto-triggering-technologies. (accessed October 2022).

2.   *Taser Use in CCRB Complaints, 2014–2017* (New York: Civilian Complaint Review Board, 2019), pg. 11, www1.nyc.gov/assets/ccrb/downloads/pdf/policy _pdf/issue_based/20191205_TaserReport.pdf.

3.   *Strengthening Accountability: The Impact of the NYPD's Body-Worn Camera Program on CCRB Investigations* (New York: Civilian Complaint Review Board, 2020), www1.nyc.gov/assets/ccrb/downloads/pdf/policy_pdf/issue _based/20200227_BWCReport.pdf.

4.   Miguel Richards, "How Police Body Cams Failed Us," *New York Times*, December 13, 2023, www.nytimes.com/2023/12/13/magazine/police-body -cameras-miguel-richards.html. Body cams "may do more to serve police interests than those of the public they are sworn to protect."

CHAPTER 7: NOTORIOUS

1. https://data.cityofnewyork.us/Public-Safety/NYPD-Arrest-Data-Year-to-Date-/uip8-fykc/about_data; https://www.vitalcitynyc.org/articles/the-truth-about-youth-crime-rates-in-nyc; *Adult Arrests 18 and Older: 2011–2020*; https://www.criminaljustice.ny.gov/crimnet/ojsa/arrests/nyc.pdf New York Police Department Fiscal Budget 2019; https://council.nyc.gov/budget/wp-content/uploads/sites/54/2018/03/FY19-New-York-Police-Department.pdf.
2. NYPD MOS Lookup (November 2024).
3. http://www.nydailynews.com/new-york/nypd-cops-probed-thefts-no-warrant-drug-raids-article-1.1405353.
4. Public NYPD MOS Database, November 2024, https://www.50-a.org/officer/LQSM.
5. Public NYPD MOS Database, November 2024.
6. https://www.nydailynews.com/2022/03/06/settlements-top-1m-for-much-sued-nypd-sergeant-accused-of-unwarranted-stops-arrests-and-raids/.
7. https://www.nydailynews.com/2013/07/22/criminal-cases-in-jeopardy-as-nypd-cops-probed-in-thefts-no-warrant-drug-raids/.
8. https://www.50-a.org/officer/LPQK.
9 https://www.50-a.org/officer/LPQK.
10. https://ecf.nysd.uscourts.gov/doc1/12714132489 Gumbs SDNY Settlement available via PACER Case 1:07-cv-02160-DC.
11. Joseph, "NYPD Detective with a Shady Past."
12. www1.nyc.gov/assets/ccrb/downloads/pdf/investigations_pdf/pg208-05-strip-search.pdf.
13. [Public NYPD MOS Database, May 2022] https://www.50-a.org/officer/DHWT.
14. [Public CCRB MOS Database, May 2022].
15. https://legalaidnyc.org/law-enforcement-look-up/.
16. Ganeva, "NYPD's Culture of Impunity Sees an Officer Repeatedly Accused of Physical and Sexual Abuse Rising Through the Ranks." https://theintercept.com/2020/07/06/nypd-culture-of-impunity/.

CHAPTER 8: THE BLACK HOLE

1. Title 38-A Civilian Complaint Review Board, New York City Rules, these rules have been amended multiple times since 2018.
2. https://www.nyc.gov/assets/operations/downloads/pdf/mmr2023/ccrb.pdf.
3. CCRB Annual Reports 2019, 2023.
4. https://www.nyc.gov/assets/ccrb/downloads/pdf/about_pdf/news/press-releases/2022/PR_2022_Rule_Changes_October2022.pdf.

5. https://www.nytimes.com/2021/10/29/nyregion/nypd-officer-hitman-sentenced.html; https://www.justice.gov/usao-edny/pr/two-new-york-city-police-department-detectives-and-two-others-charged-paycheck.
6. Campisi, *Blue on Blue*. https://www.nyc.gov/assets/ccpc/downloads/pdf/Performance-Study-The-Internal-Affairs-Bureaus-Integrity-Testing-Program-March-2000.pdf; https://www.nydailynews.com/2017/08/16/disgraced-cop-sacked-for-his-20-fib-in-integrity-test-sues-nypd-in-bid-to-get-his-dismissal-reversed/; Campisi, Blue on Blue, 112–126.
7. *Best Practice: Citywide Merchandise Licensing Program* (New York: New York City Global Partners, 2010), www1.nyc.gov/assets/globalpartners/downloads/pdf/NYC_Tourism%20Marketing_CMLP.pdf.
8. NYC City Charter Section 440 https://www.nyc.gov/html/ccrb/downloads/pdf/enabling_legislation.pdf.
9. https://www.nyc.gov/assets/ccrb/downloads/pdf/policy_pdf/annual_bi-annual/2019CCRB_AnnualReport.pdf, page 8.
10. *Annual Report 2019* (New York: Civilian Complaint Review Board, 2019), www1.nyc.gov/assets/ccrb/downloads/pdf/policy_pdf/annual_bi-annual/2019CCRB_AnnualReport.pdf.
11. CCRB 2019 Annual Report pg. 31; CCRB 2020 Annual Report pg. 27.
12. *James Blake Fellow Report*, 10.
13. Conlon, Blue Blood, pg. 490.
14. https://www.nyc.gov/site/ccrb/policy/annual-bi-annual-reports.page, 2020, 2021, 2023 Annual Reports.
15. https://www.documentcloud.org/documents/20692760-ccrb-policy-unit-flip-memo-2020.
16. https://www.nyc.gov/site/ccrb/about/board/salvatore-carcaterra.page.
17. https://www.nyc.gov/site/ccrb/about/board/frank-dwyer.page; https://consentdecree.baltimorecity.gov/files/whiteford-taylor-and-prestonpdf.
18. https://www.cbsnews.com/newyork/news/the-hard-conversation-jennifer-jones-austin-of-the-federation-of-protestant-welfare-agencies-and-the-new-york-urban-leagues-arva-rice-on-nypd-reforms/.
19. https://www.nyc.gov/assets/ccrb/downloads/pdf/about_pdf/apu_mou.pdf.
20. https://www.propublica.org/article/nypd-commissioner-edward-caban-police-discipline-retention-eric-adams.

CHAPTER 9: THE ACADEMY

1. "New York City Police Academy," Perkins&Will, perkinswill.com/project/new-york-city-police-academy. Accessed 2022.
2. https://web.archive.org/web/20240320233650/; https://www.independentpanelreportnypd.net/assets/report.pdf.
3. Ta-Nehisi Coates, "Worst Movie of the Decade," *The Atlantic*, December 30, 2009, www.theatlantic.com/entertainment/archive/2009/12/worst-movie-of-the-decade/32759.

4. Eli Rosenberg, "Stonewall Inn Named National Monument, a First for the Gay Rights Movement," *New York Times*, June 25, 2016, www.nytimes.com /2016/06/25/nyregion/stonewall-inn-named-national-monument-a-first-for -gay-rights-movement.html; http://www.nytimes.com/2016/06/25/nyregion /stonewall-inn-named-national-monument-a-first-for-gay-rights-movement .html.

CHAPTER 10: FROM IRELAND TO THE NYPD

1. Tom Wolfe, *The Bonfire of the Vanities*, 43.
2. Ian N. Gregory, Niall A. Cunningham, Paul S. Ell, Christopher D. Lloyd, Ian G. Shuttleworth, *Troubled Geographies: A Spatial History of Religion and Society in Ireland* (Bloomington, IN: University of Indiana Press, 2013).
3. Conn Malachi Hallinan, *The Subjugation and Division of Ireland: Testing Ground for Colonial* Policy, Crime and Social Justice, No. 8 (fall-winter 1977), 53.
4. Hallinan, 53.
5. M. S. Kumar and L. A. Scanlon, "Ireland and Irishness: The Contextuality of Postcolonial Identity," *Annals of the Association of American Geographers* 109, no. 1 (2019): 202–22, pureadmin.qub.ac.uk/ws/files/153662440/Ireland _and_Irishness_The_Contextuality_of_Postcolonial_Identity.pdf; Martin Forker, "The use of the 'cartoonist's armoury' in manipulating public opinion: anti-Irish imagery in 19th century British and American periodicals," *Journal of Irish Studies* 27 (2012): 58–71.
6. https://hilo.hawaii.edu/campuscenter/hohonu/volumes/documents/From OppressiontoNationalism-TheIrishPenalLawsof1695SamanthaHowell.pdf.
7. https://defector.com/let-me-tell-you-about-my-secret-pride-irish-dance.
8. Noel Ignatiev, *How the Irish Became White* (London: Routledge, 1995), 41.
9. Samantha Howell, "From Oppression to Nationalism: The Irish Penal Laws of 1695," *Hohonu* 14 (2016): 21–23, hilo.hawaii.edu/campuscenter/hohonu /volumes/documents/FromOppressiontoNationalism-TheIrishPenalLawsof 1695SamanthaHowell.pdf.
10. Hallinan, 53.
11. Ignatiev, *How the Irish Became White*, 2.
12. Blessing, Patrick J. (1980). "Irish". In Thernstrom, Stephan (ed.). *Harvard Encyclopedia of American Ethnic Groups*. Cambridge, MA: Harvard University Press, 528; Rouse, Parke Jr. (1992). *The Great Wagon Road: From Philadelphia to the South* (1st ed.). Dietz Press.
13. "Indentured Servants in the U.S.," PBS, www.pbs.org/opb/historydetectives /feature/indentured-servants-in-the-us; "History and Demographics of the Irish Coming to America," Macaulay Honors College at CUNY, macaulay .cuny.edu/seminars/gardner-irish/articles/h/i/s/History_and_Demographics _of_the_Irish_Coming_to_America_248e.html. (accessed 2022).

14. https://www.nantucketatheneum.org/wp-content/uploads/Irish-Immigration
-to-America.pdf; https://www.ucc.ie/en/emigre/history/.

15. Tim Hitchcock, "A Population History of London," Proceedings of the Old
Bailey, Autumn 2023, www.oldbaileyonline.org/static/Population-history
-of-london.jsp#a1715-1760 (accessed 2022); "Population 1801 to 2021,"
Office of National Statistics, data.london.gov.uk/dataset/historic-census
-population; Tertius Chandler, *Four Thousand Years of Urban Growth: An
Historical Census* (Lewiston, NY: Edwin Mellen Press, 1987).

16. Nick Pinto, "The Point of Order," *The New York Times*, January 18, 2015,
www.nytimes.com/2015/01/18/magazine/the-point-of-order.html.

17. Pinto, "The Point of Order."

18. https://www.nytimes.com/2014/04/16/nyregion/sir-robert-peels-nine
-principles-of-policing.html; https://web.archive.org/web/20140428135157
/http://www.nyc.gov/html/nypd/html/administration/commissioners_corner
.shtml (accessed 2022).

19. Pinto, "The Point of Order."

20. William G. Powderly, "How Infection Shaped History: Lessons from
the Irish Famine," *Transactions of the American Clinical and Climatological
Association* 130 (2019): 127–35, www.ncbi.nlm.nih.gov/pmc/articles/PMC
6735970; "Fleeing the Famine: North America and Irish Refugees,
1845–1851," page 1. *publisher.abc-clio.com*; https://www.bbc.com/news/world
-us-canada-19892837.

21. https://www.archives.gov/publications/prologue/2017/winter/irish-births#
:~:text=The%20online%20database%20shows%208%2C075,among%202
%2C883%20total%20reported%20fatalities.; https://teachdemocracy.org
/index.php?option=com_content&view=article&id=805#:~:text=Between
%201845%20and%201855%20more,crops%2C%20leaving%20millions%20
without%20food.

22. Mark Holan, "Ireland's Famine Children 'Born at Sea,'" *Prologue Magazine*
49, no. 4 (Winter 2017–2018), www.archives.gov/publications/prologue
/2017/winter/irish-births; Stephan Thernstrom, ed., *Harvard Encyclopedia of
American Ethnic Groups* (Cambridge: Belknap Press, 1980), archive.org/details
/harvardencyclope00ther/page/529/mode/2up?view=theater. (accessed 2022).

23. Hallinan, 57.

24. Livia Gershon, "How Stereotypes of the Irish Evolved from 'Criminals' to
Cops," History, last modified June 1, 2023, www.history.com/news/how
-stereotypes-of-the-irish-evolved-from-criminals-to-cops.

25. Kevin Cullen, "Erin go Barney," *Boston Globe*, March 15, 2011, archive
.boston.com/news/local/massachusetts/articles/2011/03/15/boston
_celebrates_first_irish_police_officer_in_us; "Barney McGinnisken" *Boston
Pilot*, October 1851. https://nleomf.org/barney-mcginniskin-the-first-irish
-american-cop/.

26. "Young Friends of Ireland," *New York Times*, March 20, 1855, timesmachine
.nytimes.com/timesmachine/1855/03/20/87573760.pdf.

27. Patrick Markey, "The beat goes on: new breed of Irish cops in New York," *The Irish Echo*, February 16, 2011, group.irishecho.com/2011/02/the-beat-goes-on-new-breed-of-irish-cops-in-new-york-2.

28. Daniel J. Czitrom, *New York Exposed: The Gilded Age Police Scandal that Launched the Progressive Era* (New York: Oxford University Press, 2016), 33.

29. Czitrom, *New York Exposed*, 35.

30. Lawrence M. Friedman, *A History of American Law*, 4th ed. (Oxford: Oxford University Press, 2019), 3.

31. *Total and Foreign-born Population, New York City, 1700–2000* (New York: New York City Department of City Planning Population Division), www1.nyc.gov/assets/planning/download/pdf/data-maps/nyc-population/historical-population/1790-2000_nyc_total_foreign_birth.pdf; Czitrom, *New York Exposed*, xii; https://virtualny.ashp.cuny.edu/EncyNYC/Irish.html; https://newspapers.bc.edu/?a=d&d=irishliterary20010901-01.2.34&e=-------en-20--1--txt-txIN-------.

32. Lady Morgan, *Florence Macarthy: An Irish Tale* (London: Henry Colburn, 1818), 35.

33. https://time.com/4384963/nypd-scandal-history/, https://www.nytimes.com/1900/02/02/archives/gambling-in-brooklyn-chief-devery-as-reported-will-again-make.html.

34. Street Justice, A History of Police Violence in New York City, Marilynn S. Johnson, pg. 51.

35. https://sabr.org/bioproj/person/bill-devery/#sdendnote2sym; Island of Vice: Theodore Roosevelt's Quest to Clean Up Sin-Loving New York, Richard Zacks, p. 25.

36. https://www.americanheritage.com/well-what-are-you-going-do-about-it.

37. https://www.nydailynews.com/2017/01/08/a-look-at-the-bombastic-corrupt-tammany-hall-police-commissioner-william-big-bill-devery/.

38. https://guides.lib.jjay.cuny.edu/nypd/Commissioners.

39. John Timoney, "More Than the Usual Suspects: The Complex and Colorful NYPD," *Observer*, June 19, 2000, observer.com/2000/06/more-than-the-usual-suspects-the-complex-and-colorful-nypd.

40. Richard Bessel and Clive Emsley. Patterns of Provocation: Police and Public Disorder. (2000), 87.

41. https://www.urbandictionary.com/define.php?term=Irish%20welfare; https://www.glocktalk.com/threads/police-slang-in-your-area-what-you-got.1293001/page-5.

42. Nathan Glazer and Daniel P. Moynihan, *Beyond the Melting Pot: The Negroes, Puerto Ricans, Jews, Italians, and Irish of New York City* (Cambridge: MIT Press, 1963), archive.org/stream/beyondmeltingpot1963glaz/beyondmeltingpot1963glaz_djvu.txt.

43. *Crime and the Cities*, May 17, 1964 (TV program), Behind the Shield, 143.

44. Tom Wolfe, *The Bonfire of the Vanities*, (New York: Farrar, Straus and Giroux, 1987), 43; Dwight Garner, "Tom Wolfe Kept a Close, Comical and

Astonished Eye on America," *New York Times*, May 15, 2018, www.nytimes
.com/2018/05/15/books/tom-wolfe-appraisal.html.

45. Independent research done examining dozens of NYPD Commissioner
obituaries through the New York Times Archive.

46. Saki Knafo, "Bridging the Divide Between the Police and the Policed," *The
New Yorker*, April 28, 2021, www.newyorker.com/news/our-local
-correspondents/bridging-the-divide-between-the-police-and-the-policed.

47. The Cultural Geography of the United States, Zelinsky, 20, 23, 24, 25, 28, 127.

48. *Final Report of the President's Task Force on 21st Century Policing Report*
(Washington, DC: Office of Community Oriented Policing Services, 2015),
cops.usdoj.gov/pdf/taskforce/taskforce_finalreport.pdf.

49. *CompStat: Its Origins, Evolution, and Future in Law Enforcement Agencies*
(Washington, DC: Police Research Forum, 2013), vii, bja.ojp.gov/sites/g/files
/xyckuh186/files/Publications/PERF-Compstat.pdf.

50. Ali Winston, "Stationed Overseas, but Solving Crimes in New York City,"
New York Times, August 21, 2018, www.nytimes.com/2018/08/21/nyregion
/terrorism-nypd-intelligence-crime.html.

CHAPTER 11: TOUGH ON CRIME

1. Maggie Koerth and Amelia Thomson-DeVeaux, "Many Americans Are
Convinced Crime Is Rising in the U.S. They're Wrong," FiveThirtyEight,
August 3, 2020, fivethirtyeight.com/features/many-americans-are-convinced
-crime-is-rising-in-the-u-s-theyre-wrong.

2. https://www.nyc.gov/site/nypd/news/p0527/nypd-citywide-crime-statistics
-august-2024.

3. John A. Eterno and Eli B. Silverman, *The Crime Numbers Game: Management
by Manipulation* (London: Routledge, 2012), 26.

4. Franklin E. Zimring, "The City that Became Safe: New York and the Future
of Crime Control" (working paper, Joseph and Gwendolyn Straus Institute for
the Advanced Study of Law & Justice, New York University School of Law,
New York, 2011), www.law.nyu.edu/sites/default/files/siwp/WP9Zimring.pdf.

5. *Seven Major Felony Offenses*, NYPD. (accessed 2022) www1.nyc.gov/assets
/nypd/downloads/pdf/analysis_and_planning/historical-crime-data/seven
-major-felony-offenses-2000-2021.pdf.

6. https://kinginstitute.stanford.edu/wallace-george-corley-jr.

7. Gabriel Sherman, *The Loudest Voice in the Room: How the Brilliant, Bombastic
Roger Ailes Built Fox News—and Divided a Nation* (New York: Random
House, 2014).

8. "Does Treatment Work?" PBS, www.pbs.org/wgbh/pages/frontline/shows
/drugs/buyers/doitwork.html. (accessed 2022).

9. Dan Baum, "Legalize It All: How to Win the War on Drugs," *Harper's
Magazine*, April 2016, harpers.org/archive/2016/04/legalize-it-all.

10. John Schwartz, "Seven Things About Ronald Reagan You Won't Hear at the Reagan Library GOP Debate," The Intercept, September 16, 2015, theintercept.com/2015/09/16/seven-things-reagan-wont-mentioned-tonight -gops-debate; Reagan Library Campaign Travel Summary, July 19, 1980– November 4, 1980 (provided directly from Reagan Library).

11. Ian Haney-Lopez, "The racism at the heart of the Reagan presidency," Salon, January 11, 2014, www.salon.com/2014/01/11/the_racism_at_the_heart_of _the_reagan_presidency.

12. Daniel S. Lucks, "Op-Ed: Donald Trump, a True Reagan Republican," *Los Angeles Times*, July 19, 2020, www.latimes.com/opinion/story/2020-07-19 /ronald-reagans-racism-cleared-the-way-for-trump.

13. "Politic Talk: The 'Wallace Vote,'" *Washington Post*, April 5, 1980, www .washingtonpost.com/archive/politics/1980/04/05/politic-talk-the-wallace -vote/5d0e9097-785c-4f46-abf7-1be02233ba76; Joel Kotkin, "The Reagan Democrats Return," *Wall Street Journal*, June 9, 1998, www.wsj.com/articles /SB897338802645399000.

14. "'Lock the S.O.B.s Up': Joe Biden and the Era of Mass Incarceration," Sheryl Gay Stolberg and Astead W. Herndon, *New York Times*, June 25, 2019, www.nytimes.com/2019/06/25/us/joe-biden-crime-laws.html.

15. Christopher Patrella, "On Stone Mountain," *Boston Review*, March 30, 2016, bostonreview.net/articles/christopher-petrella-stone-mountain-white -supremacy-modern-democratic-party.

16. https://www.presidency.ucsb.edu/documents/address-accepting-the -presidential-nomination-the-democratic-national-convention-new-york.

17. *Violent Crime Control and Law Enforcement Act of 1994—Conference Report*, Congressional Record 140, no. 122, August 23, 1994, www.govinfo.gov /content/pkg/CREC-1994-08-23/html/CREC-1994-08-23-pt1-PgS16.htm.

18. *Violent Crime Control and Law Enforcement Act of 1994: U.S. Department of Justice Fact Sheet* (Washington, DC: Department of Justice, 1994), www .ncjrs.gov/txtfiles/billfs.txt.

19. *Violent Crime Control and Law Enforcement Act of 1994: U.S. Department of Justice Fact Sheet*; Violent Crime Control and Law Enforcement Act of 1994, P. L. No. 103–322, 108 Stat. 1796 (1994), www.congress.gov/103/statute /STATUTE-108/STATUTE-108-Pg1796.pdf.

20. "'Lock the S.O.B.s Up.'"; https://ewuarexosayande.medium.com/biden owes -black-voters-a-police-reform-executive-order-as-an-act-of-redemption -2da9dd3e2970.

21. Gary Fields, "White House Czar Calls for End to 'War on Drugs,'" *Wall Street Journal*, May 14, 2009, www.wsj.com/articles/SB124225891527617397.

22. https://www.washingtonpost.com/politics/2020/06/07/over-past-60-years -more-spending-police-hasnt-necessarily-meant-less-crime/, "Police cannot and do not prevent crime." Police for the Future, David Bayley. https://www .reuters.com/legal/government/police-are-not-primarily-crime-fighters

-according-data-2022-11-02/#:~:text=In%202016%2C%20a%20group%20
of,Studies%20and%20Business%20Ethics%20Department.

23.   https://crime-data-explorer.app.cloud.gov/pages/explorer/crime/crime-trend
       (accessed August 2022); newer FBI Crime Data link: https://cde.ucr.cjis.gov
       /LATEST/webapp/#/pages/home.

24.   Politico Staff, "Full text: 2017 Donald Trump inauguration speech
       transcript," Politico, January 20, 2017, www.politico.com/story/2017/01/full
       -text-donald-trump-inauguration-speech-transcript-233907.

25.   https://www.reuters.com/article/us-usa-crime-fbi/violent-crime-in-u-s-rose
       -in-2016-vs-2015-justice-department-idUSKCN1C025V/.FBI UCR Crime
       Data (Access Date August 2022).

26.   FBI UCR Crime Data (Access Date August 2022).

27.   FBI UCR Crime Data (Access Date August 2022).

28.   Justin McCarthy, "Perceptions of Increased U.S. Crime Highest Since 1993,"
       Gallup, November 13, 2020, news.gallup.com/poll/323996/perceptions
       -increased-crime-highest-1993.aspx.

29.   Martin Kaste, "Nationwide Crime Spike Has Law Enforcement Retooling
       Its Approach," NPR, July 1, 2015, www.npr.org/2015/07/01/418555852
       /nationwide-crime-spike-has-law-enforcement-retooling-their-approach.

30.   Ashley Gold, "Why had the murder rate in some US cities suddenly spiked?"
       BBC News, June 5, 2015, www.bbc.com/news/world-us-canada-32995911.;
       https://www.cnn.com/2015/06/02/us/crime-in-america/index.html

31.   https://www.nytimes.com/2015/09/01/us/murder-rates-rising-sharply-in
       -many-us-cities.html.

32.   The study was sponsored by the United States Department of Health and
       Human Services and United States Department of Justice. Margaret T.
       Gordon and Linda Heath, "Reactions to crime: Institutions react: The news
       business, crime, and fear," *Sage Criminal Justice System Annals* 16 (1981):
       227–50, psycnet.apa.org/record/1982-29994-001; https://www.ojp.gov/ncjrs
       /virtual-library/abstracts/news-business-crime-and-fear-reactions
       -crime-p-227-250-1981-dan.; Koerth and Thomson-DeVeaux, "Many
       Americans Are Convinced Crime Is Rising in the U.S. They're Wrong."

33.   https://bjs.ojp.gov/content/pub/pdf/bgpcdes.pdf; https://www.themarshall
       project.org/2023/07/13/fbi-crime-rates-data-gap-nibrs.

34.   *2021 Year-End Crime Report: Crime, Computer-Aided Dispatched (CAD)
       Events and Community Feedback* (Seattle: Seattle Police Department, 2022),
       www.seattle.gov/Documents/Departments/Police/Reports/2021_SPD
       _CRIME_REPORT_FINAL.pdf.

35.   *2019 Annual Report* (Towson: Baltimore County Police Department, 2020),
       resources.baltimorecountymd.gov/Documents/Police/2020pdfs/2019
       annualreport.pdf.

36.   "Violent Crime Decreases Significantly Since Operation Legend," Kansas
       City Missouri Police Department, August 25, 2020, www.kcpd.org/media
       /news-releases/violent-crime-decreases-significantly-since-operation-legend.

37. *CompStat Report Covering the Week 8/26/2024 Through 9/1/2024.*

38. https://www.pacificresearch.org/all-crime-is-local-why-national-crime-statistics-dont-matter/; https://ucr.fbi.gov/crime-in-the-u.s/2019/crime-in-the-u.s.-2019/topic-pages/methodology#:~:text=Following%20audit%20standards%20established%20by,procedures%20once%20every%203%20years; Weihua Li, "What Can the FBI Data Say About Crime in 2021? It's Too Unreliable to Tell," Marshall Project, June 14, 2022, www.themarshallproject.org/2022/06/14/what-did-fbi-data-say-about-crime-in-2021-it-s-too-unreliable-to-tell; https://www.newsweek.com/fbi-crime-data-violence-biden-trump-1911383.

39. Tim Hrenchir, "News conference highlights decreased crime, increased 'sense of hope' in Topeka community," *Topeka Capital-Journal*, last modified October 11, 2021, www.cjonline.com/story/news/2021/10/11/news-conference-spotlights-decreased-crime-topeka-shawnee-county/6090902001.

40. Tim Hrenchir, "News conference highlights decreased crime, increased 'sense of hope' in Topeka community," *Topeka Capital-Journal*, last modified October 11, 2021, www.cjonline.com/story/news/2021/10/11/news-conference-spotlights-decreased-crime-topeka-shawnee-county/6090902001.

41. Tim Hrenchir, "News conference highlights decreased crime, increased 'sense of hope' in Topeka community," *Topeka Capital-Journal*, last modified October 11, 2021, www.cjonline.com/story/news/2021/10/11/news-conference-spotlights-decreased-crime-topeka-shawnee-county/6090902001.

42. API Team, "Personal News Cycle study methodology and background," American Press Institute, March 17, 2014, www.americanpressinstitute.org/publications/reports/survey-research/personal-news-cycle-methodology.

43. https://www.nature.com/articles/s41562-024-02067-4.

44. Jerry Ratcliffe, "Year-to-date comparisons and why we should stop doing them," Jerry Ratcliffe: Crime and Policing, July 13, 2017, www.jratcliffe.net/post/year-to-date-comparisons-and-why-we-should-stop-doing-them.

45. Larry Celona and Jorge Fitz-Gibbon, "Crime up 60 percent in the past week, NYPD stats show," *New York Post*, last modified February 7, 2022, nypost.com/2022/02/07/crime-up-60-percent-citywide-in-the-past-week-nypd-stats; https://www.nbcnews.com/news/us-news/inside-look-system-cut-crime-new-york-75-percent-n557031; Maple, *The Crime Fighter*; https://nymag.com/intelligencer/2018/03/the-crime-fighting program-that-changed-new-york-forever.html.

46. Jack Maple, *The Crime Fighter: Putting the Bad Guys Out of Business* (New York: Doubleday, 1999), 93.

47. From surveys conducted by Eterno and Silverman throughout 2000s of then-current and former NYPD Captains, Eterno and Silverman, *The Crime Numbers Game*, 111.

48. Eterno and Silverman, *The Crime Numbers Game*, 109.

49. "A Little Computing Money for Cops," *Today in Montclair, 94611*, December 13, 2009, montclairoak.com/2009/12/13/a-little-computing-money

-for-cops; *CompStat: Its Origins, Evolution, and Future in Law Enforcement Agencies*; https://www.ojp.gov/ncjrs/virtual-library/abstracts/compstat -los-angeles-police-department; https://www.kqed.org/news/96767/bratton -report-a-serious-indictment-of-oakland-police-department; https://www .chicagopolice.org/statistics-data/statistical-reports/#:~:text=Since%202011 %2C%20the%20Chicago%20Police,similarities%20between%20Comp Stat%20and%20UCR; https://nopdnews.com/post/august-2016/sneak -preview-nopd-replacing-current-comstat-proc/ https://bja.ojp.gov/sites/g /files/xyckuh186/files/Publications/PERF-Compstat.pdf; https://www.miami -police.org/field_operations.html#:~:text=FOD%20also%20manages%20 the%20COMPSTAT,Auxiliary/Reserve%20Police%20Officer%20program.

50. https://urbanomnibus.net/2018/06/the-compstat-evangelist-consultant -world-tour/; FBI UCR Crime Data Explorer (access date January 2025) https://cde.ucr.cjis.gov/.

51. Robert Zink, "The Trouble with Compstat," *The PBA Magazine*, Summer 2004, web.archive.org/web/20040822141857/http://www.nycpba.org /publications/mag-04-summer/compstat.html.

CHAPTER 12: BROKEN BONES AND STITCHES

1. https://ballotpedia.org/New_York_City_Ballot_Question_2,_Civilian_ Complaint_Review_Board_Charter_Amendment_(November_2019).
2. https://www.nytimes.com/2018/03/19/nyregion/new-york-police-perjury -promotions.html.
3. [Public NYPD MOS Database, July 2022].
4. [Public NYPD MOS Database, July 2022].
5. https://www.nyc.gov/html/ccrb/downloads/pdf/pg203-08-making-false -statements.pdf (Accessed December 2024).
6. Former NYPD commissioner Bill Bratton, *The Profession: A Memoir of Policing in America* (New York: Penguin Press, 2021), 359; https://www .latinojustice.org/en/pressreport/shielded-accountability-how-nypd-officers -get-away-lying-ccrb.
7. https://www.latinojustice.org/sites/default/files/2023-08/CCRB%20 Report_v4_4-9%20%2811%29.pdf.
8. Rocco Parascandola, "NYPD quietly shuts down controversial trespass program," *New York Daily News*, last modified October 2, 2020, www .nydailynews.com/new-york/nyc-crime/ny-nypd-trespass-tactic-ended -20201002-abh5q5nanzeu3enk53q2hy7dzy-story.html; "Settlement Will End Unconstitutional NYPD Stops, Frisks and Arrests in Clean Halls Buildings," NYCLU, February 2, 2017, www.nyclu.org/en/press-releases /settlement-will-end-unconstitutional-nypd-stops-frisks-and-arrests-clean -halls.
9. *Local Law 25 of 2018 Report* (New York: Mayor's Office of Criminal Justice, 2021), criminaljustice.cityofnewyork.us/wp-content/uploads/2021/02/LL25

-Warrants-Report-CY2020-.pdf; https://criminaljustice.cityofnewyork.us
/wp-content/uploads/2023/03/CY-2022-LL25-Warrants-Report.pdf.

10. "Stop-and-Frisk Data"; "NYCLU Releases Report Analyzing NYPD
Stop-and-Frisk Data," ACLU, March 14, 2019, www.aclu.org/press-releases
/nyclu-releases-report-analyzing-nypd-stop-and-frisk-data.

11. Gersh Kuntzman, "NYPD Targets Blacks and Latinos for 'Jaywalking'
Tickets," *Streetsblog NYC*, January 8, 2020, nyc.streetsblog.org/2020/01/08
/nypd-targets-blacks-and-latinos-for-jaywalking-tickets; Gersh Kuntzman,
"NYPD's Racial Bias in 'Jaywalking' Tickets Continues into 2020,"
Streetsblog NYC, May 7, 2020, nyc.streetsblog.org/2020/05/07/nypds-racial
-bias-in-jaywalking-tickets-continues-into-2020; https://www.nyc.gov/assets
/ccrb/downloads/pdf/policy_pdf/issue_based/CCRB_YouthReport.pdf.

12. "Article 240—NY Penal Law," Law Firm of Andrew M. Stengel, ypdcrime
.com/penal.law/article240.php#p240.20. (accessed 2022).

13. *Article 181: Protection of Public Health Generally*, NYC Department of
Health. www1.nyc.gov/assets/doh/downloads/pdf/about/healthcode/health
-code-article181.pdf.

14. Shaun Ossei-Owusu, "Police Quotas," *New York University Law Review* 96
(May 2021): 529–605, www.nyulawreview.org/wp-content/uploads/2021/05
/Ossei-Owusu.pdf.

15. Joel Rose, "Despite Laws and Lawsuits, Quota-Based Policing Lingers,"
NPR, April 4, 2015, www.npr.org/2015/04/04/395061810/despite-laws-and
-lawsuits-quota-based-policing-lingers.

16. Saki Knafo, "A Black Police Officer's Fight Against the NYPD," *New York
Times*, February 21, 2016, www.nytimes.com/2016/02/21/magazine/a-black
-police-officers-fight-against-the-nypd.html; FindLaw Staff, "New York
Consolidated Laws, Labor Law—LAB § 215-a. Discrimination against
employees for failure to meet certain ticket quotas," FindLaw, last modified
January 1, 2021, codes.findlaw.com/ny/labor-law/lab-sect-215-a.html;
https://www.nbcnewyork.com/news/local/nypd-quota-tickets-summonses
-minority-nyc-neighborhoods/1823761/.

17. https://taser.com/?; https://www.nyc.gov/assets/ccrb/downloads/pdf/policy
_pdf/issue_based/20191205_TaserReport.pdf; https://abc11.com/taser-stun
-gun-deaths-nc-nationwide-raleigh-police/12719372/.

18. Greg B. Smith, "De Blasio's 'Stalled' Pet NYPD Neighborhood Policing
Plan Draws Outside Look," The City, July 23, 2020, www.thecity.nyc/2020/7
/23/21336402/de-blasios-nypd-neighborhood-policing-plan-draws-outside
-look.

19. Public NYPD MOS Database, November 2024.

20. City of Houston v. Hill, 482 U.S. 451 (1987).

21. Law Enforcement, Police Unions, and the Future, pg. 70.

CHAPTER 13: THE CHOKEHOLDS

1. Karen O. Anderson, Carmen R. Green, and Richard Payne, "Racial and ethnic disparities in pain: causes and consequences of unequal care," *Journal of Pain* 10, no. 12 (2009): 1187–204; V.L. Bonham, "Race, ethnicity, and pain treatment: striving to understand the causes and solutions to the disparities in pain treatment," *Journal of Law, Medicine & Ethics* 29, no. 1 (2001): 52–68; C. S. Cleeland, R. Gonin, L. Baez, P. Loehrer, and K. J. Pandya, "Pain and treatment of pain in minority patients with cancer. The Eastern Cooperative Oncology Group Minority Outpatient Pain Study," *Annals of Internal Medicine* 127, no. 9 (1997): 813–16.

2. Robert J. Sampson and Dawn Jeglum Bartusch, "Legal Cynicism and (Subcultural?) Tolerance of Deviance: The Neighborhood Context of Racial Differences," *Law & Society Review* 32, no. 4 (1998): 777–804, scholar.harvard .edu/files/sampson/files/1998_lsr_bartusch.pdf.

3. Arthur Niederhoffer, *Behind the Shield: The Police in Urban Society* (New York: Doubleday, 1967), 95.

4. Monica C. Bell, "Situational Trust: How Disadvantaged Mothers Reconceive Legal Cynicism," *Law & Society Review* 50, no. 2 (2016): 314–47, scholar .harvard.edu/files/bell/files/bell-2016-law_society_review.pdf. "Research using administrative data on police reporting has shown that—even controlling for crime rates—African Americans, women, and residents of high-poverty neighborhoods are equally or more likely to call the police than other groups."

5. Bell, "Situational Trust."

6. Bell, "Situational Trust."

7. "TASER 7 Cartridge Characteristics," Axon, my.axon.com/s/article/TASER -7-Cartridge-Characteristics?language=en_US. (accessed 2022); https:// www.thetrace.org/newsletter/nypd-tasers-efficacy-shooting-subway/#:~:text =One%20possible%20reason%20for%20the%20failures:%20The,sued%20 the%20manufacturer%20over%20the%20reduced%20efficacy.

8. "Drive-stun backup," Axon, my.axon.com/s/article/Drive-stun-backup ?language=en_US; "Warning arc display," Axon, my.axon.com/s/article /Warning-arc-display?language=en_US. (accessed 2022).

9. Harry Stevens, "Under intense pressure, young and largely inexperienced staff at CCRB tasked with investigating police misconduct," *New York World*, June 25, 2015, thenewyorkworld.org/2015/06/25/intense-scrutiny-young -untested-staff-ccrb-tasked-investigating-police-misconduct.

10. https://www1.nyc.gov/assets/ccrb/downloads/pdf/policy_pdf/annual_bi -annual/2019CCRB_AnnualReport.pdf. *Annual Report 2019*.

11. https://www.nytimes.com/2019/06/09/nyregion/eric-garner-case-pantaleo -trial.html.

12. https://nycpba.org/news-items/wall-street-journal/2019/defense-medical -examiner-offers-alternate-theory-in-eric-garner-s-death/.

CHAPTER 14: THE SHOOTINGS

1. Arthur Niederhoffer, *The Police Family: From Station House to Ranch House* (Lanham, MD: Lexington Books, 1978), 41.

2. https://www.newyorker.com/news/news-desk/kalief-browder-1993-2015; https://www.newyorker.com/magazine/2014/10/06/before-the-law.

3. https://www.chicagocopa.org/about-copa/rules-regulations/#:~:text=By%20 ordinance%2C%20COPA%20is%20required,federal%20or%20state%20 criminal%20investigation.

4. https://civilrights.justice.gov/report/.

5. Niederhoffer, *Behind the Shield*, 96.

6. Niederhoffer, *Behind the Shield*, 97.

7. *Behind the Shield*, pgs. 99–100.

8. *Behind the Shield*, pg. 99

9. Westley, "The Police: A Sociological Study of Law, Custom, and Morality," op. cit., p. ii.

10. Hernandez, David (6 July 2020). "The thin blue line: The history behind the controversial police emblem". *San Diego Union-Tribune*; Day, Meagan (14 July 2016). "The problem with the 'thin blue line.' Cops aren't the army". *Timeline (Medium)*; Anderson, N. D. (1911). The Voice of the Infinite. Sherman, French, 6; Shaw, David (25 May 1992). "Chief Parker Molded LAPD Image—Then Came the '60s : Police: Press treated officers as heroes until social upheaval prompted skepticism and confrontation". *Los Angeles Times*; https://www.washingtonpost.com/sf/opinions/2016/10/24/how-police -censorship-shaped-hollywood/; https://www.versobooks.com/blogs/news /4756-how-lapd-chief-william-h-parker-influenced-the-depiction-of -policing-on-the-tv-show-dragnet?; Jason Mittell (2004). Genre and Television: From Cop Shows to Cartoons in American Culture. Routledge. ISBN 0-415-96903-4; Buntin, John (2009). *L.A. Noir: The Struggle for the Soul of America's Most Seductive City*. New York: Harmony Books. ISBN 9780307352071. OCLC 431334523.

11. Niederhoffer, *Behind the Shield*, 103–4.

12. https://www.nytimes.com/2015/03/14/nyregion/playing-police-officers-with -a-car-as-part-of-the-costume.html.

13. NYPD Patrol Guide 202-05 (accessed November 2024).

14. Conlon, *Blue Blood*, 127–128.

15. https://www.nyc.gov/assets/nypd/downloads/pdf/use-of-force/use-of-force -2021.pdf, NYPD 2023 Annual Use of Force Data Tables - Incidents by Force Category, NYPD Force Dashboard, NYC Open Data (access date November 2024); https://www.nyc.gov/site/nypd/stats/reports-analysis /firearms-discharge.page; https://www.thecity.nyc/2023/12/21/nypd -shootings-force-report/; https://data.cityofnewyork.us/Public-Safety /NYPD-Shooting-Incident-Data-Historic-/833y-fsy8/data_preview.

CHAPTER 15: SLAVE PATROLS

1. Peter H. Wood, *Black Majority: Negroes in Colonial South Carolina from 1670 through the Stono Rebellion* (New York: W.W. Norton Company, 1974), p.24.
2. https://finesandfeesjusticecenter.org/articles/investigation-ferguson-police-department/.
3. https://www.supremecourt.gov/DocketPDF/19/19-292/132289/20200207110826521_19-292%20Amicus%20Brief%20of%20NAACP%20LDF.pdf.
4. https://www.newyorker.com/magazine/2020/07/20/the-invention-of-the-police; https://time.com/4779112/police-history-origins/; https://www.npr.org/2020/06/13/876628302/the-history-of-policing-and-race-in-the-u-s-are-deeply-intertwined.
5. Sally Hadden, Law and Violence in Virginia and the Carolinas, 5.
6. Woodard, American Nations, "Founding the Deep South," 82.
7. The late regulations respecting the British colonies on the continent of America considered, in a letter from a gentleman in Philadelphia to his friend in London, page 14. John Dickenson.
8. Barbados: The Rise of the Planter Class, 72.
9. *Barbados: Just Beyond Your Imagination*. Hansib Publishing (Caribbean) Ltd. 1997, 46, 48.
10. In 1650, there were approximately 30 African slaves in the entire colony of Virginia. In 1680, there were approximately 3,000. https://www.washingtonpost.com/history/2019/02/06/virginia-is-birthplace-american-slavery-segregation-it-still-cant-escape-that-legacy/.
11. American Nations, 85.
12. American Nations, p.85.
13. The Police Control of the Slave in South Carolina, H. M. Henry (1913); Philip L. Reichel, Southern Slave Patrols as a Transitional Police Type, 7 Am. J. Police 51, 66 (1988); North and South had not yet been officially divided, and was still owned by allies of the British crown.
14. Alan Taylor, *American Colonies: The Settlement of North America* (New York: Penguin Books, 2001), 226; https://www.carolana.com/Carolina/thesplit.html; https://www.ushistory.org/us/5c.asp#:~:text=As%20the%20two%20locales%20evolved,this%20peaceful%20divorce%20took%20effect.
15. Sally Hadden, *Slave Patrols: Law and Violence in Virginia and the* Carolinas. 8–28.
16. https://nationalhumanitiescenter.org/pds/becomingamer/peoples/text4/stonorebellion.pdf.
17. Calling Out Liberty: The Stono Slave Rebellion and the Universal Struggle for Human Rights, Jack Schuler.
18. https://history.state.gov/milestones/1784-1800/haitian-rev.
19. https://www.africanamericancharleston.com/places/the-citadel/.
20. https://www.ccpl.org/records-charleston-police-department-1855-1991.

21. Hadden, 1–5.
22. Hadden, 4.
23. Hadden, 203–220.
24. https://www.statista.com/statistics/195324/
gender-distribution-of-full-time-law-enforcement-employees-in-the-us
/#:~:text=In%202023%2C%2059.9%20percent%20of,law%20enforcement
%20officers%20were%20male.

CHAPTER 16: THE PROTESTS

1. Law Enforcement, Police Unions, and the Future, pg. 74
2. Below is the full quote: "Oh, my goodness. I have squirters. Bro, like no exaggeration I got like thirty different sheets because every bitch I fuck, if they're not bleeding all over the place, they're fucking squirting all over the place. Regardless, it's always wet. I always have to change my sheets. One bitch was coming, it was like fucking toothpaste. I'm like, 'What the fuck?' Jesus. God damn, man. I can't have fucking girls in my house. If they don't invite me to theirs, I'm like, 'Fuck it.' It's not even worth it anymore. I'm tired of being in the laundromat. All the little Mexican girls are looking at me like, 'What the fuck is with this guy? He must have a huge dick.' And then I got one bitch. It's like every time I touch her, she's squirting in the fucking car. I'm like, 'This is a brand-new car. Fuck you. Don't fuck up my car.'"
3. https://nypost.com/2020/03/27/more-than-500-members-of-the-nypd-have
-coronavirus/; https://www.cdc.gov/mmwr/volumes/69/wr/mm6913e2.htm.
4. https://www.nytimes.com/2020/04/03/nyregion/coronavirus-nypd.html.
5. https://www.cnn.com/2020/04/19/us/new-york-city-police-covid-19-deaths
/index.html; https://abc7ny.com/nypd-death-doris-kirkland-covid-deaths
-coronavirus-in-the/6208730/.
6. https://www.nyc.gov/assets/ccrb/downloads/pdf/policy_pdf/issue_based
/2020NYCProtestReport.pdf.
7. https://ag.ny.gov/sites/default/files/filed_complaint_ny_v_nypd_1.14.2021.
pdf.
8. https://theintercept.com/2020/07/06/nypd-culture-of-impunity/?utm
_source=twitter&utm_medium=social&utm_campaign=theintercept.
9. Ice Cube (@icecube), "Very sick people," Twitter (now X), July 6, 2020, twitter.com/icecube/status/1280346369685741568?s=20&t=JijR-N2yZo TaBBZe1xkE6A.
10. "US: New York Police Planned Assault on Bronx Protesters," Human Rights Watch, September 30, 2020, www.hrw.org/news/2020/09/30/us-new-york -police-planned-assault-bronx-protesters.
11. Nick Pinto, "NYC Gives Arrested Legal Observers a Check and a 'Middle Finger' to Make Their NYPD Lawsuit Go Away," Hell Gate, July 21, 2022, hellgatenyc.com/legal-observers-nypd-mott-haven-settlement.

12. Reuven Blau, "City Brass Net Over $21 Million in Retirement Payouts for Workaholic Tendencies," The City, October 5, 2022, www.thecity.nyc/work /2022/10/5/23388144/city-brass-net-21-million-retirement-payouts -workaholic-tendencies.

13. https://www.nbcnewyork.com/news/local/nearly-400-nypd-officers-hurt -during-nycs-two-weeks-of-protest-over-george-floyds-death/2455285/.

14. https://www.nytimes.com/2020/06/04/nyregion/De-blasio-protests-curfew .html.

15. Rocco Parascandola, "See It: NYPD commissioner bashes city leaders as 'cowards' in police brass meeting: 'They are failing at every possible measure to be leaders,'" New York Daily News, last modified July 18, 2020, www.nydaily news.com/new-york/nyc-crime/ny-nypd-commissioner-dermot-shea-calls -city-leaders-cowards-20200718-jqh3qagax5cjda73izzuq3t4xu-story.html.

16. Steven Long and Justin McCarthy, "Two in Three Americans Support Racial Justice Protests," Gallup, July 28, 2020, news.gallup.com/poll/316106/two -three-americans-support-racial-justice-protests.aspx; Amanda Barroso and Rachel Minkin, "Recent protest attendees are more racially and ethnically diverse, younger than Americans overall," Pew Research Center, June 24, 2020, www.pewresearch.org/fact-tank/2020/06/24/recent-protest-attendees -are-more-racially-and-ethnically-diverse-younger-than-americans-overall.

17. Dean Balsamini, "Overtime for uniformed NYPD soared 24 percent in fiscal year 2020," New York Post, November 28, 2020, nypost.com/2020/11/28/nypd -overtime-for-uniformed-cops-rose-24-percent-in-fiscal-year.

18. Michael Elsen-Rooney, "Plan to transfer NYC school safety agents from the NYPD to the Education Dept. is reversed," New York Daily News, last modified March 3, 2022, www.nydailynews.com/new-york/education/ny -budget-reverses-school-safety-transfer-to-doc-20220303-37k4a22s2 fahfpdu4nvhfs7ngu-story.html.

19. "A Watchdog Accused Officers of Serious Misconduct. Few Were Punished.," New York Times, November 15, 2020, www.nytimes.com/2020/11 /15/nyregion/ccrb-nyc-police-misconduct.html; Stephon Johnson, Amsterdam News, June 11, 2020, "Inez and Charles Barron: scrap the CCRB and form a new, elected oversight board," amsterdamnews.com/news/2020 /06/11/inez-and-charles-barron-scrap-ccrb-and-form-new-el.

20. https://www.nytimes.com/2020/11/15/nyregion/ccrb-nyc-police-misconduct .html, Ashley Southall, Ali Watkins and Blacki Migliozzi.

21. For example: https://www.nyc.gov/assets/ccrb/downloads/pdf/about_pdf /bwc_mou.pdf.

22. https://www.nytimes.com/2024/09/23/us/murder-crime-rate-fbi.html# :~:text=The%20F.B.I.'s%20report%2C%20which,a%20decline%20of%2011 .6%20percent; https://counciloncj.org/homicide-trends-report/#:~:text =The%20U.S.%20homicide%20rate%20began,before%20the%20COVID%2 D19%20pandemic.

23. https://www.vice.com/en/article/police-are-telling-shotspotter-to-alter
    -evidence-from-gunshot-detecting-ai/.

24. https://igchicago.org/wp-content/uploads/2021/08/Chicago-Police
    -Departments-Use-of-ShotSpotter-Technology.pdf; https://apnews.com
    /article/technology-business-chicago-1d62906b0c4b4dc67886da89596b1f12.

25. https://bds.org/assets/files/Brooklyn-Defenders-ShotSpotter-Report.pdf.

26. https://cbcny.org/research/seven-facts-about-nypd-budget; https://council
    .nyc.gov/budget/wp-content/uploads/sites/54/2019/03/056-NYPD-2020
    .pdf; https://council.nyc.gov/budget/wp-content/uploads/sites/54/2024/03
    /056-NYPD.pdf.

27. https://www.discoverpolicing.org/about-policing/financial-stability-and
    -benefits/; https://www.researchgate.net/profile/David-Lester-3/publication
    /290810192_Why_do_people_become_police_officers_A_study_of_reasons
    _and_their_predictions_of_success/links/593bfabc0f7e9b331749f32b/Why
    -do-people-become-police-officers-A-study-of-reasons-and-their-predictions
    -of-success.pdf; https://digitalcommons.unomaha.edu/cgi/viewcontent.cgi
    ?article=1090&context=criminaljusticefacpub.

28. Campisi, *Blue on Blue*, 68–69.

29. Campisi, *Blue on Blue*, 68.

30. Campisi, *Blue on Blue*, 68.

31. https://nyassembly.gov/Press/files/20200608a.php#:~:text=Assembly%20
    Passes%20Eric%20Garner%20Anti%2DChokehold%20Act&text=Speaker
    %20Carl%20Heastie%20and%20Assemblymember,6144%2DB%2C%20
    Mosley.

32. https://nypost.com/2022/06/09/ex-nypd-cop-gets-up-to-4-years-for-firing
    -gun-into-ocean/.

33. https://www.nbcnewyork.com/news/local/nypd-officer-charged-with-using
    -chokehold-banned-after-george-floyds-death/5688870/.

34. https://nysfocus.com/2022/03/03/nypd-plainclothes-anti-crime-unit
    -neighborhood-safety-team-ccrb-complaints-lawsuits.

35. https://www.nyclu.org/commentary/complaints-nypd-abuse-are-way-under
    -mayor-adams.

CHAPTER 17: TERMINATION

1. https://nysfocus.com/2024/10/31/new-york-police-misconduct-employment
   -records.

2. https://www.washingtonpost.com/politics/2020/06/16/what-happens-when
   -police-officer-gets-fired-very-often-another-police-agency-hires-them/.

3. https://www.pbs.org/newshour/nation/cleveland-police-office-shot-tamir
   -rice-unfit-duty-years-ago-police-reports-show.

4. https://www.sfchronicle.com/projects/2024/police-clean-record-agreements/.

5. https://indypendent.org/2022/12/army-of-snitches/#:~:text=30%2C000%
20informants%20currently%20work%20for,police%20at%20any%20given
%20time.

6. https://www.copsandkidsboxing.com/news#:~:text=%E2%80%9CBoxing
%20is%20a%20carrot%20on%20a%20stick,be%20part%20of%20a%20
positive%20program.%E2%80%9D%20https://www.silive.com/news/2022
/07/nyc%2Dcops%2Dkids%2Dboxing%2Dexpands%2Dstaten%2Disland
%2Dfacility%2Dto%2Doffer%2Dfree%2Dfitness%2Dgym%2Dto%2
Dyouth.html.

7. https://hls.harvard.edu/today/falling-in-love-with-your-rat-the-criminal
-informant-system-in-the-u-s/; https://www.cato.org/commentary
/criminally-confidential#.

8. https://www.thecity.nyc/2022/09/19/nypd-eric-dym-civilian-complaints
-retires/.

9. Daria Roithmayr, "The Dynamics of Excessive Force," *University of Chicago
Legal Forum* 2016, no. 1 (2016): 407–36.

10. George Wood, Daria Roithmayr, and Andrew V. Papachristos, "The Network
Structure of Police Misconduct," *Socius: Sociological Research for a Dynamic
World* 5 (2019).

11. https://scholarworks.gsu.edu/cgi/viewcontent.cgi?article=1008&context
=cj_facpub.

12. https://journals.plos.org/plosone/article?id=10.1371/journal.pone.0267217.

13. https://archive.ph/20230915075636/https://gothamist.com/news/most
-expensive-nypd-lawsuits-2021-2022.

14. (NYPD MOS Database).

15. [Public NYPD MOS Database, July 2022].

16. McGoldrick, "Irish American NYPD Commissioner couldn't be prouder
this St. Patrick's Day."

CHAPTER 18: A BETTER WORLD

1. https://news.gallup.com/poll/647303/confidence-institutions-mostly-flat
-police.aspx.

2. https://www.reuters.com/legal/government/
police-are-not-primarily-crime-fighters-according-data-2022-11-02/;
https://www.nytimes.com/2024/01/27/world/canada/canada-letter-police
-spending-crime.html#:~:text=Spending%20More%20Money%20on%20
Police%20Shows%20No,Crime%20Levels%20%2D%20The%20New%20
York%20Times; https://journals.sagepub.com/doi/10.1177/00111287
10382263.

3 Scott, Liz (Dec 2001). "Jack Maple: 'The Fat Man' as Crime Fighter". *New
Orleans Magazine* 1. (16–18).

4. https://boltsmag.org/a-police-stop-is-enough-to-make-someone-less-likely-to
-vote/.

5. Reginald Young-Drake, Temitope Aladetimi, Alexis Chambers, and Brooke Radford, *A Growing Dilemma: How Police Brutality Affects Mental Health in Black Communities* (Washington, DC: Movement Lawyering Clinic, 2021), thurgoodmarshallcenter.howard.edu/sites/tmcrc.howard.edu/files/2021-05/A%20Growing%20Dilemma%20-%20How%20Police%20Brutality%20Affects%20Mental%20Health%20in%20the%20Black%20Communities.pdf; Jacob Bor, Atheendar S. Venkataramani, David R. Williams, Alexander C. Tsai, "Police killings and their spillover effects on the mental health of black Americans: a population-based, quasi-experimental study," *Lancet* 392, no. 10144 (2018): 301–10, www.ncbi.nlm.nih.gov/pmc/articles/PMC6376989/pdf/nihms-1007736.pdf.

6. https://bja.ojp.gov/sites/g/files/xyckuh186/files/Publications/PERF-Compstat.pdf.

7. https://www.nytimes.com/1993/11/01/opinion/why-good-cops-turn-rotten.html.

8. https://nymag.com/nymetro/news/anniversary/35th/n_8551/.

9. https://www.vitalcitynyc.org/articles/civic-life-can-create-safety.

10. The Crime Machine, Reply All podcast, Part II.

11. "COMPSTAT, which was a system of accountability that was brought down from New York, was really transformed in the Baltimore Police Department from an accountability tool into score-keeping, crude score-keeping. The fortunes of supervisors in the department were driven by the numbers that they and their squads produced. And the greater the productivity that the squad showed, the less the supervision, because there was no incentive to kill the goose that was laying the golden egg. That led to coddling, promoting and protecting productive members of the department. Productive measured in pure numerical term. And a numbers mentality to an ends justify the means mentality. If you're putting the numbers on the board, there was just not a lot of inquiry into how you were doing it."—Michael R. Bromwich, February 2022; https://www.youtube.com/watch?v=dNrWwN4UcUs (44:49).

12. https://eji.org/news/study-finds-increased-incarceration-does-not-reduce-crime/; https://www.sentencingproject.org/publications/one-in-five-how-mass-incarceration-deepens-inequality-and-harms-public-safety/; https://nij.ojp.gov/topics/articles/hidden-consequences-impact-incarceration-dependent-children.

13. https://daily.jstor.org/rethinking-prison-as-a-deterrent-to-future-crime/; https://www.pewtrusts.org/en/research-and-analysis/issue-briefs/2018/03/more-imprisonment-does-not-reduce-state-drug-problems; https://www.vera.org/publications/for-the-record-prison-paradox-incarceration-not-safer; https://daily.jstor.org/rethinking-prison-as-a-deterrent-to-future-crime/.

14. https://laist.com/shows/take-two/paying-people-not-to-commit-crimes-could-it-work-in-socal; https://www.sfchronicle.com/bayarea/justinphillips/article/richmond-crime-homicides-progressive-reform-18626585.php;

https://www.brookings.edu/articles/should-we-pay-people-not-to-commit
-crime/.

CHAPTER 19: SIX PROPOSALS

1. Niederhoffer, *Behind the Shield*, 160.
2. https://www.policechiefmagazine.org/beyond-recruitment/.
3. https://30x30initiative.org/; https://bja.ojp.gov/news/blog/30x30-initiative
   -positive-impacts-women-law-enforcement.
4. https://theappeal.org/more-black-cops-will-not-solve-police-violence/;
   https://journals.sagepub.com/doi/10.1177/00938548241227551.
5. DeLord and York, *Law Enforcement, Police Unions, and the Future*, 188.
6. https://michellawyers.com/wp-content/uploads/2010/06/
   Report-of-the-Independent-Commission-on-the-LAPD-re-Rodney-King
   _Reduced.pdf.
7. https://www.ojp.gov/pdffiles1/nij/252963.pdf.
8. https://www.nyc.gov/site/ccrb/policy/annual-bi-annual-reports.page; https://
   www.nyc.gov/site/ccrb/policy/data-transparency-initiative.page.
9. Harrington et al. 1998.
10. Marie Ouellet, Sadaf Hashimi, Jason Gravel, and Andrew Papachristos,
    titled "Network Exposure and Excessive Use of Force: Investigating the
    Social Transmission of Police Misconduct.
11. Dave Hickey, "The Heresy of Zone Defense" in *Air Guitar: Essays on Art &
    Democracy* (Los Angeles: Art Issues Press, 1997).
12. Dale Gieringer, "State's war on drugs a 100-year-old bust/Rate of addiction
    has doubled since crackdown on use," SFGate, March 4, 2007, www.sfgate
    .com/opinion/article/State-s-war-on-drugs-a-100-year-old-bust-Rate
    -2644479.php.
13. Conlon, *Blue Blood*, 172.
14. https://www.nytimes.com/2023/08/08/nyregion/drug-overdoses-supervised
    -consumption-nyc.html; https://www.cato.org/briefing-paper/overdose
    -prevention-centers-successful-strategy-preventing-death-disease; https://
    pmc.ncbi.nlm.nih.gov/articles/PMC5685449/; https://jamanetwork.com
    /journals/jamanetworkopen/fullarticle/2811766.
15. https://www.newyorker.com/magazine/2024/01/22/a-new-drug-war-in
    -oregon.
16. https://www.nbcnews.com/meet-the-press/data-download/costs-war-drugs
    -continue-soar-rcna92032.
17. Weihua Li and Jamiles Lartey, "As Murders Spiked, Police Solved About
    Half in 2020," Marshall Project, January 12, 2022, www.themarshallproject.
    org/2022/01/12/as-murders-spiked-police-solved-about-half-in-2020;
    https://www.statista.com/statistics/194213/crime-clearance-rate-by-type-in
    -the-us/; https://www.npr.org/2023/04/29/1172775448/

people-murder-unsolved-killings-record-high; https://hellgatenyc.com/nypd
-clearance-reports-are-nowhere-to-be-found/.

18.   Blue View Podcast, episode #26, 10:30 (accessed August 2022).

19.   Associated Press, "Most police never shoot, study finds: In N.Y., chief says
well over 95% never fire weapons," *Deseret News*, February 21, 2000, www
.deseret.com/2000/2/21/19492101/most-police-never-shoot-study-finds-br
-in-n-y-chief-says-well-over-95-never-fire-weapons.

20.   https://www.policinginstitute.org/wp-content/uploads/2019/05/2.-OIS_off
_sub_8.28.19.pdf; Rich Morin and Andrew Mercer, "A closer look at
police officers who have fired their weapon on duty," Pew Research Center,
February 8, 2017, www.pewresearch.org/fact-tank/2017/02/08/a-closer-look
-at-police-officers-who-have-fired-their-weapon-on-duty.

21.   Hassan Kanu, "Police are not primarily crime fighters, according to the data,"
Reuters, November 2, 2022, www.reuters.com/legal/government/police-are
-not-primarily-crime-fighters-according-data-2022-11-02; "911 Analysis:
Our Overreliance on Police by the Numbers," Vera, April 2022, www.vera
.org/publications/911-analysis.

22.   *Media Guide 2020* (Eugene: CAHOOTS, 2020), whitebirdclinic.org/wp
-content/uploads/2020/07/CAHOOTS-Media.pdf.

23.   Matt DeLaus, "Alternatives to Police as First Responders: Crisis Response
Programs," Government Law Center, November 16, 2020, www.albanylaw
.edu/government-law-center/alternatives-police-first-responders-crisis
-response-programs#_bookmark126.

24.   https://www.themarshallproject.org/2024/07/25/police-mental-health
-alternative-911.

25.   https://oaklandside.org/2024/09/09/holly-joshi-oakland-ceasefire-violence
-prevention/.

26.   https://cao-94612.s3.amazonaws.com/documents/Oakland-Ceasefire
-Evaluation-Final-Report-May-2019.pdf.

27.   Sharon Gray, *Community Safety Workers: An Exploratory Study of Some
Emerging Crime Prevention Occupations* (International Collegiate
Programming Contest, 2006), cipc-icpc.org/wp-content/uploads/2019/08
/Community_Safety_Workers._An_exploratory_Study_of_Some_Emerging
_Crime_Prevention_Occupations2_ANG.pdf.

28.   Maple, *The Crime Fighter*, 244.

29.   Campisi, *Blue on Blue*, 73.

30.   https://nypost.com/2020/06/28/cop-suing-nypd-for-racial-profiling-running
-for-city-council/.

31.   https://nypost.com/2021/03/17/rampant-corruption-in-nypds-internal
-affairs-bureau-lawsuit/; https://nypost.com/2015/09/01/cop-suing-over
-minority-arrest-quotas-says-he-faced-retaliation/.

32.   https://www.themarshallproject.org/2024/08/03/police-congress-corruption
-whistleblower.

33. https://www.nydailynews.com/2018/01/09/two-anonymous-cops-set-up
-comedic-website-the-hairbag-times-to-spoof-nypd/; https://www.cbsnews
.com/news/investigator-of-police-misconduct-claims-chicago-cops-abused
-him/; https://nypost.com/2024/05/25/us-news/whistleblower-cop-jailed
-with-killers-at-rikers/; https://www.themarshallproject.org/2024/08/03
/police-congress-corruption-whistleblower.
34. NYS Assemby Transcript 6-9-2020 for Bill A10611, 80.
35. https://www.courthousenews.com/nypd-lose-appeal-to-keep-disciplinary
-records-under-lock-key/; https://www.courthousenews.com/wp-content
/uploads/2021/02/nypd-discipline-ca2.pdf.
36. https://le.fbi.gov/file-repository/about-the-ucr-program.pdf.
37. https://ucr.fbi.gov/data_quality_guidelines#:~:text=In%20addition%20to
%20the%20initial,2)%20the%20principle%20of%20transparency.
38. https://www.cdc.gov/nchs/data/databriefs/db492.pdf.
39. Kenneth D. Kochanek, Jiaquan Xu, and Elizabeth Arias, *Mortality in the
United States, 2019* (Washington, DC: U.S. Department of Health and
Human Services, 2020), www.cdc.gov/nchs/data/databriefs/db395-H.pdf;
https://www.kff.org/key-data-on-health-and-health-care-by-race-and
-ethnicity/?entry=health-status-and-outcomes-life-expectancy.
40. "The Truth and Reconciliation Commission (TRC)," Apartheid Museum,
www.apartheidmuseum.org/exhibitions/the-truth-and-reconciliation
-commission-trc. (accessed August 2022).
41. "Chile recognizes 9,800 more victims of Pinochet's rule," BBC News,
August 18, 2011, www.bbc.com/news/world-latin-america-14584095.
42. "History of Chicago's Reparations Movement," Chicago Torture Justice
Center, www.chicagotorturejustice.org/history.
43. Niederhoffer, *Behind the Shield*, 100.
44. Ian Kullgren and Robert Iafolla, "Cities, States Prevail in Early Legal
Clashes with Police Unions," Bloomberg Law, November 18, 2020, news
.bloomberglaw.com/daily-labor-report/cities-states-prevail-in-early-legal
-clashes-with-police-unions; https://www.nationalaffairs.com/publications
/detail/the-trouble-with-police-unions.

EPILOGUE

1. https://urbanomnibus.net/2018/06/the-compstat-evangelist-consultant
-world-tour/; https://nacla.org/news/2015/10/26/giuliani-rio; https://www
.nytimes.com/2001/12/13/nyregion/giuliani-plans-own-business-with-top
-aides-in-consulting.html; https://theintercept.com/2018/10/05/rudy
-giuliani-amazon-contract-brazil-election/.

About the Authors

MAC MUIR was raised in Oakland, California. After his time as a supervising investigator at New York City's Civilian Complaint Review Board, Mac served as the executive director of Oakland's Community Police Review Agency. He's old enough to remember when Oakland had three professional sports teams. Those were the days.

GREG FINCH was raised in Queens, New York. Greg was a senior investigator at the CCRB. He has never been ticketed for speeding.